Advanced Blazor Architecture with .NET 10 and Azure OpenAI

Enterprise-Grade Design Patterns, AI Integration, and Cloud-Ready Solutions

Amit Prasad
Harvendra Singh

Apress®

Advanced Blazor Architecture with .NET 10 and Azure OpenAI: Enterprise-Grade Design Patterns, AI Integration, and Cloud-Ready Solutions

Amit Prasad
Louisville, KY, USA

Harvendra Singh
Lakeland, FL, USA

ISBN-13 (pbk): 979-8-8688-2517-0
ISBN-13 (electronic): 979-8-8688-2518-7
https://doi.org/10.1007/979-8-8688-2518-7

Managing Director, Apress Media LLC: Welmoed Spahr
Acquisitions Editor: Ryan Byrnes
Editorial Project Manager: Gryffin Winkler

Cover designed by eStudioCalamar

Cover image designed by Freepik (www.freepik.com)

Distributed to the book trade worldwide by Springer Science+Business Media New York, 1 New York Plaza, New York, NY 10004. Phone 1-800-SPRINGER, fax (201) 348-4505, e-mail orders-ny@springer-sbm.com, or visit www.springeronline.com. Apress Media, LLC is a Delaware LLC and the sole member (owner) is Springer Science + Business Media Finance Inc (SSBM Finance Inc). SSBM Finance Inc is a **Delaware** corporation.

For information on translations, please e-mail booktranslations@springernature.com; for reprint, paperback, or audio rights, please e-mail bookpermissions@springernature.com.

Apress titles may be purchased in bulk for academic, corporate, or promotional use. eBook versions and licenses are also available for most titles. For more information, reference our Print and eBook Bulk Sales web page at http://www.apress.com/bulk-sales.

Any source code or other supplementary material referenced by the author in this book is available to readers on GitHub. For more detailed information, please visit https://www.apress.com/gp/services/source-code.

If disposing of this product, please recycle the paper

Dedicated to our parents, who gave us the roots to grow and the wings to soar, and to our families whose love, patience, and constant encouragement made this work possible.

Table of Contents

About the Authors

Amit Prasad is a technology professional focused on designing and delivering scalable, secure, and high-performance solutions. He has contributed to numerous technology initiatives that promote innovation, improve operational efficiency, and create meaningful business value. His work spans modern cloud platforms, enterprise architecture, and emerging technologies, helping organizations build resilient and future-ready systems. Amit is passionate about solving complex technical challenges and fostering collaboration to deliver impactful and reliable solutions.

Harvendra Singh is a technology professional and leader specializing in cloud engineering, enterprise architecture, and AI-driven systems. He focuses on designing scalable, secure, and high-performance platforms that help organizations build modern digital solutions and make better use of data. Over the years, he has worked extensively with cloud-native technologies and distributed systems, developing applications and platforms that support large-scale digital transformation initiatives. His work centers on applying practical architectural principles to build systems that are resilient, efficient, and well suited for enterprise environments. Harvendra is passionate about continuous learning and knowledge sharing within the global technology community, and through technical writing, research, mentoring, and speaking engagements, he actively contributes to advancing modern cloud and AI architectures.

About the Technical Reviewer

Venkata Vemuri is a Senior Principal Front-End Engineer at Oracle, working at the intersection of front-end engineering, accessibility, and AI. He is a W3C member contributing to the drafting of WCAG 3 standards and is passionate about shaping more inclusive digital experiences. He is also an author committed to teaching, mentoring, and sharing practical knowledge with the broader engineering community.

Acknowledgments

Writing *Advanced Blazor Architecture with .NET 10 and Azure OpenAI* has been an exciting and rewarding journey for both of us, and we are deeply grateful to the many people who supported us along the way.

First and foremost, we would like to thank our families for their unwavering encouragement, patience, and understanding throughout the long hours of research, writing, and revisions. Their support and belief in us made it possible to bring this book to completion.

We would also like to extend our sincere appreciation to the editorial and publishing team for their guidance, professionalism, and continuous support during the development of this book. Their thoughtful feedback, coordination, and dedication helped shape this manuscript into a polished and valuable resource for developers and architects.

Our gratitude also goes to the technical reviewers and colleagues who shared their insights and constructive suggestions, helping us improve the clarity and depth of the content.

Finally, we are thankful to the global developer community whose shared knowledge and innovation continue to inspire learning and progress. We hope this book contributes meaningfully to that community.

Introduction

The way we build modern applications is changing rapidly. Today's users expect applications that are fast, interactive, scalable, and increasingly intelligent. At the same time, developers and architects are looking for tools and frameworks that simplify development while still allowing them to build powerful enterprise-grade solutions. Technologies such as Blazor, modern .NET platforms, cloud-native services, and artificial intelligence are playing a major role in shaping this new landscape.

Blazor has emerged as a compelling framework within the .NET ecosystem, enabling developers to build rich, interactive web applications using C# instead of JavaScript. By allowing developers to share skills, libraries, and architectural patterns across the entire stack, Blazor simplifies development while maintaining flexibility and performance. With the advancements introduced in .NET 10, developers now have access to improved performance, enhanced tooling, and new capabilities that make building scalable and maintainable applications easier than ever.

At the same time, artificial intelligence is becoming an integral part of modern software systems. Platforms such as Azure OpenAI are making it possible to embed intelligent features directly into applications, from conversational interfaces and intelligent assistants to advanced data analysis and automation. When combined with modern web architectures, these technologies open up exciting opportunities to build applications that are not only functional but also adaptive and intelligent.

This book, *Advanced Blazor Architecture with .NET 10 and Azure OpenAI*, is written for developers, architects, and technology professionals who want to go beyond basic application development and explore how to design robust, scalable, and intelligent systems. Rather than focusing only on coding techniques, this book emphasizes architectural thinking about how to design applications that are maintainable, secure, and ready to evolve as technology continues to advance.

Throughout the chapters, we explore architectural patterns, performance optimization strategies, cloud integration techniques, and practical approaches for incorporating AI capabilities using Azure OpenAI. Real-world examples and practical guidance are included to help readers understand not only how to implement these solutions but also why certain architectural decisions matter in modern enterprise environments.

Our goal is to provide a resource that helps readers build a deeper understanding of modern Blazor architecture and how it can be combined with cloud and AI technologies to create innovative applications. Whether you are a developer looking to expand your technical skills or an architect designing next-generation systems, we hope this book provides valuable insights and practical knowledge to support your journey.

CHAPTER 1

Introduction to Modern Blazor

Evolution of Blazor

Blazor's evolution from a bold experiment to a mainstream enterprise framework is one of the most notable journeys in modern web development. When Microsoft first introduced the idea in 2017, web application development was almost entirely dominated by JavaScript frameworks such as Angular, React, and Vue. Developers who built their back-end services in .NET often faced the challenge of maintaining two separate technology stacks: C# for the server side and JavaScript for the browser. Microsoft's engineers wondered whether it was possible to eliminate that split by running .NET code directly inside the browser. With the advent of WebAssembly, Microsoft began experimenting with running .NET directly in the browser, an effort that eventually became the Blazor project. The breakthrough that made this feasible was WebAssembly (WASM), a compact bytecode format capable of running at near-native speed within all major browsers without plug-ins. Early Blazor prototypes introduced a streamlined .NET runtime compiled to WebAssembly, enabling developers to execute C# securely within the browser while interacting directly with the DOM. These early explorations established the architectural groundwork for what would later mature into Blazor's two primary hosting models: Blazor Server and Blazor WebAssembly.

The initial demonstrations were intentionally simple, a "Hello World" page featuring a small Razor component and some C# logic, but they proved the concept that a .NET application could run entirely within the browser. Razor, already familiar to ASP.NET developers as a concise and expressive templating syntax, provided a natural foundation for building interactive UI components in this new environment. This capability

A. Prasad and H. Singh, *Advanced Blazor Architecture with .NET 10 and Azure OpenAI*,
https://doi.org/10.1007/979-8-8688-2518-7_1

attracted attention because it meant that developers could write client-side code in the same language as their server logic, reuse existing .NET libraries, and avoid the overhead of switching between C# and JavaScript. Community feedback was enthusiastic, and Microsoft quickly formalized the project under the name "Blazor," a blend of "Browser" and "Razor," the existing ASP.NET templating engine.

C#

```
using BlazorApp1.Components;

var builder = WebApplication.CreateBuilder(args);

// Add services to the container.
builder.Services.AddRazorComponents()
    .AddInteractiveServerComponents();

var app = builder.Build();

// Configure the HTTP request pipeline.
if (!app.Environment.IsDevelopment())
{
    app.UseExceptionHandler("/Error", createScopeForErrors: true);
    // The default HSTS value is 30 days. You may want to change this for production
    app.UseHsts();
}

app.UseHttpsRedirection();

app.UseStaticFiles();
app.UseAntiforgery();

app.MapRazorComponents<App>()
    .AddInteractiveServerRenderMode();

app.Run();
```

The first production-ready version arrived with .NET Core 3.0 in 2019 as **Blazor Server**, which kept the application's logic and rendering engine on the server while maintaining a persistent SignalR connection to the client. In this model, when a user clicked a button or changed a form field, the event traveled back to the server, where the corresponding C# code executed and generated a small UI diff that was sent back to the browser. This architecture offered the interactivity of a single-page application while avoiding the need to download a large .NET runtime to the client. For many enterprise intranet scenarios, where a stable network connection is standard and central data control is important, Blazor Server quickly became an attractive option. It also simplified security and state management because all business logic remained on the server side, leveraging ASP.NET Core's mature middleware for authentication and authorization.

The below snippet defines the standard startup sequence for a Blazor WebAssembly application. The WebAssemblyHostBuilder initializes the runtime and configures the application environment. The root App component is registered and mapped to the #app element in index.html. An HttpClient instance is added to the dependency injection container with its base address set to the application's hosting environment. Finally, the host is built, and the application is executed in the browser using WebAssembly.

C#

```
var builder = WebAssemblyHostBuilder.CreateDefault(args);
builder.RootComponents.Add<App>("#app");
builder.Services.AddScoped(sp =>
    new HttpClient { BaseAddress = new Uri(builder.HostEnvironment.BaseAddress) });
await builder.Build().RunAsync();
```

Building on that success, Microsoft released Blazor WebAssembly in 2020, fulfilling the original vision of running .NET code directly in the browser. Blazor WebAssembly applications download a small runtime along with the application assemblies and execute entirely on the client, enabling offline capabilities and reducing server load. This model unlocked scenarios such as progressive web apps and high-performance dashboards that could work even when the network connection was intermittent. Developers could share code seamlessly between the client and the server, for example, using the same C# validation logic both when data is entered in the browser and when it is processed on the server's API layer. Although early versions faced criticism for relatively large download sizes and slower startup compared with traditional JavaScript Single Page Applications (SPAs), each subsequent .NET release introduced optimizations, including Intermediate Language (IL) trimming, lazy loading, and Ahead-of-Time compilation, to improve performance and reduce payload sizes.

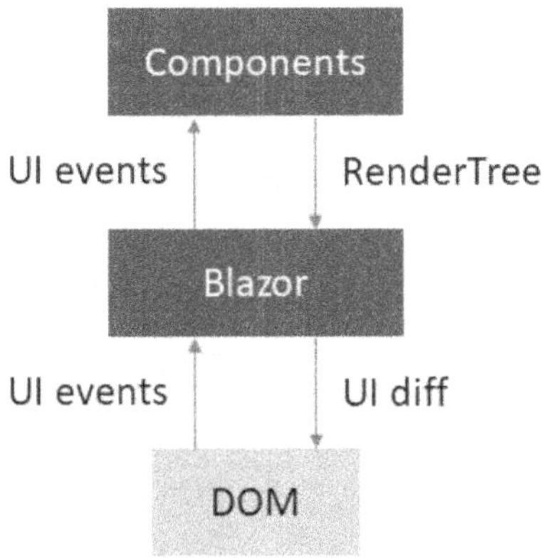

Figure 1-1. *Architecture of Blazor*

Over the next few years, the Blazor ecosystem expanded rapidly. Microsoft added features such as Hot Reload for near-instant feedback during development, improved debugging tools, and tight Visual Studio and Visual Studio Code integration. Third-party vendors released mature UI component libraries offering grids, charts, and advanced form controls tailored for Blazor, while open source contributors provided state management solutions, testing frameworks, and performance utilities. This vibrant ecosystem meant that developers could adopt Blazor without fear of being locked into proprietary tooling or limited support. Enterprises already invested in the Microsoft stack began to migrate new projects to Blazor because it reduced the learning curve for C# developers and lowered long-term maintenance costs by consolidating the technology stack.

The release of **.NET 10** marks another milestone in Blazor's growth. Features such as Ahead-of-Time (AOT) compilation produce native WebAssembly binaries, dramatically improving load times and runtime performance. Support for newer WebAssembly proposals, threads, SIMD (single instruction, multiple data) instructions, and host bindings opens the door to multithreaded workloads and efficient numerical computations directly in the browser. Combined with better security defaults, package signing, and automatic vulnerability scanning, .NET 10 enhances Blazor's appeal for mission-critical enterprise applications. These advancements position Blazor not just as a competitor to JavaScript frameworks but as a first-class, enterprise-ready platform for building secure, scalable, and high-performance web applications.

Today, Blazor stands as a mature and versatile framework that lets developers build interactive web interfaces entirely in C#, share code across client and server, and integrate seamlessly with cloud services such as Azure OpenAI. Its journey from a simple experimental demo to a fully supported part of the .NET ecosystem illustrates Microsoft's commitment to unifying web development under a single, powerful language and runtime. For organizations seeking to modernize their web solutions while maximizing productivity and leveraging existing .NET skills, Blazor's growth story demonstrates that it is no longer an alternative experiment but a proven path to building the next generation of enterprise applications.

Blazor Evolution Timeline

- **2017**: Steve Sanderson's prototype introduced WebAssembly-based .NET in the browser.
- **2018**: First public preview announced at Build.

- **2019**: Blazor Server released with .NET Core 3.0.
- **2020**: Blazor WebAssembly GA with .NET 5.
- **2021**: Integrated into unified .NET 6/8 LTS platform.

.NET 10 Highlights: AOT and WebAssembly Improvements

The release of .NET 10 represents a major milestone for developers working with Blazor, marking a significant evolution in speed, security, and developer productivity. Each previous iteration of .NET has refined the framework's capabilities, but .NET 10 includes updates aimed at improving startup behavior and stronger security across the stack.

ML

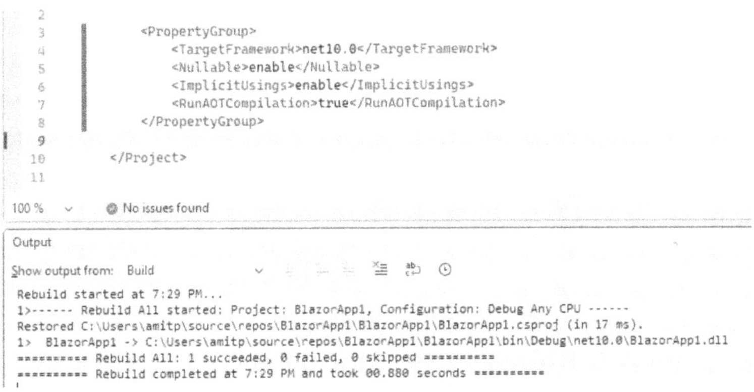

One of the most influential improvements is the introduction of Ahead-of-Time (AOT) compilation as a first-class feature for Blazor WebAssembly. Earlier versions of Blazor WebAssembly, from the original 3.2 release through .NET 7, depended on runtime IL interpretation rather than Ahead-of-Time compilation, resulting in JIT-like execution inside the browser, meaning that the application's intermediate language code was converted to native instructions only after it had been downloaded to the browser. This process added noticeable startup delays, particularly for large or complex applications. .NET 10 includes the capability to precompile assemblies into optimized WebAssembly binaries, which can be performed during the build process, allowing the browser to run native instructions immediately. AOT delivers faster runtime performance, but it typically requires a larger initial memory footprint because the browser must load precompiled WebAssembly binaries at startup. Combined with enhanced IL trimming, which automatically removes unused code, AOT helps ensure that production builds are as lean and efficient as possible.

WebAssembly threads bring multithreading capabilities to Blazor applications, further improving performance in scenarios that benefit from parallel execution. Through support for WebAssembly threads, compute-intensive tasks such as data analytics, image manipulation, or advanced mathematical processing can now run on separate worker threads without blocking the user interface. This enables developers to take full advantage of multi-core processors, allowing heavy background work to proceed smoothly while maintaining an interactive front end. Another related feature is the addition of SIMD (single instruction, multiple data) capabilities, which allow the runtime to perform operations on multiple pieces of data simultaneously. In workloads such as large dataset processing, scientific computations, or on-device machine learning, SIMD may offer improvements by enabling more efficient parallel operations.

C#

```
await Task.Run(() =>
{
    Parallel.For(0, 1_000_000, i =>
    {
        // Heavy CPU-bound work
    });
});
```

Beyond raw speed, .NET 10 places a strong emphasis on developer productivity. Hot Reload, which allows developers to apply code changes to a running application without restarting it, has been refined for greater reliability and faster feedback loops. This capability dramatically shortens development cycles, enabling rapid experimentation and iteration. The accompanying tooling in Visual Studio and Visual Studio Code has also matured, offering improved debugging, more accurate IntelliSense suggestions, and clearer diagnostics. These enhancements provide a smoother, more unified experience across Windows, macOS, and Linux, ensuring that teams can work efficiently regardless of their operating system of choice.

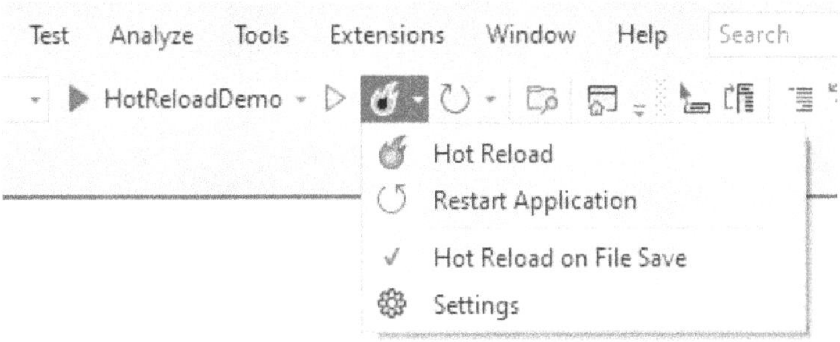

Figure 1-2. *Hot Reload Feature*

Security receives equal attention in .NET 10. The framework now enforces stronger default encryption protocols, including widespread adoption of TLS 1.3, which safeguards data in transit using modern cryptographic standards. The NuGet ecosystem benefits from improved package signing and integrated vulnerability scanning, helping teams identify outdated or risky dependencies before they reach production. For enterprises that manage sensitive data—such as financial services, healthcare providers, or government agencies—these measures reduce the risk of supply chain attacks and simplify compliance with regulations like GDPR and HIPAA.

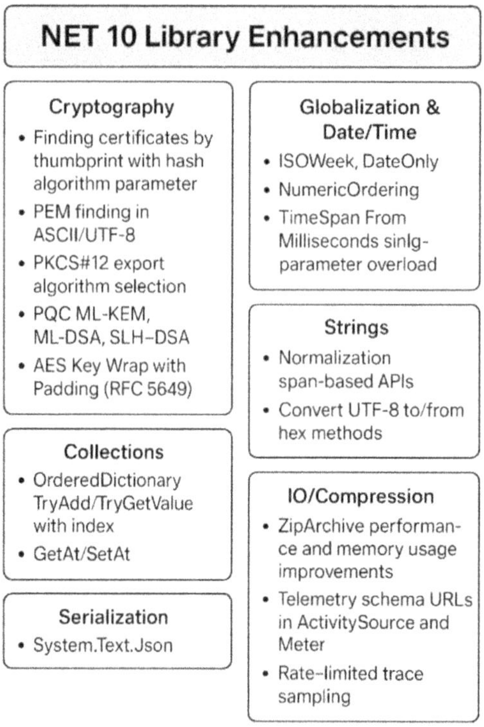

Figure 1-3. *.NET 10 Libraries Enhancement*

Configuration and secrets management have also been strengthened. Integration with Azure Key Vault and other secure storage mechanisms is more seamless than ever, allowing developers to keep API keys, database connection strings, and other sensitive credentials out of source control. This approach aligns with Zero-Trust security principles and makes it easier to rotate or revoke credentials without code changes. The result is a safer deployment pipeline and a reduced risk of accidental exposure of critical information.

Cloud-native deployment scenarios gain benefits from .NET 10. The runtime and its associated container images have been optimized for smaller size and faster cold starts, which is especially valuable when running Blazor applications on platforms such as Azure Kubernetes Service or Azure App Service. Enhanced garbage collection and memory management further improve stability and scalability, which is crucial for Blazor Server applications that may need to maintain thousands of concurrent SignalR connections over long periods of time.

The hosting model introduced in earlier versions of .NET has been refined to simplify application startup. Minimal hosting APIs allow developers to configure services, middleware, and routing with less boilerplate, producing cleaner and more maintainable code bases. Even with these streamlined patterns, developers retain the flexibility to incorporate advanced features such as dependency injection, authentication, and cloud service integrations without added complexity. The improved interoperability with JavaScript also stands out. Although Blazor allows developers to stay in C# for most tasks, there are occasions where a specialized JavaScript library is needed. .NET 10 reduces the overhead of JavaScript interop calls and makes communication between C# and JavaScript more efficient, ensuring that mixed-technology applications remain responsive.

These enhancements have practical implications for integrating advanced capabilities like Azure OpenAI. Faster client-side performance means that Blazor applications can deliver real-time AI experiences—such as intelligent chat interfaces or natural language search—without frustrating delays, even when complex language model queries run in the background. Strengthened security features ensure that the API keys and tokens used to access Azure OpenAI remain protected. WASM threads and SIMD offer the potential to accelerate lightweight preprocessing tasks, including filtering, formatting, and simple numerical transformations, prior to forwarding data to cloud services.

Taken together, the improvements in .NET 10 make Blazor an even more compelling choice for building sophisticated, enterprise-grade web applications. Ahead-of-Time compilation can accelerate execution once the application is running, even though the generated WebAssembly binaries are usually larger, while WebAssembly threads and SIMD empower high-performance computing directly in the browser. Developers benefit from faster iteration through Hot Reload and richer tooling support, and organizations gain confidence from the framework's stronger security posture and streamlined secrets management. For teams aiming to combine the flexibility of web development with the power of cloud-hosted AI, .NET 10 provides a foundation that is not only faster and more secure but also easier to maintain and scale.

In essence, .NET 10 is more than a routine update: it is a strategic enabler for modern Blazor applications. By uniting performance gains, developer productivity, and enterprise-grade security, it positions Blazor as a first-choice framework for businesses that require cutting-edge capabilities and seamless integration with services like Azure OpenAI. These advancements ensure that applications built today will remain performant, secure, and maintainable well into the future, giving organizations the confidence to invest in Blazor as the core of their web development strategy.

Why Blazor Is Enterprise Ready

Blazor has matured from an experimental web framework into a robust, enterprise-grade platform capable of powering mission-critical applications. Its ability to let developers build interactive client-side web interfaces entirely in C# without the need for JavaScript as the primary language makes it especially attractive to organizations that already invest heavily in the Microsoft ecosystem. When considering enterprise adoption, decision-makers look for a combination of stability, scalability, security, and a productive developer experience. Blazor now delivers convincingly on all these fronts, particularly when paired with .NET 10 and modern cloud infrastructure such as Azure.

A key advantage of Blazor in enterprise scenarios is the unified technology stack. Large organizations often struggle with maintaining separate teams for front-end JavaScript frameworks and back-end .NET services. Blazor eliminates this divide by enabling full-stack development in a single language and runtime. This not only streamlines hiring and training but also encourages code sharing between client and server, leading to fewer bugs and faster development cycles. For example, validation logic, data models, and even certain business rules can be written once and reused across the entire application. This reduction in duplication lowers maintenance costs and helps keep large code bases consistent.

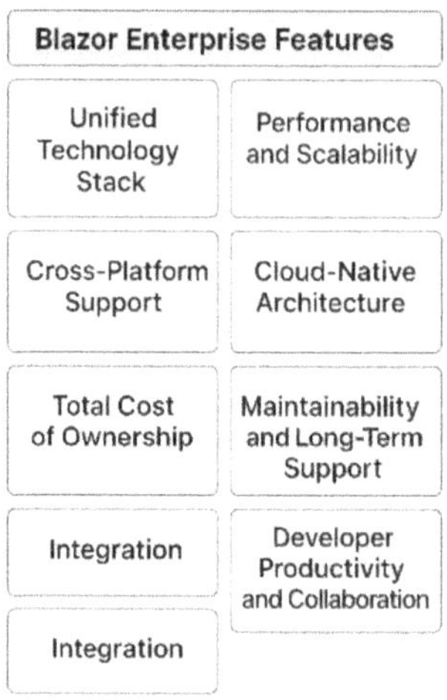

Figure 1-4. *Blazor for Enterprise Use*

Enterprises also demand a high degree of flexibility in deployment models, and Blazor offers multiple approaches to meet different architectural needs [1]. Blazor Server runs on the server side and communicates with the browser over a real-time SignalR connection. This model allows for very thin clients and easy integration with existing .NET back-end systems, making it ideal for internal business tools, dashboards, and line-of-business applications where reliable connectivity is the norm. On the other hand, Blazor WebAssembly runs client-side in the browser using WebAssembly, enabling fully offline scenarios and reducing server load, perfect for customer-facing apps that must function with intermittent connectivity. Enterprises can even blend the two, adopting a hybrid strategy where certain modules run server-side while others execute in the browser, providing fine-grained control over performance and resource utilization.

Performance and scalability are critical for enterprise adoption, and the features introduced in .NET 10 address these requirements directly. Ahead-of-Time (AOT) compilation dramatically improves startup speed and increases payload size for WebAssembly deployments. WebAssembly threads and SIMD instructions allow for parallel computation and efficient data processing, ensuring that even complex applications remain responsive under heavy user loads. On the server side, improved garbage collection and asynchronous APIs enable Blazor Server apps to scale to thousands of concurrent connections with predictable resource usage. These enhancements give enterprises confidence that Blazor can handle everything from small departmental tools to global customer portals.

Security is another decisive factor for large organizations, and Blazor benefits from the **comprehensive security infrastructure of the .NET platform**. Built-in support for strong encryption protocols such as TLS 1.3, integrated identity management via ASP. NET Core Identity, and smooth interoperability with Azure Active Directory make it easier to implement enterprise-grade authentication and authorization. Developers can use role-based or policy-based security to protect sensitive pages and APIs, while improved secrets management, integrating seamlessly with Azure Key Vault, ensures that credentials and tokens never reside in source code or configuration files. Because security updates to .NET automatically apply to Blazor applications, enterprises also benefit from Microsoft's ongoing investment in patching vulnerabilities and providing long-term support releases.

Modern enterprises increasingly rely on **cloud-native architecture**, and Blazor aligns naturally with this trend. Applications can be containerized and deployed to Azure Kubernetes Service, Azure App Service, or other cloud platforms with minimal configuration. The leaner container images and faster cold-start times in .NET 10 make horizontal scaling more efficient and cost-effective. Furthermore, Blazor integrates smoothly with other Azure services that enterprises commonly adopt, including Azure SQL Database, Cosmos DB, Event Grid, and Azure Functions. When paired with Azure OpenAI, organizations can build sophisticated AI-driven features, such as intelligent search, natural language chatbots, and predictive analytics, directly into their Blazor applications, while keeping data secure and compliant with corporate governance requirements.

Maintainability and long-term support are equally important in enterprise contexts, where applications often remain in production for many years. Microsoft provides clear road maps and extended support lifecycles for .NET releases, giving organizations the assurance that Blazor will be maintained and compatible with future .NET versions. The strong typing and mature tooling of C# help teams avoid many common runtime errors, while advanced debugging tools, Hot Reload, and integrated testing frameworks reduce the cost of ongoing maintenance. Enterprises benefit from a rich ecosystem of NuGet packages, third-party component libraries, and community resources that further accelerate development and ensure that applications remain adaptable as business needs evolve.

Another compelling factor is **developer productivity and team collaboration**. By leveraging familiar tools such as Visual Studio, Visual Studio Code, and GitHub Actions, development teams can implement continuous integration and delivery pipelines with ease. Hot Reload allows developers to see UI and logic changes instantly, reducing context switching and increasing iteration speed. The unified .NET ecosystem supports strong typing and comprehensive refactoring tools, enabling large, distributed teams to work on complex applications without fear of breaking functionality. This productivity translates directly into faster time-to-market and lower overall development costs, both of which are crucial for competitive enterprises.

Blazor also excels in **user experience and modern interface design**. The component-based architecture encourages reusable UI elements, consistent styling, and dynamic data binding, enabling developers to build rich, interactive web interfaces that rival those of popular JavaScript frameworks. Advanced routing capabilities allow for sophisticated single-page applications, while integration with CSS frameworks and responsive design tools ensures that applications work seamlessly across desktops, tablets, and mobile devices. Enterprises can therefore deliver a polished, consumer-grade experience to customers and employees alike, reinforcing brand reputation and improving user satisfaction.

From an **integration perspective**, Blazor supports multiple communication patterns, including REST APIs, SignalR, and gRPC-Web. While browsers cannot use full gRPC due to protocol limitations, gRPC-Web offers a compatible alternative for calling gRPC-based back-end services [2]. Enterprises rarely operate in green-field environments; they often need to integrate new applications with existing ERP, CRM, or supply chain systems. Blazor's seamless interoperability with JavaScript also allows organizations to leverage existing JavaScript libraries or UI widgets when required, protecting prior investments and easing gradual migration strategies.

C#

```
// Add authentication and authorization
builder.Services.AddAuthentication(CookieAuthenticationDefaults.AuthenticationScheme)
    .AddCookie(options =>
    {
        options.LoginPath = "/Account/Login";
    });

builder.Services.AddAuthorization(options =>
{
    options.AddPolicy("AdminOnly", policy =>
        policy.RequireRole("Admin"));
});
// Add Blazor Server services
builder.Services.AddRazorPages();
builder.Services.AddServerSideBlazor();
var app = builder.Build();
// Middleware pipeline
if (!app.Environment.IsDevelopment())
{
    app.UseExceptionHandler("/Error");
    app.UseHsts();
}
app.UseHttpsRedirection();
app.UseStaticFiles();
app.UseRouting();
app.UseAuthentication();
app.UseAuthorization();
app.MapBlazorHub();
app.MapFallbackToPage("/_Host");
app.Run();
```

When evaluating the total cost of ownership, many organizations find that **Blazor offers compelling economics**. By enabling full-stack C# development, it reduces the need to maintain separate front-end and back-end skill sets, lowering recruitment and training expenses. The simplified deployment pipeline and the ability to share code across tiers mean less duplication and fewer maintenance headaches. Additionally, because Blazor apps can run in standard web browsers without plug-ins, organizations avoid the licensing fees and distribution challenges associated with proprietary client technologies.

The growing adoption of **open standards and cross-platform support** further cements Blazor's place in the enterprise landscape. Applications built with Blazor can run on Windows, macOS, and Linux servers, and WebAssembly ensures compatibility across all major browsers [3]. This cross-platform nature allows enterprises to deploy the same application across diverse infrastructures—on-premises, in the cloud, or in hybrid environments, without rewriting core logic. Such flexibility is particularly valuable for multinational corporations with heterogeneous IT ecosystems.

Ultimately, Blazor has proven that it is ready for enterprise use by combining performance, security, maintainability, and developer efficiency within a single cohesive framework. The advancements introduced in .NET 10, ranging from Ahead-of-Time compilation to improved containerization and enhanced security defaults, amplify these strengths and make Blazor an even more compelling choice. Organizations can confidently build mission-critical systems knowing that the platform is backed by Microsoft's long-term support and an active global community. Whether the goal is to create internal business tools, customer-facing portals, or AI-enhanced applications integrated with Azure OpenAI, Blazor provides a modern, future-proof foundation that aligns with enterprise demands for scalability, compliance, and rapid innovation.

Blazor has rapidly transformed from an experimental framework into a mature, enterprise-grade platform for building rich web applications with C#. Its evolution mirrors the broader growth of the .NET ecosystem, culminating in the powerful features introduced with .NET 10. Today, Blazor provides developers with a modern, high-performance, and secure foundation for creating everything from small internal tools to large, customer-facing enterprise systems [4]. It began as a bold experiment in 2018, when Microsoft set out to answer a simple but ambitious question: Could developers write full-stack web applications entirely in C#, without relying heavily on JavaScript? Early versions relied on a server-centric approach where the application logic ran on the server and communicated with the browser through a persistent SignalR connection. This allowed developers to reuse .NET skills for web development, but required a constant network connection and could suffer from latency under heavy load.

The next major leap came with Blazor WebAssembly, which enabled true client-side execution by compiling C# code into WebAssembly (WASM). This breakthrough meant developers could ship a single-page application that ran entirely in the browser, eliminating the need for a constant server connection. Users benefited from faster interactions and offline capabilities, while developers enjoyed the productivity of the

.NET ecosystem and the ability to share code between client and server. Over time, both hosting models matured. Server-side Blazor gained better scalability through efficient SignalR management and smarter state handling, while WebAssembly support improved with smaller download sizes, better debugging, and richer JavaScript interoperability. Microsoft also introduced unified project templates, component libraries, and deeper Azure integration, which helped Blazor become a first-class citizen in the .NET world and a serious contender for enterprise projects.

By the time .NET 6 and .NET 7 were released, Blazor was already powering production workloads in finance, healthcare, government, and ecommerce. Enterprises valued its ability to reuse existing C# skills, its strong typing and tooling, and its tight integration with established .NET investments. Yet developers continued to ask for faster startup times, improved runtime performance, and stronger security goals that directly influenced the road map for .NET 10. The release of .NET 10 represents a major milestone for Blazor, delivering dramatic improvements in speed, developer productivity, and security. Perhaps the most impactful change is the introduction of Ahead-of-Time (AOT) compilation as a first-class feature for Blazor WebAssembly. In earlier versions, applications were delivered as Intermediate Language code and compiled to machine instructions in the browser at runtime. This just-in-time process caused noticeable startup delays, particularly for large or complex apps. With AOT, developers can precompile assemblies into optimized WebAssembly binaries before deployment, allowing the browser to run native instructions immediately after the application loads. Although AOT increases download size and initial memory usage, it provides more predictable runtime performance once the application is running. Complementing AOT is enhanced IL trimming, which removes unused code during the build process so that production builds are smaller and more efficient.

Performance gains continue with WebAssembly multithreading, which lets Blazor applications run compute-intensive tasks—such as image processing, data analysis, or complex calculations on separate worker threads, fully exploiting multi-core processors. Coupled with new SIMD (single instruction, multiple data) capabilities, these changes allow the runtime to process multiple pieces of data simultaneously, an advantage for applications handling large datasets, scientific computations, or on-device machine learning. Developer productivity also benefits from .NET 10. Hot Reload has been refined to let developers apply code changes to a running application without restarting it, drastically shortening feedback loops and encouraging rapid iteration. Visual Studio and Visual Studio Code provide improved IntelliSense, debugging, and diagnostics, while cross-platform consistency ensures a smooth workflow on Windows, macOS, and Linux alike.

.NET adopts modern TLS defaults, leveraging up-to-date encryption protocols to maintain strong protections for data transmitted over the network. The NuGet ecosystem gains integrated vulnerability scanning and improved package signing to guard against supply chain attacks. These measures simplify compliance with regulations like GDPR and HIPAA and give enterprises greater confidence in the integrity of their dependencies. Secrets management also sees notable improvements. Integration with Azure Key Vault and other secure storage providers is more seamless, allowing developers to keep API keys and database connection strings out of source control. This aligns with Zero-Trust principles and makes rotating or revoking credentials easier without code changes.

Cloud-native scenarios also benefit from ongoing improvements to container image size and startup efficiency. Much of this work began in .NET 8 and .NET 9, with .NET 10 providing further refinements rather than major new features. They are especially valuable for applications running on Azure Kubernetes Service, Azure App Service, or other container platforms. Memory management and garbage collection have been tuned to handle thousands of concurrent SignalR connections in Blazor Server scenarios, ensuring stability and scalability under enterprise workloads. The minimal hosting model introduced in recent .NET versions simplifies application startup and configuration. Developers can implement advanced features such as dependency injection, authentication, and custom middleware with less boilerplate code, leading to cleaner, more maintainable solutions. Improved JavaScript interoperability reduces overhead and makes communication between C# and JavaScript more efficient, so mixed-technology applications remain responsive and easy to extend.

All of these advances translate directly into enterprise value. Thanks to AOT compilation, IL trimming, multithreaded WebAssembly, and SIMD balanced against the increased payload size that comes with AOT, Blazor applications start faster and handle complex computations directly in the browser, enabling rich, interactive experiences such as real-time dashboards or on-device AI preprocessing. Built-in TLS 1.3 support, secure package signing, and vulnerability scanning provide a hardened foundation, while seamless integration with Azure Key Vault ensures sensitive secrets remain protected—an essential requirement for industries like healthcare, finance, and government. The ability to share C# code across client and server reduces duplication and eases long-term maintenance, while Hot Reload and improved tooling speed up development cycles. When JavaScript is needed, developers can easily interoperate with existing libraries without leaving the strongly typed .NET environment.

Blazor's synergy with Azure services further strengthens its enterprise appeal. Features such as Azure Active Directory authentication, Azure Functions, and Azure OpenAI integrate smoothly with Blazor, allowing developers to build intelligent, cloud-connected applications with minimal friction. For example, a Blazor front end can securely call Azure OpenAI endpoints to power natural language search, generate real-time reports, or provide conversational interfaces, while API keys remain safely stored in Azure Key Vault. Microsoft's long-term support for .NET gives enterprises confidence that their applications will remain stable and supported for years, and the vibrant community ensures ongoing innovation, extensive documentation, and a wide range of libraries.

Summary

Modern Blazor, strengthened by the innovations of .NET 10, represents a powerful convergence of performance, security, and productivity. From its origins as an ambitious experiment in client-side C#, it has grown into a robust, enterprise-ready framework capable of delivering sophisticated, high-performance web applications. Ahead-of-Time compilation, WebAssembly multithreading, enhanced tooling, and fortified security measures position Blazor as a top choice for organizations seeking to build scalable, future-proof solutions. For development teams, this means the ability to create responsive, interactive applications with a familiar language and a unified technology stack. For enterprises, it means confidence that those applications will be fast, secure, maintainable, and ready to integrate with cutting-edge cloud services such as Azure OpenAI. As the demands of modern web development continue to grow, Blazor and .NET 10 provide a foundation that is not only current but forward-looking, equipping businesses to meet the challenges of today and the opportunities of tomorrow.

CHAPTER 2

.NET 10 Enhancements for Blazor

Deep Dive into Minimal APIs

The release of .NET 10 brings a renewed focus on making the development experience more concise, maintainable, and approachable, and the centerpiece of this effort for Blazor developers is the refinement of Minimal APIs. In earlier versions of ASP.NET Core, creating web endpoints typically required multiple files, extensive boilerplate code, and complex configuration steps. Developers typically defined controllers, applied routing attributes, and configured supporting infrastructure even for simple endpoints, a model that, while powerful for larger applications due to its conventions around filters, versioning, and validation, introduced more structure than necessary for basic scenarios. Although this traditional model offered flexibility and powerful features, it often felt heavy, especially for teams building microservices or small services to complement their Blazor front ends.

Minimal APIs cut through this complexity by allowing developers to define endpoints using a straightforward, functional style. At its core, a Minimal API application begins with a single Program file in which routes, middleware, and configuration are expressed in a few readable lines. This is not merely syntactic sugar; while the new patterns simplify syntax by reducing the ceremony around routing, dependency injection, and endpoint registration, they also reflect a broader philosophical shift toward convention over configuration and toward aligning back-end development more closely with the modern, component-driven patterns used in Blazor itself. Developers can spin up an HTTP endpoint to serve data to a Blazor app without worrying about controllers, attributes, or excessive scaffolding, reducing mental overhead and accelerating iteration cycles.

A. Prasad and H. Singh, *Advanced Blazor Architecture with .NET 10 and Azure OpenAI*,
https://doi.org/10.1007/979-8-8688-2518-7_2

For Blazor developers, the implications of this are profound. A Blazor application, whether using WebAssembly or Server hosting, often needs lightweight API endpoints for tasks like fetching user profile data, saving form submissions, or retrieving product lists. With Minimal APIs, those endpoints can be defined inline next to the app's startup logic, reducing the separation between back-end and front-end teams. A single developer can quickly create a complete full-stack feature in one sitting, moving seamlessly from Blazor's Razor components to Minimal API endpoints. This alignment of client and server fosters a unified development workflow in which shared models, validation logic, and dependency injection can flow smoothly between layers. Developers new to full-stack .NET often benefit from seeing how this sharing works at the project and compilation level. Common patterns include

1. **Shared Class Libraries**

   - A dedicated shared project (e.g., MyApp.Shared) contains data models, DTOs, validation attributes, enums, and utility classes.
   - Both the Blazor client and the ASP.NET Core server reference this library.
   - When compiled, both layers use the same .NET types, eliminating duplication and serialization mismatches.

2. **Shared Validation Logic**

   - Validation attributes (e.g., [Required], [EmailAddress], custom ValidationAttribute classes) live in the shared project.
   - The Blazor UI can perform client-side validation using the same rules the server enforces, ensuring consistent business logic across tiers.

3. **Shared Dependency Injection Contracts**

   - Interfaces for services (e.g., IWeatherService, IProductRepository) are defined in the shared project.
   - The server provides the concrete implementation.
   - The client consumes the interface, allowing tools like gRPC-Web, REST clients, or SignalR to bind seamlessly.

4. **Shared API Shapes and Serialization**

    - Record types or DTO classes are shared so the client and server agree on
    - Property names
    - Types
    - Serialization schema
    - This reduces API contract drift, a common source of bugs in multi-language stacks.

5. **Common Build and Tooling Environment**

    - Both layers use the same .NET SDK, project structure, analyzers, logging patterns, and configuration mechanisms.
    - Developers move between front-end and back-end code without context switching to a different language or ecosystem.

Minimal APIs in .NET 10 build on the foundation introduced in .NET 6 and .NET 7. While the core programming model is not new, .NET 10 refines the dependency injection experience through features such as source-generated service activation, improved analyzers, and more predictable startup behavior across hosting scenarios which further benefits Blazor applications. Services like database contexts, logging, and caching can be registered and consumed in a concise manner, eliminating the verbose startup classes of the past. When building microservices to support a large Blazor-based enterprise portal, this reduction in boilerplate helps teams maintain clarity across dozens of services. Each microservice can remain small, self-contained, and easy to understand, which is crucial in large organizations where different teams own different slices of the architecture.

The benefits extend beyond development speed to runtime performance and scalability. The Minimal API pipeline is lightweight by design, with fewer abstractions between incoming HTTP requests and the code that handles them. These optimizations can improve memory efficiency and request throughput, but the degree of improvement varies based on the middleware pipeline and how the application is configured, which directly improves the responsiveness of Blazor apps that rely on these endpoints for dynamic data. When paired with modern cloud infrastructure such as Azure App Service or Kubernetes, Minimal API services can scale efficiently, supporting high-traffic scenarios with predictable resource consumption.

Another key advantage is how naturally Minimal APIs integrate with modern security practices. In enterprise environments, APIs must be secured using techniques such as JWT-based authentication, OAuth2, or Azure Active Directory. .NET 10's Minimal APIs include first-class support for authentication and authorization middleware, enabling developers to protect endpoints with just a few lines of configuration. For a Blazor application that must comply with stringent corporate or regulatory standards, this simplicity lowers the risk of misconfiguration while keeping security robust.

Minimal APIs also enhance the developer experience when testing and documenting services. They work seamlessly with tools like Swashbuckle to generate OpenAPI specifications, making it easy to produce interactive API documentation for front-end developers or external partners. Unit testing and integration testing benefit as well, since endpoints are defined as straightforward methods that can be invoked directly without a heavy controller infrastructure. For teams practicing continuous integration and continuous delivery (CI/CD), this reduces the friction in writing automated tests, which is critical for maintaining quality as applications grow.

Notably, the adoption of Minimal APIs does not mean abandoning the rich ecosystem of ASP.NET Core. Developers can mix and match; complex projects can still use controllers and MVC patterns alongside Minimal APIs. This hybrid approach is valuable in real-world Blazor applications where some modules, perhaps legacy systems or highly complex domains, demand the structure of controllers, while others thrive with the agility of Minimal APIs. .NET 10's tooling makes it easy to choose the right pattern for each part of an application without compromise.

From an architectural perspective, Minimal APIs empower teams to embrace microservices and serverless computing. A Blazor front end might consume dozens of specialized endpoints distributed across microservices or Azure Functions. The lightweight nature of Minimal APIs fits perfectly with containerized deployments, allowing developers to spin up small, focused services that start quickly and scale horizontally. This aligns with the cloud-native strategies that many enterprises are adopting, where agility, cost efficiency, and resilience are paramount.

C#

```
// Program.cs

var builder = WebApplication.CreateBuilder(args);
var app = builder.Build();

// -------------------- ENDPOINTS --------------------

// Health check endpoint (useful for monitoring tools, e.g. Kubernetes, load balancers).
app.MapGet("/api/health", () => Results.Ok(new { status = "Healthy", timestamp = DateTime.UtcNow }));

// Greeting endpoint (example of using a route parameter).
// Example: GET /api/users/Alex → "Welcome, Alex!"
app.MapGet("/api/users/{username}", (string username) =>
    Results.Ok(new { message = $"Welcome, {username}!" }));

// Data submission endpoint (simulate saving posted JSON or text data).
// Example: POST /api/messages with body "Hello World!" → returns confirmation.
app.MapPost("/api/messages", async (HttpContext context) =>
{
    using var reader = new StreamReader(context.Request.Body);
    var body = await reader.ReadToEndAsync();
    return Results.Ok(new { received = body, length = body.Length });
});

// -------------------- RUN APP --------------------
app.Run();
```

Minimal API Sample Code

For organizations investing in AI and advanced analytics, particularly those integrating Azure OpenAI capabilities with Blazor Minimal APIs, provide an ideal gateway. AI-driven features often require rapid prototyping of endpoints that handle natural language queries, deliver predictive results, or manage real-time chat interactions. With Minimal APIs, developers can experiment quickly, deploying new services that connect Blazor's interactive components with AI back ends without weeks of setup or configuration.

The broader developer ecosystem also benefits. Teams that include junior developers or those new to the .NET stack can onboard more quickly, thanks to the intuitive syntax and reduced conceptual overhead of Minimal APIs. This lowers training costs and accelerates team ramp-up, which is critical in large enterprises where staffing needs evolve rapidly. By simplifying the entry point to back-end development, .NET 10 ensures that more developers can contribute effectively to Blazor projects from day one.

In terms of long-term maintainability, Minimal APIs shine because of their explicitness and readability. Routes, parameters, and handlers are declared in a single, easily scanned location. This transparency makes it simpler to review code during audits, identify potential security issues, and understand application flow months or years after initial development. Enterprises with strict compliance requirements appreciate this clarity, as it simplifies code reviews and reduces the likelihood of hidden vulnerabilities.

Ultimately, the enhancements to Minimal APIs in .NET 10 represent more than just syntactic convenience. They embody a strategic vision of unifying front-end and back-end development around a lean, modern architecture. For Blazor developers, this means that building, securing, and scaling data services is faster and less error-prone, enabling them to focus on delivering rich, interactive user experiences. Whether powering internal dashboards, global ecommerce platforms, or AI-driven customer portals, the combination of Blazor and Minimal APIs offers a compelling, future-proof approach that balances agility with enterprise-grade robustness.

Ahead-of-Time Compilation and Performance Improvements

Ahead-of-Time (AOT) compilation plays a significant role in optimizing modern .NET applications. Building on the capabilities introduced in .NET 7 and enhanced in .NET 8, .NET 10 delivers incremental runtime and tooling improvements that further strengthen AOT workflows for Blazor applications. Traditionally, .NET applications rely on Just-in-Time (JIT) compilation: when a .NET app starts, its Intermediate Language (IL) code is compiled into machine code on the fly, right when the method is first executed. While this provides flexibility and enables dynamic scenarios such as runtime code generation or reflection, it introduces a delay at startup because the runtime must perform compilation tasks before code can run. This overhead can be noticeable in client-side BlazorWebAssembly applications where the entire application downloads to the browser and executes inside a constrained environment. Every extra millisecond of startup time can affect user experience, especially on mobile devices or networks with high latency. Ahead-of-Time compilation offers a powerful alternative by shifting that compilation step to build time, producing native machine code ahead of execution and dramatically reducing or eliminating runtime compilation costs.

The core principle of AOT is deceptively simple: instead of packaging IL and relying on the JIT compiler to convert IL into CPU instructions at runtime, the application is compiled to platform-specific binary code before deployment. This seemingly small change has a cascade of benefits for Blazor developers. First, startup performance improves significantly because there is little or no JIT work to perform when the application begins. This is critical for WebAssembly (WASM), where the .NET runtime itself is running inside a browser sandbox. In .NET 10, the AOT toolchain has been refined to produce smaller, faster WebAssembly modules that can be delivered to users more quickly and parsed more efficiently by the browser. By generating optimized machine code in advance, .NET 10 minimizes the warm-up time and allows the Blazor application to render interactive components with remarkable speed almost immediately after download.

Performance gains from AOT are not limited to startup. Because the compiler can analyze the entire application at build time, it can apply aggressive optimizations that are difficult or impossible for a JIT compiler working under strict runtime constraints. For example, the AOT compiler can perform global inlining of methods, dead-code elimination, and advanced link-time optimizations. It can tailor the generated code to the target architecture, leveraging specific CPU instruction sets like AVX2 or ARM64 vector instructions without worrying about cross-platform compatibility, because the build pipeline can produce distinct binaries for each platform. This means that critical hot paths in Blazor applications—such as rendering logic, data binding, and complex computations—benefit from finely tuned machine instructions that execute more efficiently than their JIT-compiled counterparts.

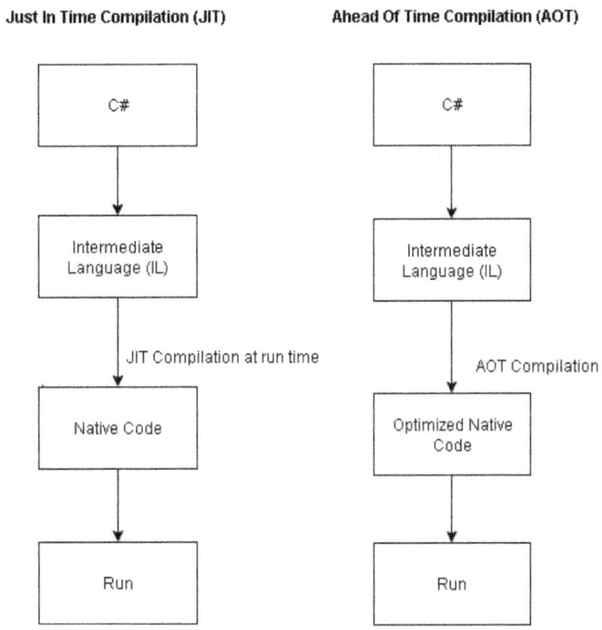

Figure 2-1. *Comparison of Just-in-Time vs. Ahead-of-Time Compilation Pipelines*

JIT	AOT/NativeAOT
Compilation Timing (Runtime vs. Build time)	
When your app runs for the first time, the Just-In-Time (JIT) compiler kicks in and compiles code on demand. That means the very first request is slower, but once warmed up, it flies.	Ahead-of-Time (AOT) compilation pre-builds everything into native code before you even start the app. The result: lightning-fast startup and predictable performance.
Startup Speed (Slow warm-up vs. Instant)	
The runtime loads Intermediate Language (IL) assemblies and compiles them as needed. It's flexible and adaptive; the JIT can tune the code based on your actual workload and CPU.	AOT compilation can help reduce runtime memory pressure because the runtime no longer needs to allocate resources for JIT compilation or related metadata structures.
Compatibility (High flexibility vs. Restricted reflection)	
You'll see a slightly larger memory footprint during startup, since the runtime needs the JIT compiler and metadata in memory. But it also means you get dynamic optimizations like tiered JIT and profile-guided tuning.	AOT apps typically use less memory and have a smaller runtime footprint. Because the code is pre-optimized, there's no warm-up phase; what you ship is exactly what runs.
Use Case (Dev/Server vs. Cloud/Wasm)	
Ideal for development and iterative builds. You can use reflection, dynamic code generation, and Hot Reload without worrying about linker restrictions.	Best for production, especially in cloud or edge scenarios, where startup time and memory efficiency matter most. Some reflection or dynamic features may need linker hints to keep them alive.
Errors in dynamic paths may only appear when the app runs those paths.	AOT catches many issues at build time, but reflection-based features can still fail at runtime. JSON serialization often requires System.Text.Json source generation, making source generators essential for reliable AOT applications.

(*continued*)

JIT	AOT/NativeAOT
Common commands: dotnet run, or dotnet publish -c Release -p:PublishReadyToRun=true for partial precompilation.	Common commands include dotnet publish -c Release -r linux-x64 -p:PublishAot=true -p: StripSymbols=true for server-side or containerized workloads. For Blazor WebAssembly, AOT is typically enabled in the project file rather than through RID-specific CLI commands.
Output: compiled DLLs plus the dotnet host portable but requires the runtime.	Output: a self-contained native EXE, no dotnet runtime needed. Great for containers and standalone tools.
Best when the app runs long enough to warm up and stay hot—like web servers or long-lived background services.	Best for workloads needing instant start and predictable performance—like microservices, CLIs, and serverless functions.

JIT vs. AOT in .NET 10: Performance, Deployment, and Development Trade-Offs

Memory efficiency is another area where AOT shines. JIT compilation requires memory overhead to store generated code and associated metadata during execution. By contrast, an AOT-compiled application arrives at runtime with all necessary machine code embedded, reducing the dynamic memory footprint. This lower memory usage is especially valuable in WebAssembly, where the runtime operates within a fixed memory boundary enforced by the browser. Devices with limited RAM, such as older smartphones or low-end tablets, can run complex Blazor applications more comfortably when memory pressure is reduced. Additionally, the smaller memory footprint contributes indirectly to performance by decreasing garbage collection frequency and enabling more predictable latency, which translates into smoother user interfaces.

Security considerations also favor AOT compilation. Because the final deployed artifact contains native code rather than IL, reverse engineering becomes more difficult. IL can be decompiled relatively easily with widely available tools, exposing business logic or proprietary algorithms. Native code, while not impossible to analyze, raises the bar for potential attackers. Moreover, eliminating JIT compilation reduces the runtime attack surface, as there is no need for components that dynamically generate and execute code. Fewer moving parts at runtime mean fewer potential vulnerabilities, aligning well with enterprise security policies that demand robust defense against code injection and runtime tampering.

The improvements in .NET 10's AOT pipeline build on years of incremental progress. Earlier versions of Blazor WebAssembly introduced experimental AOT modes, but they required long build times and produced relatively large binaries, sometimes offsetting performance gains with heavier network payloads. .NET 10 addresses these concerns with a more efficient crossgen2 compiler and a refined linker that performs better tree-shaking to remove unused code paths. As a result, developers can now expect smaller download sizes even when AOT is enabled. The tooling has also matured to integrate seamlessly with Visual Studio and the .NET CLI, allowing developers to enable AOT with a simple configuration setting in the project file. This ease of use lowers the barrier to adoption and encourages teams to embrace AOT as a default for production builds.

For server-side Blazor, AOT delivers different but equally valuable benefits. While server-side Blazor does not rely on WebAssembly in the browser, it still profits from precompiled code that reduces startup latency and boosts throughput under heavy load. High-traffic web applications hosted on ASP.NET Core can handle more concurrent users when CPU cycles are not consumed by JIT compilation. Reduced latency during application warm-up is particularly important in environments that scale dynamically, such as cloud deployments using Kubernetes or Azure App Service. When new instances of a Blazor application spin up to handle spikes in demand, precompiled native binaries ensure that those instances become responsive almost immediately, leading to a more elastic and cost-effective infrastructure.

AOT in .NET 10 is complemented by a host of other performance-oriented enhancements that together create a compelling story of speed and efficiency. The runtime itself has been optimized for lower overhead in critical paths, from garbage collection improvements to more efficient thread pooling. The JIT compiler, still relevant for scenarios that require runtime flexibility, has received its own set of optimizations, ensuring that applications mixing AOT and JIT can achieve balanced performance. The base class libraries have been profiled and tuned, reducing allocations and leveraging span-based APIs to minimize copying and improve cache locality. Collectively, these runtime and tooling improvements mean that even code paths that are not themselves compiled with AOT can benefit from a faster, leaner execution environment.

One of the hallmark advantages of the .NET 10 AOT strategy is its synergy with Blazor WebAssembly. WebAssembly itself is a low-level bytecode designed for fast execution and small size, enabling near-native performance in the browser. However, running a large IL payload atop WebAssembly previously required a runtime to interpret or JIT compile .NET assemblies within the WASM sandbox, creating additional overhead. By emitting native WebAssembly instructions ahead of time, the .NET 10 AOT toolchain effectively merges the .NET compilation pipeline with the WebAssembly format, delivering pre-optimized WASM modules that the browser can instantiate directly. This eliminates the double layer of translation and allows Blazor apps to start as quickly as comparable applications written in C++ or Rust, traditionally the languages of choice for high-performance WebAssembly modules.

From a developer's perspective, adopting AOT does not require a dramatic shift in workflow. Most of the complexity is handled by the build system, which invokes the crossgen2 compiler and linker behind the scenes. Developers primarily need to decide when to enable AOT, typically for production releases, and ensure that their code avoids patterns incompatible with full Ahead-of-Time compilation. For instance, extensive use of reflection or dynamic code generation can pose challenges because the AOT compiler needs to know at build time exactly which types and methods to include. Fortunately, .NET 10 provides clear diagnostics and linker configuration options to help developers annotate code paths and preserve necessary metadata. With these tools, teams can continue using familiar Blazor component patterns while taking advantage of AOT's performance benefits.

The economic impact of these performance boosts should not be underestimated. Faster startup and execution can contribute to better user retention and higher conversion rates for consumer-facing applications, especially on slower networks or devices. In enterprise environments, more efficient CPU utilization translates directly to lower cloud hosting costs and improved scalability. When applications require less memory and fewer compute resources, organizations can serve more users with the same hardware or reduce their infrastructure footprint without sacrificing responsiveness. These advantages compound over time, delivering tangible savings and a better return on investment for projects built on the Blazor platform.

It is also important to recognize that AOT is not a one-size-fits-all solution. Some applications may prioritize rapid iteration, dynamic plug-in architectures, or heavy runtime reflection, for which JIT remains a better fit. The strength of .NET 10 lies in its flexibility: developers can choose full AOT, partial AOT (compiling only specific assemblies ahead of time), or pure JIT according to the needs of each project. This adaptability allows teams to adopt AOT incrementally, starting with performance-critical modules and expanding coverage as they optimize their code base. Over time, as the ecosystem evolves and best practices emerge, the balance between AOT and JIT will continue to shift toward the former, but the coexistence of both approaches ensures that developers are never locked into a single strategy.

Looking ahead, Ahead-of-Time compilation is more than a performance optimization; it represents a broader philosophical shift in the .NET ecosystem. By enabling developers to produce self-contained native binaries for a wide array of platforms—desktop, mobile, browser, and cloud—.NET 10 blurs the lines between traditional managed runtimes and compiled languages like C++ or Rust. This empowers Blazor to compete not just with other web frameworks but with native technologies, bringing the productivity of C# and the richness of the .NET libraries to performance-sensitive domains previously considered out of reach for managed code. Whether delivering blazing-fast single-page applications, real-time dashboards, or interactive 3D experiences, Blazor with .NET 10 and Ahead-of-Time compilation stands ready to meet the demands of modern users and enterprises alike.

Integration with Blazor Apps

Integrating .NET 10 into a Blazor application is not always a complex process. Many projects can be upgraded by adjusting project files and rebuilding, particularly if they are not adopting new runtime or hosting features. However, scenarios involving WebAssembly AOT, updated interop patterns, hosting model changes, or deeper trimming requirements may require broader architectural alignment. Large enterprise applications often benefit from reviewing the full stack to ensure consistency, while small and medium projects may migrate with minimal modifications. The new version of .NET brings an array of performance optimizations, security reinforcements, and development workflow improvements, all of which can influence how modern Blazor solutions are planned, implemented, and maintained. To realize the full value of these improvements, teams need a thoughtful strategy that begins with architectural choices and extends through testing, deployment, and ongoing operations.

A natural starting point is evaluating the hosting model. Blazor continues to support WebAssembly, Server, and Auto (hybrid) hosting models, and each model benefits differently from .NET 10's enhancements. Blazor WebAssembly can now take full advantage of Ahead-of-Time compilation and IL trimming which were introduced in earlier .NET releases; however, .NET 10 extends these capabilities with more granular trimming, smaller AOT binaries, improved startup performance, and enhanced WebAssembly multithreading. These features combine to shorten application startup times, lower memory consumption, and unlock true parallel processing in the browser, making it ideal for highly interactive or computation-heavy applications. Blazor Server applications, by contrast, experience substantial gains from the runtime's improved memory management, smaller container images, and faster cold-start times critical when sustaining thousands of SignalR connections across a distributed infrastructure. Some organizations even adopt a hybrid approach, running most of the interface in WebAssembly for responsiveness while relying on server-side components for workloads that require secure data access or heavy back-end integration. Choosing the right combination early ensures that subsequent integration work is aligned with performance and scalability goals.

Once the hosting model is set, the build pipeline becomes the next focus. .NET 10 makes AOT compilation a first-class feature, allowing developers to produce precompiled WebAssembly binaries that execute directly as native instructions in the browser. This eliminates the just-in-time compilation delays that plagued earlier versions and offers a noticeably faster initial load experience for end users. Integrating AOT requires updating project configurations, release profiles, and continuous integration scripts to support the longer compile times and to monitor output sizes. At the same time, the improved IL trimming capability automatically removes unused code paths, helping keep download packages lean. Careful testing is important here; aggressive trimming can inadvertently strip libraries or reflection-based features if not configured correctly. A disciplined build process that incorporates automated load time benchmarking ensures that the gains from AOT and trimming translate into measurable real-world performance.

.NET 10 also introduces additional APIs that facilitate working with spans, thereby helping you to reduce unnecessary allocations, as shown in the following code snippet:

```
public static class StringNormalizationExtensions
{
    // Returns the expected length of the normalized text without allocating memory
    0 references
    public static int GetNormalizedLength(this ReadOnlySpan<char> source,
        NormalizationForm normalizationForm = NormalizationForm.FormC)
    {
        return source.ToString().Normalize(normalizationForm).Length;
    }

    // Checks if the given text is already normalized
    1 reference
    public static bool IsNormalized(this ReadOnlySpan<char> source,
        NormalizationForm normalizationForm = NormalizationForm.FormC)
    {
        return source.IsNormalized(normalizationForm);
    }

    // Tries to normalize the text directly into a destination span without creating new strings
    1 reference
    public static bool TryNormalize(this ReadOnlySpan<char> source,
        Span<char> destination, out int charsWritten,
        NormalizationForm normalizationForm = NormalizationForm.FormC)
    {
        return source.TryNormalize(destination, out charsWritten, normalizationForm);
    }
}
```

```
ReadOnlySpan<char> input = "Some text".AsSpan();

// Convert to string for normalization checks
string inputString = input.ToString();

// 1) Check whether the string is already normalized (Form C is a common default).
if (!inputString.IsNormalized(NormalizationForm.FormC))
{
    // 2) Normalize the string
    string normalizedText = inputString.Normalize(NormalizationForm.FormC);

    // 3) Work with it as a span if needed
    ReadOnlySpan<char> normalized = normalizedText.AsSpan();

    // Example usage: print normalized text
    Console.WriteLine(normalizedText);
}
else
{
    Console.WriteLine("Already normalized: " + inputString);
}
```

.NET 10: Span-Based String Normalization Extensions

Performance tuning goes beyond compilation. .NET 10 further enhances and stabilizes WebAssembly multithreading and Single Instruction Multiple Data (SIMD) capabilities, instructions that allow Blazor apps to use multiple cores and process multiple data points in a single CPU instruction. For developers, this means architecting components and services with concurrency in mind. Data structures must be thread-safe, and UI logic needs to account for asynchronous updates when background tasks complete. When implemented carefully, these features can transform client-side capabilities; intensive operations such as real-time analytics, image filtering, or on-device machine learning inference can run smoothly in parallel, while the main interface remains responsive. Although the runtime handles much of the low-level optimization, teams still benefit from profiling tools to identify bottlenecks and confirm that multithreading and SIMD produce the expected gains on different devices and browsers.

Alongside performance enhancements, .NET 10 greatly improves the developer experience, and integrating these changes can significantly shorten feedback loops. Teams that fully embrace Hot Reload during development cycles can experiment with UI layouts, styling, and business logic in real time, reducing the need for frequent rebuilds and redeployments. Similarly, the evolution of Minimal APIs streamlines the creation of lightweight endpoints for Blazor applications. By adopting the minimal hosting model, developers can configure routing, middleware, and services with a fraction of the boilerplate previously required, resulting in cleaner, more maintainable code. When integrating these APIs, organizations should establish consistent patterns for validation, logging, and authentication so that the simplicity of Minimal APIs does not lead to a fragmented back end.

Security is another pillar where .NET 10 offers tangible improvements, and weaving these features into Blazor projects is critical for enterprise scenarios. The framework now enforces stronger default encryption protocols, including TLS 1.3, and provides improved support for secrets management through services such as Azure Key Vault. Integrating these features means revisiting the entire authentication and authorization strategy. Sensitive credentials database connection strings, API keys, and OAuth tokens should never be hard-coded or stored in source control. Instead, they can be managed through secure vault services with automated rotation and revocation. Additionally, NuGet's enhanced package-signing and vulnerability scanning must be incorporated into the continuous integration pipeline so that any risky dependencies are flagged long before they reach production. Adopting these security measures not only protects data in transit and at rest but also simplifies compliance with regulatory frameworks like GDPR or HIPAA, which many enterprise customers require.

The improvements to .NET 10's cloud-native deployment model deserve special attention. While runtime container image size reductions began in .NET 8, .NET 10 extends these efforts with more aggressive trimming, smaller AOT outputs, and continued base image optimization which is a major advantage when hosting Blazor applications on services such as Azure Kubernetes Service or Azure App Service.

To integrate these benefits, development teams should update Docker files and Helm charts to use the new lightweight base images and then run stress tests to verify startup performance under heavy load. Smaller images also translate to quicker rollouts and lower bandwidth costs during scaling events. Advanced garbage collection algorithms and improved memory management further enhance the stability of long-running Blazor Server applications, where thousands of concurrent SignalR connections must remain stable for extended periods.

Integration is not purely technical; it also demands organizational readiness. Because .NET 10 introduces multithreading and more aggressive code trimming, team members across development, QA, and operations need to understand the new paradigms. Code reviews should specifically examine concurrency handling, while QA teams design tests that simulate real-world parallel workloads. Documentation must be updated to reflect changes in build steps, deployment scripts, and runtime behavior so that future developers can maintain the application confidently. Training sessions and internal demos can accelerate adoption and help avoid pitfalls such as race conditions or performance regressions.

Comprehensive testing is the final step to ensure successful integration. Automated performance benchmarks should measure first-paint times, memory usage, and frame rates on a variety of devices. Security testing—static analysis, penetration testing, and dependency checks—confirms that stronger encryption and secret management policies are in place. Functional testing verifies that Hot Reload updates behave correctly and that Minimal API endpoints return accurate results under load. Observability tools such as Azure Application Insights or Prometheus should be configured to monitor CPU usage, thread activity, and request latency so that teams can validate the improvements of .NET 10 in production and quickly identify anomalies.

A real-world example highlights the payoff. Imagine an enterprise analytics dashboard that previously suffered from slow initial load times and laggy data visualizations. By enabling AOT compilation, the team cuts first-load latency dramatically, while IL trimming keeps bundle sizes minimal. Implementing WebAssembly threads (where supported and when COOP/COEP headers are enabled) allows complex client-side calculations to run in the background without freezing the interface. Hot Reload improves developer productivity by allowing faster UI refinement during development, without affecting application runtime performance, and .NET 10 enhances Minimal APIs with faster routing, endpoint filters, and improved JSON binding. Azure Key Vault integration ensures that database credentials and API tokens remain secure, and updated container images reduce cold-start times when scaling to meet traffic spikes. The end result is a responsive, secure, and maintainable application that showcases the cumulative benefits of .NET 10 when its features are carefully integrated.

In sum, integrating .NET 10 features into Blazor applications is an end-to-end process encompassing architecture, build configuration, performance engineering, security hardening, and team enablement. The process begins with deliberate choices about hosting models, including auto where appropriate, and continues through enabling AOT compilation, exploiting WebAssembly threads and SIMD, adopting Hot Reload and Minimal APIs, and strengthening security posture with modern encryption and secret management. Organizations that approach integration systematically, backed by automated testing, clear documentation, and cross-team education, unlock a platform that is faster, more secure, and easier to evolve. This not only elevates the immediate user experience but also future-proofs applications against the rapidly changing demands of modern web development, positioning Blazor and .NET 10 as a robust foundation for enterprise-grade solutions well into the coming years.

The capabilities introduced in .NET 10 collectively redefine what developers can expect from Blazor applications. Through Ahead-of-Time (AOT) compilation, Blazor WebAssembly can achieve faster runtime execution and improved startup performance, at the cost of larger download sizes, longer build times, and potentially higher memory usage while enabling richer, more demanding user experiences directly in the browser. In Blazor WebAssembly scenarios, performance improvements such as multithreading, SIMD instructions, and garbage collection refinements can improve execution behavior, and leaner runtime images ensure that even large enterprise solutions can scale gracefully and run efficiently on a wide range of devices.

Equally important, these advances do not come at the cost of developer productivity or maintainability. The streamlined Minimal API approach, enhanced Hot Reload, and refined tooling in Visual Studio and Visual Studio Code let teams iterate rapidly, shorten release cycles, and maintain cleaner code bases. Stronger security defaults at the hosting and infrastructure level, including broader adoption of TLS 1.3, improved package signing, and seamless integration with

Azure Key Vault offers enterprises confidence that their applications meet stringent compliance and data protection requirements.

For organizations aiming to integrate intelligent cloud services such as Azure OpenAI, .NET 10 provides the ideal foundation. Faster client-side performance supports real-time AI features, while secure secrets management protects critical API keys and tokens. Whether deploying to Azure Kubernetes Service, Azure App Service, or other cloud platforms, the optimized runtime and smaller container images lower operating costs and accelerate cold starts, making cloud-native Blazor solutions both cost-effective and highly responsive.

Taken together, these improvements reflect Blazor's evolution into a mature, enterprise-ready platform, supported by long-term support (LTS) releases, significantly improved tooling and diagnostics in Visual Studio and the .NET CLI, expanded hosting options across Azure and containerized environments, and measurable performance gains in startup time, memory usage [5-8], and throughput, particularly for Blazor WebAssembly workloads. By marrying the versatility of .NET with cutting-edge performance and security, .NET 10 provides measurable improvements in startup latency, payload size, rendering efficiency, and deployment scalability for modern web applications. In a landscape where speed, reliability, and security are paramount, the enhancements in this release empower teams to innovate with confidence and to meet the evolving demands of modern, data-driven businesses.

CHAPTER 3

Enterprise-Grade Blazor Architecture

Clean Architecture

Clean Architecture has become a cornerstone of modern software development because it helps teams build applications that are maintainable, testable, and resilient to change. When applied to Blazor, a web UI framework within ASP.NET Core that enables building interactive web applications using C# and .NET, the principles of Clean Architecture help separate concerns, simplify testing, and support long-term scalability. Clean Architecture is especially valuable for enterprise-grade Blazor projects, where multiple developers collaborate on complex code bases that may live for many years and need to adapt quickly to changing business requirements.

At its core, Clean Architecture revolves around the idea of independence of layers. The application is structured so that the core business logic is independent of external frameworks, UI technologies, or databases. Robert C. Martin (Uncle Bob), who popularized Clean Architecture, describes it as a set of concentric circles with the innermost layer representing the enterprise's business rules and the outermost representing infrastructure concerns such as databases, web frameworks, and third-party services. The key rule is that dependencies always point inward. For Blazor developers, this translates into designing the application so that the UI components (Razor components, including routed pages) depend on the Application and Domain layers, but those layers never depend on the UI.

A. Prasad and H. Singh, *Advanced Blazor Architecture with .NET 10 and Azure OpenAI*,
https://doi.org/10.1007/979-8-8688-2518-7_3

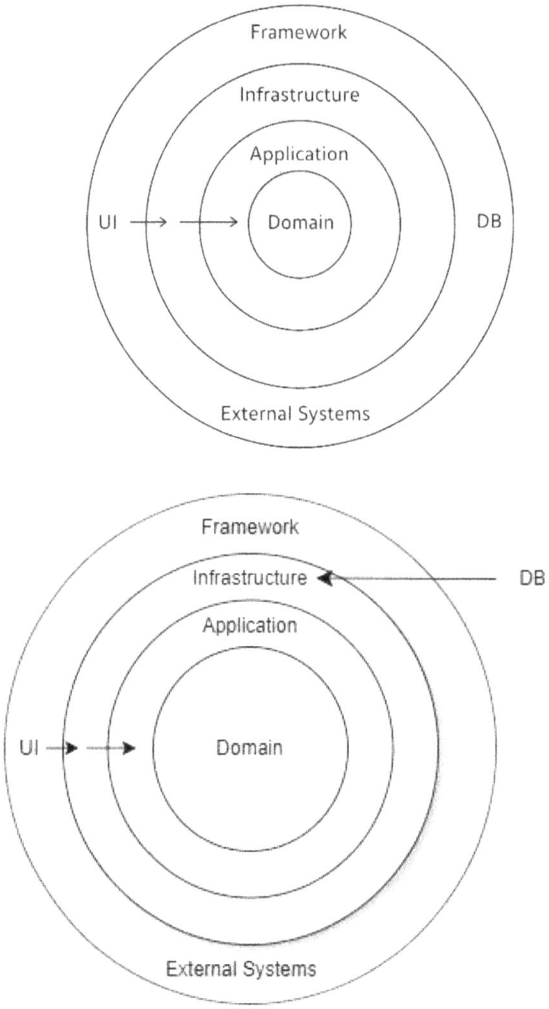

Figure 3-1. *Layered Architecture for a Blazor Application*

A typical Clean Architecture solution for Blazor consists of four major layers: Domain, Application, Infrastructure, and Presentation (UI). The Domain layer contains the core business logic entities, value objects, and domain services that express the ubiquitous language of the business. This layer is pure C# code and knows nothing about Blazor or any database. For example, in an ecommerce Blazor application, domain entities might include classes such as Order, Product, and Customer, each encapsulating business rules like validating order totals or applying discounts. Because this layer has no dependencies on external technologies, it is easily testable and stable over time.

The Application layer sits just outside the domain and coordinates the flow of data between the UI and the domain. It contains use cases or service classes that implement application-specific logic, orchestrating domain entities to fulfill user requests. This layer might include command and query handlers, interfaces for repositories, and abstractions for external services. For example, an Order Service could coordinate placing an order by validating input, creating the Order entity, and calling a repository to persist it. Crucially, the Application layer depends only on the Domain layer and abstractions, not on Blazor or a specific database.

The Infrastructure layer provides the actual implementations for the abstractions defined in the Application layer. Here is where we put Entity Framework Core (EF Core) DbContexts, database migrations, file system access, external API calls, and email-sending services. This layer is allowed to depend on external libraries and frameworks because it is the most replaceable. For instance, if the team decides to move from SQL Server to PostgreSQL, the change occurs here without altering the Domain or Application layers.

Finally, the Presentation layer is where Blazor lives. This layer represents the application's UI, composed of Razor components, including routable components, along with any JavaScript interop code. It is responsible solely for interacting with the user and relaying requests to the Application layer. For example, a Blazor OrderForm.razor component collects user input and calls an IOrderService interface defined in the Application layer to process the order. The Presentation layer depends on the Application layer but not the other way around, ensuring that the UI can evolve independently of the business logic.

One of the most important benefits of Clean Architecture in Blazor is testability. Because the Domain and Application layers contain all the critical logic and are free of UI and infrastructure concerns, they can be unit-tested without starting a web server or connecting to a database. Developers can write automated tests for complex business rules, ensuring that changes in the UI or infrastructure do not inadvertently break the core logic. This capability dramatically improves confidence in the system and reduces long-term maintenance costs.

Implementing Clean Architecture in Blazor also encourages the Dependency Inversion Principle (DIP), a key part of the SOLID guidelines. Instead of the Application layer depending on a concrete data access class, it depends on an interface such as IOrderRepository [9]. The Infrastructure layer provides an EF Core implementation of this interface, but the Application layer remains agnostic. This design allows developers to swap implementations, for instance, using an in-memory repository for testing or a different database provider without changing the application code. Dependency injection (DI), which is built into ASP.NET Core and by extension Blazor, makes this pattern straightforward. By registering interfaces and their concrete implementations in the service container, the framework automatically injects the required dependencies at runtime.

Another advantage is maintainability. In large Blazor solutions, UI requirements often change quickly due to evolving design trends or user feedback. With Clean Architecture, developers can redesign the UI, replace components, or even move from Blazor Server to Blazor WebAssembly without affecting business rules. Similarly, the Infrastructure layer can evolve, for example, migrating from REST APIs to gRPC without altering the domain model or application services. This separation of concerns ensures that each layer can change independently, making the overall system far easier to maintain over time.

Clean Architecture also supports cross-cutting concerns such as logging, caching, and validation. Instead of sprinkling these concerns throughout the UI or application logic, they can be implemented using decorators or middleware-like patterns. For example, a caching decorator could wrap a query handler interface in the Application layer, ensuring that frequently requested data is served quickly while keeping the core logic clean and focused.

When applying Clean Architecture in a Blazor Server application, developers must consider state management. Because Blazor Server maintains a persistent SignalR connection, careful design is required to avoid memory leaks and to keep domain logic free of UI-specific state. By isolating business logic in the Application and Domain layers, stateful components can remain thin and focus solely on UI rendering and event handling. For Blazor WebAssembly, which runs entirely in the browser, Clean Architecture provides similar benefits by allowing offline-first features and client-side caching to be implemented in the Infrastructure layer without polluting core logic.

Moreover, Clean Architecture facilitates continuous integration and deployment (CI/CD). Since the layers are well defined, teams can build and test the Domain and Application layers independently from the UI, enabling faster pipelines and more reliable deployments. Static code analysis and automated testing can verify that no layer violates dependency rules—for example, ensuring that the Domain layer does not reference Infrastructure classes.

In an enterprise context, these advantages translate directly into business value. Clean Architecture reduces the risk of technical debt, making the application easier to extend with new features, integrate with other systems, or onboard new developers. The clear separation of responsibilities allows different teams to work in parallel: UI/UX designers focus on the Presentation layer, back-end specialists work on Infrastructure, and business analysts refine the Domain layer, all with minimal risk of stepping on each other's work.

Sample Blazor component syntax:

```
@page "/hello"
<h3>Hello, @name!</h3>
<input @bind="name" placeholder="Type your name" />
<button @onclick="SayHello">Greet</button>
<p>@message</p>
@code {
    private string name = "";
    private string message = "";
    private void SayHello()
    {
        message = $"Welcome to Blazor, {name}!";
    }
}
```

```
@page "/hello"
@*
   Presentation Layer:
   This Razor component represents the UI layer. It should remain thin and
   delegate business logic to the Application layer rather than implement it directly.
*@
@inject IGreeterService GreeterService

<h3>Hello, @name!</h3>

<input @bind="name" placeholder="Type your name" />
<button @onclick="SayHelloAsync">Greet</button>

<p>@message</p>

@code {
    // UI state only (no business logic)
    private string name = string.Empty;
    private string message = string.Empty;

    private async Task SayHelloAsync()
    {
        // Delegates the operation to the Application layer
        message = await GreeterService.GetGreetingAsync(name);
    }
}
```

Supporting Application-layer contract (for context)

```
using System;
public interface IGreeterService
{
    Task<string> GetGreetingAsync(string name);
}
```

This example illustrates how a Blazor Razor component in the Presentation layer remains focused on UI concerns while delegating business behavior to an Application-layer service. By depending on the **IGreeterService** abstraction, the UI avoids embedding business logic directly, improving testability and maintaining a clear separation of concerns consistent with Clean Architecture principles.

Adopting Clean Architecture in a Blazor application does require discipline. Teams must resist the temptation to take shortcuts, such as directly querying the database from a Razor component or mixing UI logic with domain rules. Code reviews and automated tests can help enforce boundaries. Over time, the initial investment pays dividends as the application grows in complexity but remains manageable.

Applying Clean Architecture in Blazor provides a powerful blueprint for building enterprise-grade web applications that stand the test of time. By separating concerns into Domain, Application, Infrastructure, and Presentation layers, developers achieve a clean dependency flow, exceptional testability, and flexibility to adapt to new technologies or requirements. Whether the application is a small internal dashboard or a massive customer-facing platform, Clean Architecture ensures that the heart of the business logic remains independent, maintainable, and ready to evolve. For organizations investing in Blazor as a long-term web platform, Clean Architecture is not merely an optional pattern; it is an essential strategy for sustainable success.

Domain-Driven Design

Understanding Domain-Driven Design in the Blazor Context

Domain-driven design (DDD) is a strategic software approach that places the core business domain at the heart of the application. When combined with Blazor, a modern web UI framework within ASP.NET Core for building rich, interactive web interfaces, it creates an architecture that can grow with changing requirements while preserving clarity and maintainability. The essence of DDD is to model software around the language, processes, and rules of the actual business rather than letting technical details dominate the design.

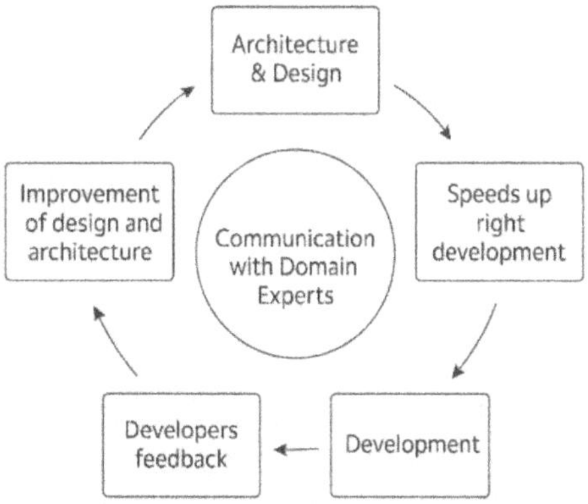

Figure 3-2. *Domain-Driven Design Application Lifecycle*

This begins with establishing a ubiquitous language that is applied consistently across the Domain, Application, UI components, and Infrastructure layers described in the "Clean Architecture" section—a shared vocabulary developed collaboratively by developers and domain experts. By using this language consistently across code, discussions, and documentation, teams ensure that entities, methods, and events accurately reflect the business. In a Blazor project, this means the Domain layer captures the business rules and behaviors independently of the web UI. The Blazor components then interact with the application layer, which orchestrates commands and queries, while the Domain layer remains pure and agnostic of infrastructure or presentation concerns. Such separation allows the business logic to remain stable even as the user interface or underlying storage evolves.

Entities, Value Objects, and Aggregates

Central to DDD is the distinction between entities, value objects, and aggregates, concepts that map well to the Domain and Application layers of a Blazor-based ecosystem. Entities are objects with a unique identity that persists over time, such as a Customer or Order, whereas value objects are immutable and defined entirely by their attributes, like an Address or a Monetary Amount type. Designing these carefully avoids duplication of logic and keeps code aligned with real-world concepts. Aggregates group related entities and value objects under a single aggregate root to enforce consistency across their boundaries. For example, in a Blazor-based ecommerce application, an Order aggregate may contain multiple OrderItems and a Payment entity, with the Order acting as the aggregate root to ensure that adding an item or processing a payment never leaves the system in an inconsistent state. This clear modeling of domain objects ensures that complex operations remain predictable and that business invariants are always respected. Blazor components, in turn, can interact with these aggregates through the application layer without needing to know their internal details.

Domain Services, Events, and Application Layer

Some business operations don't belong to a specific entity or value object. DDD handles these through domain services, which encapsulate important business actions such as calculating tax, approving a loan, or processing a complex workflow. In a Blazor application, these services stay in the Domain layer, independent of UI concerns, so they are easier to test and reuse. Domain events represent significant occurrences within the system, such as OrderPlaced or PaymentProcessed. Publishing and handling these events inside the domain allow different parts of the application to react without tight coupling. For instance, an OrderPlaced event could trigger an email confirmation, update a dashboard component, or kick off an external payment process, all without the Order entity knowing anything about the front end.

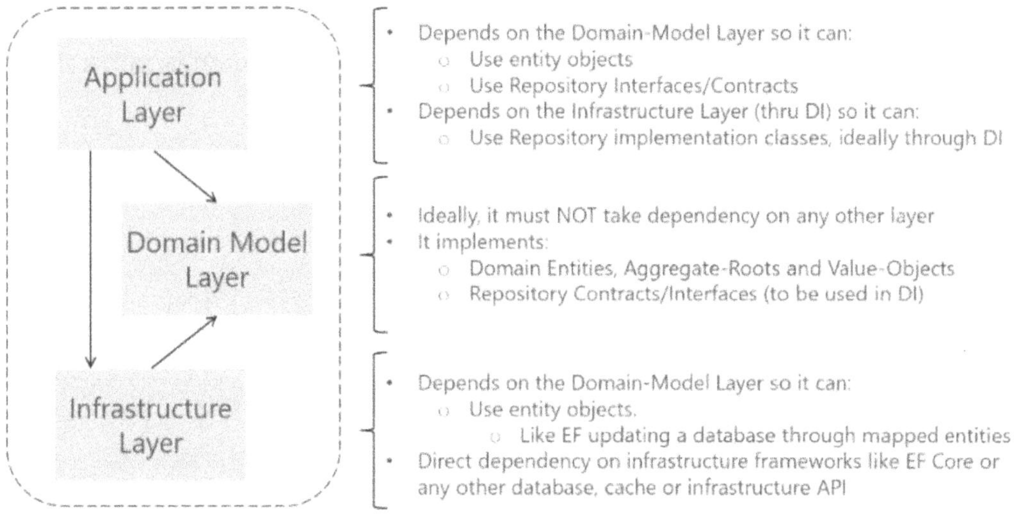

Figure 3-3. *Dependencies Between Layers in DDD*

Blazor can surface domain events to users in near real time through UI-level technologies such as SignalR or HTTP-based messaging; however, these transport mechanisms are part of the Presentation and Infrastructure layers, while the domain events themselves remain UI-agnostic, providing an interactive and responsive experience. The Application layer, sitting between the Blazor components and the domain, coordinates these interactions through commands and queries. A Place Order Command, for example, might package the necessary data, pass it to a service, and ensure the operation respects all business rules before persisting changes via a repository. This keeps the user interface focused on presentation while the domain remains the single source of truth for business logic.

Advantages for Testing, Scalability, and Long-Term Maintenance

Adopting DDD within a Blazor architecture yields substantial benefits for testing, scalability, and long-term maintenance. Because the Domain layer is decoupled from the UI, developers can unit-test entities, value objects, and services in isolation, ensuring that the core logic is correct even before the interface is complete. Integration tests can then verify that Blazor components correctly invoke application commands and display results without re-implementing business rules. This separation greatly reduces the likelihood of regressions when features evolve or when the application scales to handle more users or complex workflows. Security and compliance are reinforced through Application-layer authorization policies and infrastructure-level controls, rather than being embedded directly within domain entities.

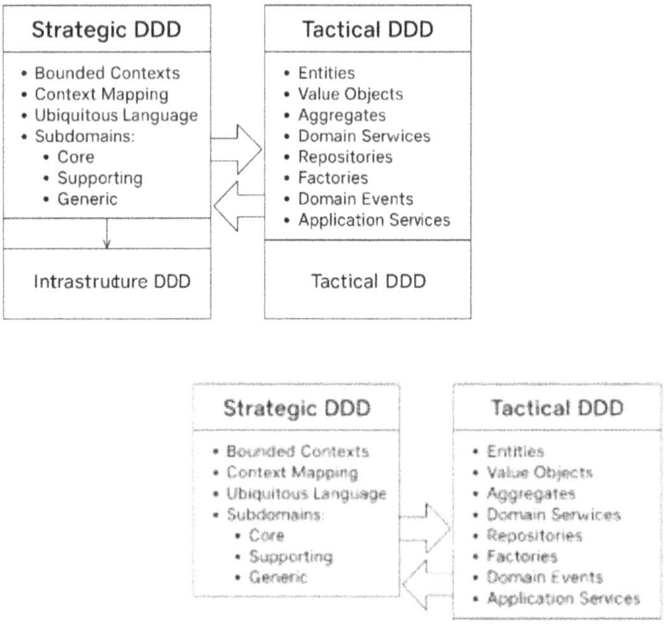

Figure 3-4. *Strategic and Tactical Domain-Driven Design*

Scaling the application, whether by deploying it to cloud environments like Azure Kubernetes Service (AKS) or App Services or by moving from Blazor Server to WebAssembly, becomes simpler because the business logic remains unchanged. Teams can refactor or redesign the UI, adopt new .NET versions, or integrate additional infrastructure services without disturbing the domain. Event-driven designs further support horizontal scaling by decoupling components and allowing asynchronous processing. Over time, as requirements shift or technology advances, a Blazor application grounded in DDD can adapt gracefully, protecting earlier investments in core business logic [10]. Domain-driven design and Blazor complement each other in building robust, enterprise-grade web applications. DDD ensures that the software model faithfully represents business processes, while Blazor provides a modern, component-based framework for delivering interactive experiences.

By emphasizing a ubiquitous language, modeling rich entities and value objects, managing operations with aggregates and domain services, and using domain events to signal significant changes, developers create a code base that is expressive, testable, and resilient. The layered architecture that DDD promotes, separating presentation, application, domain, and infrastructure, keeps the business rules at the center, unaffected by changes in technology or interface design. This combination empowers organizations to respond quickly to evolving requirements, maintain high levels of quality, and deliver user experiences that remain fast and reliable. As businesses increasingly demand applications that can evolve without losing alignment with their core processes, the synergy of domain-driven design and Blazor offers a proven path to building software that endures.

Data Persistence and Integration

In modern web application development, data persistence and integration form the backbone of any enterprise-grade solution. For applications built using Blazor and powered by .NET 10, these aspects are crucial to ensure that the application not only maintains data consistency but also communicates effectively with other systems and services. The evolution of Blazor from a client-side experimental framework to a robust platform for enterprise applications has opened the door for deeper integration patterns and sophisticated persistence strategies. In this context, data persistence involves both the temporary storage of state during a user session and long-term storage in databases or cloud-based solutions. Blazor applications benefit from .NET's Entity Framework Core through server-side components and APIs, regardless of whether the UI uses Blazor Server or Blazor WebAssembly. EF Core provides a high-level abstraction over relational databases, enabling developers to model complex domain entities while maintaining transactional consistency. When used with EF Core 8 or later in the .NET 10 ecosystem, features such as automatic migrations, change tracking, and asynchronous data access support scalable and performant server-side data operations.

Blazor applications inherently maintain a component-based architecture where state can exist at multiple levels, including local component state, cascading state across nested components, and shared application state. However, to achieve true persistence, the application must extend beyond in-memory storage. For this reason, integrating relational databases such as SQL Server or PostgreSQL, or NoSQL databases like Cosmos DB, is a common practice. Relational databases are ideal for structured data scenarios where ACID transactions are required, whereas NoSQL databases offer schema flexibility and horizontal scalability, which is particularly beneficial when dealing with large volumes of unstructured or semi-structured data. With .NET 10, developers can exploit Minimal APIs and modern ORM enhancements to seamlessly integrate database operations into Blazor components. In Blazor Server applications, components interact with Application-layer services that encapsulate data access implemented using Entity Framework Core. LINQ queries are executed within these services rather than directly in UI components, ensuring asynchronous operations do not block UI rendering while preserving Clean Architecture boundaries. This approach is particularly relevant for applications that require real-time responsiveness, such as dashboards or collaborative platforms.

Beyond traditional databases, cloud-native storage solutions play a significant role in advanced Blazor architectures. Leveraging Azure SQL Database, Azure Table Storage, or Azure Blob Storage provides high availability, automatic backups, and geographic redundancy, which are critical for enterprise-grade applications. For instance, in scenarios where large media files or AI-generated data from Azure OpenAI services are involved, Blob Storage serves as an ideal solution for cost-efficient and scalable storage. In Blazor applications, Azure Storage SDKs are typically encapsulated within infrastructure or application services, which are then consumed by Blazor components to support file uploads, streaming downloads, and progress reporting. Additionally, these storage solutions support advanced features like soft delete, data tiering, and access policies, ensuring that data management aligns with organizational governance standards. With the integration of Azure Key Vault, sensitive data such as connection strings, API keys, or cryptographic secrets can be securely managed and accessed by the Blazor application, ensuring compliance with security best practices.

Integration in modern Blazor applications is not limited to databases but extends to external services, APIs, and AI models, such as those provided by Azure OpenAI. By combining Blazor's component model with .NET 10's robust HTTP client libraries and dependency injection, developers can establish clean, maintainable service layers that encapsulate communication with REST APIs, gRPC endpoints, or AI services. For example, integrating a chatbot powered by GPT models into a Blazor application involves designing a service that handles requests, processes responses asynchronously, and updates the UI in real time. Such an architecture ensures that business logic is decoupled from UI components, which not only improves maintainability but also enhances testability. In addition, the use of GraphQL endpoints for data integration provides an efficient mechanism to retrieve exactly the data required by the client, minimizing bandwidth consumption and optimizing performance in large-scale applications.

In the realm of enterprise applications, transaction management and data consistency are critical considerations. Blazor applications integrated with distributed systems or microservices need to handle scenarios where multiple services participate in a single business transaction. In .NET 10, developers can leverage Unit of Work patterns and transaction scopes to ensure that operations across multiple repositories either succeed or fail as a single unit, reducing the risk of data anomalies. Furthermore, the async/await model in .NET allows Blazor applications to handle long-running operations, such as database migrations or AI inference calls, without blocking the user interface, thereby maintaining a seamless user experience. When integrating with external APIs, mechanisms such as retry policies, circuit breakers, and throttling can be implemented using libraries like Polly, which provide resilience and fault tolerance in distributed environments.

Another important dimension of data persistence in Blazor applications is state management, particularly for client-side Blazor WebAssembly apps. Since WebAssembly executes entirely in the browser, maintaining data consistency across sessions requires careful integration with server-side storage or cloud-backed services. Techniques such as local storage, session storage, and IndexedDB can be combined with server-side APIs to provide a hybrid persistence strategy. For instance, frequently accessed reference data or configuration settings can be cached locally for performance, while transactional or sensitive data is stored securely in a server-side database. Moreover, Blazor's cascading parameters and state containers facilitate communication of state across components, which can then be synchronized with persistent storage through well-defined service layers. This approach allows developers to create applications that are both responsive and robust, balancing performance with reliability.

Integration with machine learning and AI services, such as Azure OpenAI, adds another layer of complexity and opportunity. Data generated from user interactions, predictive models, or natural language processing must be stored, processed, and sometimes anonymized before persistence. .NET 10 provides the necessary tools to serialize complex objects, apply transformation pipelines, and persist results in both relational and NoSQL databases. For example, a recommendation engine integrated into a Blazor app can process user preferences through a GPT model, generate personalized content, and store these insights in a database for subsequent sessions. The integration pattern typically follows a layered architecture: the UI layer handles user interactions, the service layer manages communication with AI models, and the persistence layer ensures secure storage and retrieval. By following domain-driven design principles, these layers remain decoupled, ensuring that changes to AI models or data storage technologies have minimal impact on the rest of the application.

Security considerations intersect closely with data persistence and integration, but this section provides only a brief overview. The "Scalability and Security Strategies" section explores security and scalability concerns including identity, encryption, and monitoring details. In Blazor applications, especially those integrated with cloud services, developers must ensure that data at rest and in transit is encrypted, access controls are enforced, and sensitive data is never exposed inadvertently. Leveraging Azure Active Directory for authentication, role-based access control, and token-based authorization ensures that only authorized users can access or manipulate data. Furthermore, integrating Azure Application Insights or other telemetry services enables monitoring of data access patterns, API usage, and system health, which is crucial for maintaining compliance with enterprise security policies. These security considerations influence how data persistence and integration are architected, as developers need to balance performance and accessibility with privacy and regulatory compliance.

The evolution of Blazor and .NET 10 also enables hybrid integration strategies, where applications can consume data from multiple sources simultaneously. For example, a financial dashboard might combine real-time stock data from an external API, historical transaction data from a SQL database, and AI-generated forecasts from Azure OpenAI. Implementing such hybrid integrations requires careful design of the service layer, asynchronous orchestration of data retrieval, and caching strategies to optimize both performance and responsiveness. Patterns such as CQRS (Command Query Responsibility Segregation) can be employed to separate read-heavy operations from transactional writes, further optimizing database performance. In addition, event-driven architectures using Azure Event Grid or Azure Service Bus can facilitate real-time updates and notifications across integrated systems, making Blazor applications highly interactive and responsive to changes in the underlying data sources.

Data persistence and integration in advanced Blazor architectures leveraging .NET 10 and Azure OpenAI are multifaceted challenges that require careful consideration of database design, state management, cloud storage, AI integration, and security. By leveraging the powerful tools provided by .NET 10, developers can create scalable, maintainable, and secure applications that seamlessly combine local and cloud-based data, interact efficiently with external services, and incorporate cutting-edge AI capabilities. The combination of Blazor's component model, EF Core, Azure cloud services, and OpenAI integration provides a robust framework for building modern, enterprise-grade applications where data is both a strategic asset and a dynamic resource, capable of driving intelligent decision-making, personalization, and real-time interaction. Properly architected data persistence and integration not only enhance application reliability and performance but also lay the foundation for future scalability, enabling developers to extend applications to support additional services, machine learning capabilities, and global cloud deployments without significant redesign.

Scalability and Security Strategies

Scalability and security are two of the most critical considerations in modern enterprise web applications, particularly for systems built on Blazor, .NET 10, and integrated with cloud-based AI services like Azure OpenAI. In any large-scale deployment, scalability ensures that the application can handle growing workloads, user traffic, and data volumes without degradation in performance, while security ensures that sensitive information is protected, system integrity is maintained, and regulatory compliance is achieved. The architecture of a Blazor application directly impacts both these aspects, as it dictates how components interact, how data flows, and how resources are utilized. Blazor's component-based model, combined with .NET 10's runtime optimizations and Azure's cloud capabilities, provides a flexible foundation for designing systems that are both scalable and secure.

Scalability in Blazor applications can be approached at multiple levels: vertical scalability, horizontal scalability, and functional scalability. Vertical scalability involves improving the performance of a single server by increasing resources such as CPU, memory, or storage. While this can provide immediate relief for performance bottlenecks, it has inherent limits and cannot sustain exponential growth. Horizontal scalability, on the other hand, involves distributing the application across multiple servers or instances. In a Blazor Server hosting model, horizontal scaling requires careful consideration of SignalR connections in many Azure deployments; this involves enabling sticky sessions at the load balancer or offloading connection management to Azure SignalR Service to ensure that client circuits remain stable as the application scales out, which maintains real-time communication between the server and clients. Load balancers and session management strategies become essential to distribute traffic evenly, ensuring that no single server becomes a bottleneck. Using Azure App Service or Azure Kubernetes Service (AKS), developers can automatically scale instances based on

CPU usage, memory pressure, or custom metrics, allowing the system to handle sudden spikes in user demand. Horizontal scaling also improves fault tolerance, as the failure of one node does not result in a complete system outage.

In the context of Blazor WebAssembly, scalability primarily affects the back-end Application and Infrastructure layers rather than the Blazor WebAssembly client itself, since the client executes in the browser. As a result, back-end APIs, databases, and cloud services must be designed to handle concurrent requests efficiently. Implementing asynchronous programming patterns, task parallelism, and non-blocking I/O in .NET 10 ensures that server resources are utilized efficiently, reducing latency and improving throughput. The integration of caching mechanisms such as Redis or Azure Cache for Redis can further enhance scalability by storing frequently accessed data in memory, minimizing expensive database calls. For example, an AI-driven content recommendation service using Azure OpenAI can cache user preferences and previous recommendations to reduce repeated model inference calls, ensuring that the system can serve thousands of users simultaneously without significant latency.

Functional scalability is equally important in enterprise applications. This refers to the system's ability to expand functionality, integrate new modules, or adopt emerging technologies without requiring a complete redesign. Blazor's component-based architecture supports functional scalability by enabling developers to add or update components independently. Services that interact with AI models, databases, or third-party APIs can be encapsulated within well-defined interfaces, promoting modularity and ease of extension. Adopting microservices or modular service-oriented architecture ensures that different functional domains, such as authentication, reporting, or AI-driven analytics, can scale independently according to demand. This approach reduces the risk of performance bottlenecks and allows for targeted optimizations, making the application more resilient to growth and change.

Security is another cornerstone of enterprise Blazor applications. Unlike scalability, which primarily addresses performance, security focuses on protecting assets, enforcing access control, and maintaining system integrity. At the application level, authentication and authorization are fundamental. Blazor supports integration with Azure Active Directory (AAD), enabling enterprise-grade identity management. With AAD, developers can enforce role-based access control (RBAC) and claims-based authorization, ensuring that only authenticated and authorized users can access sensitive components or services. Token-based authentication, particularly using JWT (JSON Web Tokens), allows secure stateless communication between clients and APIs, which is crucial in horizontally scaled systems where session affinity may not be guaranteed.

Securing data in transit and at rest is another essential aspect. TLS/SSL encryption must be enforced for all client-server and server-service communications, ensuring that data transmitted over public networks remains confidential. For data persistence, Azure provides mechanisms such as Transparent Data Encryption (TDE) for SQL databases, server-side encryption for Blob Storage, and key management through Azure Key Vault. Key Vault allows sensitive secrets, such as API keys or encryption keys, to be securely stored and rotated regularly, reducing the risk of accidental exposure. In applications integrating Azure OpenAI, secure handling of API keys is crucial to prevent misuse or unauthorized access to AI services. By leveraging managed identities, Blazor applications can securely authenticate with cloud services without hard-coding secrets.

Application security extends beyond authentication and data encryption to include defense against common vulnerabilities. Blazor applications must be designed to resist attacks such as cross-site scripting (XSS), cross-site request forgery (CSRF), and SQL injection. In practice, this typically involves combining input validation, often implemented using data annotations and shared validation logic, with API-level protections such as anti-forgery mechanisms or token-based authentication and authorization, depending on the hosting model. Since Blazor components often generate dynamic HTML, developers need to ensure that any user-provided data is sanitized before rendering. .NET 10 provides built-in libraries and frameworks that help mitigate these vulnerabilities, such as data annotations for input validation and anti-forgery tokens for form submissions. Additionally, server-side logging and monitoring of suspicious activities using Azure Application Insights or Azure Monitor help in detecting anomalies and potential security breaches proactively.

Scaling a secure Blazor application also requires considering infrastructure security. Cloud-native deployments in Azure benefit from features such as network security groups, firewall rules, and private endpoints, which control traffic flow and restrict access to critical services. For instance, databases can be configured to only accept connections from the application's virtual network, preventing unauthorized external access. For distributed systems or microservices architectures, API gateways can enforce security policies, rate limiting, and authentication at the entry point, ensuring that downstream services remain protected from malicious traffic.

An often-overlooked aspect of scalability and security is resilience under attack or failure. Scalable systems must maintain performance during high load, while secure systems must prevent data breaches or service disruption. Techniques such as circuit breakers, retries, and graceful degradation allow Blazor applications to handle external API failures, network latency, or AI service outages without affecting the overall user experience. For example, if an Azure OpenAI endpoint becomes temporarily unavailable, the system can fall back to cached AI responses or simplified functionality, preserving continuity. Similarly, security measures such as rate limiting and anomaly detection prevent Denial-of-Service (DoS) attacks from overwhelming the system while alerting administrators in real time.

Performance monitoring and continuous optimization are crucial for both scalability and security. Azure provides tools like Azure Application Insights, Log Analytics, and Security Center, which allow developers to track application performance, detect bottlenecks, and monitor compliance with security policies. By analyzing telemetry data, developers can identify slow API calls, database query inefficiencies, or potential security incidents, enabling proactive improvements. In high-traffic Blazor applications, performance tuning may involve optimizing SignalR message throughput, reducing component re-renders, or minimizing the payload of API responses, all while ensuring that security checks remain enforced without introducing latency.

Integration with AI services introduces unique challenges for both scalability and security. Azure OpenAI models can be resource-intensive and may generate sensitive content based on user inputs. To manage scalability, developers can implement request queuing, batching, or throttling strategies to prevent overwhelming the service and to maintain predictable response times. For security, all AI requests must be validated and sanitized with appropriate authorization, auditing, and rate-limiting controls, and the system must comply with data privacy regulations such as GDPR or CCPA when processing user data. Storing AI-generated insights in secure databases or encrypted cloud storage ensures that sensitive information remains protected. Logging and auditing of AI interactions provide traceability, which is essential for accountability and compliance in regulated industries.

Finally, adopting best practices in architecture and design significantly contributes to scalability and security. Principles such as separation of concerns, modularity, and service abstraction allow Blazor applications to scale efficiently and integrate securely with other systems. Layered architectures, where presentation, business logic, and data access layers are decoupled, make it easier to apply security policies at each layer without affecting functionality. Implementing CI/CD pipelines with automated security testing, infrastructure-as-code deployment, and monitoring ensures that updates or feature additions do not compromise performance or security. Additionally, leveraging Azure DevOps or GitHub Actions with security scanning and load testing integrated into the deployment pipeline provides a continuous feedback loop for maintaining robust, scalable, and secure applications.

In conclusion, scalability and security strategies in advanced Blazor architectures using .NET 10 and Azure OpenAI are deeply interconnected and must be designed holistically. Scalability ensures that the system can grow in response to increasing demand without performance degradation, while security protects the integrity, confidentiality, and availability of data and services. Techniques such as horizontal scaling, caching, asynchronous programming, and microservices enable Blazor applications to handle high concurrency and large datasets efficiently. Security measures, including identity and access management, encryption, input validation, monitoring, and infrastructure hardening, protect the system from both internal and external threats. By combining these strategies with cloud-native services, resilient architectural patterns, and continuous monitoring, developers can build Blazor applications that are not only highly performant and reliable but also secure, compliant, and future-proof. Properly implemented, these strategies ensure that enterprise applications leveraging AI, cloud services, and real-time interactions can deliver exceptional user experiences while maintaining operational integrity and trustworthiness in increasingly complex digital environments.

CHAPTER 4

Micro-Frontends and Modular UI

Understanding Micro-Frontends in Blazor Applications

The evolution of web application architecture has seen a significant shift from monolithic front-end applications to distributed, modular designs. Among the most impactful paradigms in this evolution is the concept of micro-frontends, which extends the principles of microservices to the front-end layer. In the context of Blazor applications, in some architectures, micro-frontends can also be deployed independently, depending on the chosen composition strategy. This paradigm allows teams to break down a large Blazor application into smaller, self-contained modules, each responsible for a distinct feature or domain, while maintaining the cohesion of the overall user experience. Micro-frontends address several challenges commonly faced in enterprise applications, such as managing complex UI logic, facilitating cross-team collaboration, and scaling individual application modules independently.

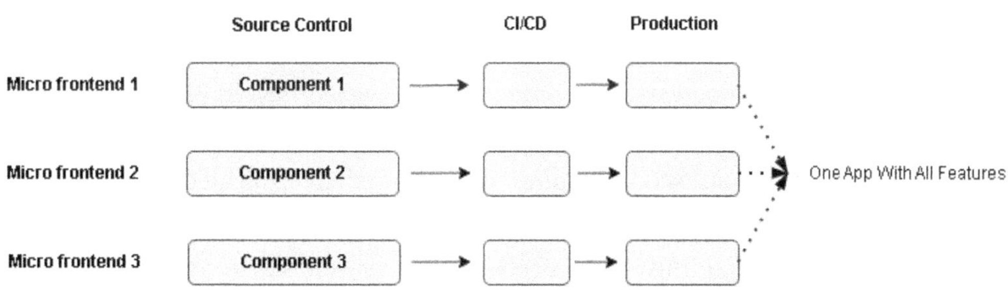

Figure 4-1. *Micro-Frontends*

A. Prasad and H. Singh, *Advanced Blazor Architecture with .NET 10 and Azure OpenAI*,
https://doi.org/10.1007/979-8-8688-2518-7_4

At its core, the micro-frontend architecture promotes decentralization of UI development [11]. Traditionally, micro front-end applications are monolithic, meaning a single code base handles all UI components, styling, routing, and business logic. As applications grow, this approach leads to tight coupling between features, increased code complexity, and longer deployment cycles. Blazor, with its component-based model, already encourages modularity at a smaller scale, but when combined with micro-frontend principles, it allows each component or module to evolve independently. Each micro-frontend can be developed and tested by a dedicated team and, depending on the architectural composition model, may also be deployed independently. In Blazor-based implementations, true independent deployment typically requires separately hosted applications, whereas component libraries within a single Blazor app share the same deployment boundary. This autonomy significantly improves development velocity, reduces integration overhead, and allows for rapid experimentation with new features.

Implementing micro-frontends in Blazor Server and Blazor WebAssembly applications requires careful architectural planning. In Blazor Server, an important consideration is the management of SignalR connections, as each client maintains a persistent connection with the server. Micro-frontend modules must be designed to efficiently share server resources while isolating state management to avoid conflicts between modules. This often involves leveraging mechanisms such as cascading parameters, where parent components provide shared values down the component tree, along with dependency injection and state containers to manage shared state. However, these techniques should be used carefully, as cascading parameters and shared state can introduce implicit coupling. Where strong isolation between micro-frontends is required, explicit contracts, well-defined interfaces, or event-based communication patterns are generally preferable. In Blazor WebAssembly, the emphasis shifts to **client-side performance** and module loading strategies. Since WebAssembly executes entirely in the browser, developers often implement lazy loading and dynamic module loading to minimize the initial download size and reduce rendering latency. In Blazor, this typically involves using assembly lazy loading (for WebAssembly) or loading feature-specific Razor class libraries and routes on demand, rather than delivering all components and dependencies in the initial application bundle. Techniques such as lazy loading and dynamic .NET assembly loading can be used to improve modularity and reduce initial load time, particularly in Blazor WebAssembly applications where feature-specific assemblies are loaded on demand.

A key benefit of micro-frontends in Blazor applications is scalability, both from a technical and organizational perspective. Technically, applications can scale by deploying individual micro-frontends on separate servers or cloud instances. These independently deployed units are then composed into a unified user experience through routing, layout shells, or host applications that dynamically integrate the micro-frontend modules at runtime, allowing load to be balanced across modules rather than overloading a single monolithic front end. Cloud platforms such as Azure App Service, Azure Kubernetes Service (AKS), or Azure Static Web Apps provide mechanisms to host micro-frontends independently, enabling horizontal scaling based on demand. Organizationally, teams can be structured around business domains, with each team owning a specific micro-frontend module. This reduces interdependencies and enables parallel development streams, allowing large organizations to deliver features faster while maintaining high-quality standards. For example, in a large ecommerce platform, the product catalog, shopping cart, and checkout flows could each be separate micro-frontends, developed and maintained by different teams, yet seamlessly integrated into a unified user experience.

Integration between micro-frontends is another critical consideration. Even though each module is independently developed, the overall application must maintain a consistent look and feel and a coherent user experience. Design systems, shared component libraries, and CSS frameworks play a crucial role in achieving UI consistency across micro-frontends. Blazor supports Razor class libraries, which allow developers to encapsulate reusable components, styling, and scripts and distribute them across multiple micro-frontends. This approach ensures that while modules are independently deployable, they adhere to the organization's design standards and provide a unified interface to users. Furthermore, shared service layers can be implemented to centralize common functionality, such as authentication, API communication, and logging, reducing duplication of effort while preserving module independence.

Communication between micro-frontends in Blazor applications can be achieved through event-driven architectures or state management patterns. Since modules are designed to be loosely coupled, direct references between them should be minimized to reduce dependencies. Instead, publish-subscribe mechanisms or message buses can facilitate inter-module communication. In Blazor, when addressing **inter-module communication** (as opposed to composition or routing), this can be implemented using custom events, .NET event handlers, or mediator-based patterns such as MediatR to propagate actions and state changes between modules. Composition concerns are typically handled through layout and routing mechanisms, while navigation is managed via the built-in Router component. For instance, in a dashboard application, a filter component in one micro-frontend could publish a selection event that other micro-frontends, such as data visualization charts or analytics panels, can subscribe to and update accordingly. This ensures that modules remain decoupled while still participating in a cohesive user experience.

Deployment and lifecycle management of micro-frontends also require careful planning. Each micro-frontend should be independently versioned, allowing teams to deploy updates without impacting unrelated modules. Continuous integration and continuous deployment (CI/CD) pipelines become essential in this scenario. Tools like Azure DevOps, GitHub Actions, or GitLab CI/CD can automate the building, testing, and deployment of each micro-frontend module. Containerization with Docker and orchestration with Kubernetes further enhance deployment flexibility, enabling blue-green or canary deployments for individual modules. This minimizes downtime, allows incremental rollouts, and facilitates rapid rollback in case of errors. By adopting micro-frontends, organizations can improve operational agility while mitigating the risks associated with large-scale modern deployments.

Security considerations in micro-frontends are equally important. Since each module can be deployed independently, developers must ensure consistent authentication and authorization policies across all micro-frontends. Blazor applications can integrate with an identity provider such as Microsoft Entra ID (formerly Azure Active Directory) using OpenID Connect for user sign-in and OAuth 2.0 for acquiring access tokens to call protected APIs to provide centralized authentication; in architectures where micro-frontends are deployed as separate applications, each module may validate access tokens and enforce role-based access control independently. In contrast, when implemented as component libraries within a single Blazor application, authentication and authorization are typically handled centrally by the host application. Additionally, communication between modules and back-end services should be encrypted using TLS/SSL, and sensitive data must be securely stored using techniques such as Azure Key Vault or encrypted databases. Adhering to security best practices ensures that the modularity provided by micro-frontends does not introduce vulnerabilities or inconsistencies in access control.

Another advantage of micro-frontends in Blazor is the ability to adopt diverse technologies within a unified application. While Blazor provides a robust .NET-based UI framework, certain modules can integrate other front-end technologies such as React or

Angular when specialized functionality is required. In practice, this is typically achieved through JavaScript interop, embedding web components, or hosting separately deployed UIs via iframe or shell-based composition. However, these approaches introduce trade-offs, including challenges around shared routing, authentication consistency, design system alignment, increased bundle size, and overall integration complexity. This hybrid approach enables organizations to leverage the strengths of different frameworks while maintaining a cohesive user experience through standard integration points, shared services, and consistent styling. Blazor's interoperability features, such as JavaScript interop, facilitate communication between Blazor components and external front-end modules, allowing micro-frontends to coexist seamlessly within a single application shell.

Testing and quality assurance in a micro-frontend architecture require dedicated strategies. Since modules are independently developed and deployed, unit testing, integration testing, and end-to-end testing must account for both isolated module behavior and overall application interactions. Tools like bUnit for Blazor component testing, Selenium for UI automation, and Postman or RestSharp for API testing help ensure that each micro-frontend meets functional requirements and integrates correctly with others. Furthermore, automated regression testing in CI/CD pipelines can detect any unintended changes introduced during module updates, ensuring that the application remains stable and reliable as new features are added.

The adoption of micro-frontends also enhances maintenance and long-term evolution of Blazor applications. Large applications often face challenges related to legacy code, outdated dependencies, and tightly coupled features. By decomposing the front end into independent modules, developers can update, refactor, or replace individual micro-frontends without affecting the entire application. This modular approach reduces technical debt and allows organizations to gradually adopt new technologies, optimize performance, and improve usability while maintaining operational continuity.

Finally, micro-frontend architectures can extend Blazor applications by consuming cloud-based AI services such as Azure OpenAI Service (or Azure OpenAI in Azure AI Foundry). Rather than the UI directly "integrating" with these services, Blazor components typically interact with back-end APIs that securely broker requests to the AI service. Each micro-frontend can interact with AI models independently, performing tasks such as natural language processing, content generation, or predictive analytics. By encapsulating AI interactions within dedicated modules, developers can scale AI workloads, monitor performance, and enforce security policies independently. This approach also facilitates experimentation and iterative improvements, as AI features can be deployed and refined in isolation without impacting unrelated modules.

Designing Reusable and Scalable Blazor Components

In modern web application development, the ability to create **reusable and scalable components** is a fundamental principle that directly impacts the maintainability, performance, and adaptability of the system. Within the Blazor framework, this principle is supported by the platform's structured component model and clear separation between UI rendering, business logic, and service layers, an inherent **component-based architecture**, which allows developers to encapsulate UI elements, business logic, and state management into discrete, modular units. Designing reusable and scalable Blazor components is not merely about breaking the UI into smaller pieces; it requires careful planning, adherence to architectural patterns, and consideration for performance, interoperability, and long-term evolution. By emphasizing modularity and scalability, organizations can ensure that Blazor applications can grow in complexity without becoming brittle, reducing technical debt and enhancing cross-team collaboration.

At its core, a **Blazor component** is a self-contained building block that combines markup, logic, and styling. Blazor components use Razor markup combined with C# for UI logic and can run either server-side (Blazor Server) or client-side (Blazor WebAssembly), depending on the chosen hosting model. Like modern JavaScript frameworks, Blazor also follows a component-based architecture, but it leverages the .NET ecosystem for application logic and tooling. The fundamental advantage of this approach is that components can maintain their own **state** while exposing clear **parameters** and **events** to parent components. To achieve reusability, developers must design components with **well-defined interfaces**. In Blazor, use parameters for component input and EventCallback<T> for output events. For editable or two-way values, follow the @bind pattern, which combines a parameter with an EventCallback<T> to support synchronized state updates. By adhering to this design pattern, components become predictable and encapsulated, allowing them to be reused across multiple views, modules, or even different applications.

Scalability, in the context of Blazor components, involves more than just performance under high user load; it also encompasses **architectural scalability**, which allows components to be extended, composed, or replaced without impacting the overall system. A scalable component is modular, loosely coupled, and adheres to the **single-responsibility principle**, ensuring that it performs a specific function without unnecessary dependencies. For example, a date picker component should handle date selection and validation internally but delegate formatting, localization, or storage responsibilities to external services or parent components. This separation of concerns makes it possible to integrate the component into various contexts without modification. Additionally, scalable components often employ **dependency injection** to acquire services dynamically, reducing hard-coded dependencies and enabling easier testing, mocking, and substitution.

One of the most critical aspects of designing reusable components in Blazor is **parameterization and templating**. By exposing configurable parameters, components can adapt their behavior, appearance, or content based on the consuming context. For instance, a data grid component can accept parameters for column definitions, sorting options, and row templates, making it versatile across multiple data sets and UI scenarios. Blazor also supports RenderFragment and RenderFragment<T>, which allow developers to define dynamic content regions that can be rendered within a component [12]. However, their use should consider component lifecycle behavior and rendering performance, as frequent re-rendering or large fragment trees can impact UI responsiveness and memory usage. Templating allows components to render custom UI elements passed from the parent component, making them highly reusable without duplicating code. This flexibility is especially valuable in enterprise applications where the same functional element such as a form, chart, or card must appear in multiple contexts with slight variations.

State management is another key factor in scalable component design. Components must manage their own local state while providing mechanisms for the application or parent components to observe and modify that state. Blazor provides several approaches for state management, including local component state, cascading parameters, and DI-backed state containers implemented through scoped or singleton services. However, the choice of pattern must account for the hosting model and render mode. In Blazor Server, scoped services are tied to the user's circuit (connection), whereas in Blazor WebAssembly, scoped services behave similarly to singletons for the lifetime of the browser session. For enterprise applications, a DI-backed state container pattern registered with the appropriate service lifetime offers a controlled and testable way to manage shared application state across components. Local state is suitable for simple, isolated components, while cascading parameters allow for the propagation of shared state across nested components. For larger applications, especially those employing **micro-frontends**, application-wide state management through service-based patterns or libraries such as **Fluxor** ensures that components remain synchronized and consistent, even when distributed across multiple modules. Proper state management prevents issues such as race conditions, redundant rendering, and inconsistent UI behavior, which can compromise both usability and performance.

Performance optimization is essential when designing scalable Blazor components. Components must minimize unnecessary re-rendering, reduce computational overhead, and manage memory efficiently. Blazor supports **component lifecycle methods**, such as `OnInitializedAsync`, `OnParametersSetAsync`, and `ShouldRender`, which allow developers to control when components render or update. Blazor allows components to override ShouldRender() to control whether a render cycle occurs; however, this is an advanced technique and should be used sparingly. Incorrect use can introduce subtle UI inconsistencies, so any overridden logic should clearly document the invariants that determine when rendering is safe to skip. In most cases, performance improvements are better achieved by reducing unnecessary state changes, splitting large components into smaller ones, using @key to preserve element identity, minimizing cascading updates, and leveraging the Virtualize component for large lists. Before applying render-level optimizations, measure actual performance using browser developer tools and .NET profiling diagnostics to ensure optimization efforts are justified. Additionally, techniques such as **virtualization**, particularly in components that display large lists or tables, allow Blazor to render only the visible subset of data, drastically reducing memory usage and improving performance. Asynchronous data fetching and event handling further ensure that long-running operations do not block the UI, maintaining a smooth user experience even under heavy load.

Styling and theming also play a critical role in reusable component design. Components should avoid tightly coupling CSS or styling to specific implementations. Instead, developers can use **CSS isolation**, **scoped CSS**, or **CSS variables** to encapsulate styling within the component while still supporting global theming. This approach ensures that components maintain a consistent appearance across different modules and applications while allowing developers to adapt the design to organizational branding or user preferences. Moreover, integrating components with a **design system** or shared component library enhances reusability and consistency, as teams can rely on standardized components that adhere to accessibility, usability, and visual guidelines.

Testing and maintainability are vital considerations in component design. Reusable components must be **unit-testable**, ensuring that their behavior remains predictable and reliable as the application evolves. Tools such as **bUnit** enable developers to write test cases for Blazor components, verifying rendering, event handling, and parameter behavior. Integration with **external services and APIs** further enhances the scalability of Blazor components. Components can be designed to interact with back-end services through **HTTP clients**, **gRPC**, or **SignalR**, abstracting the service layer from the UI logic. For example, a notification component could subscribe to real-time events from a SignalR hub, displaying alerts dynamically without coupling to a specific server implementation. By decoupling components from the underlying data sources, developers ensure that components can be reused in multiple applications or contexts while allowing back-end services to evolve independently. This separation also supports **modular architecture patterns**, where micro-frontends can compose and orchestrate reusable components dynamically.

Security considerations are integral to scalable component design, particularly in enterprise applications that handle sensitive data. Components should validate and authorize user input in alignment with the application's security model. In Blazor, this typically involves combining built-in form validation mechanisms with authorization controls such as AuthorizeView and policy-based authorization to ensure UI elements and actions are restricted appropriately. Additionally, developers should exercise caution when rendering dynamic content using MarkupString, as improper handling can introduce cross-site scripting (XSS) risks, handle authentication and authorization appropriately, and prevent vulnerabilities such as cross-site scripting (XSS) or injection attacks. Blazor's **built-in input validation**, along with data annotations and custom validation logic, ensures that components enforce proper data integrity. Additionally, components that integrate with services such as **Azure OpenAI** or other APIs must manage credentials and secrets securely, using techniques like **Azure Key Vault**, **managed identities**, or token-based authentication. By designing components with security in mind, developers reduce the risk of introducing vulnerabilities that could compromise the application or its users.

Composition and modularity are central to creating scalable Blazor components. Components should be designed to be composable, meaning that they can be combined with other components to create more complex UI elements without losing modularity.

For example, a dashboard page could compose multiple smaller components, such as charts, tables, and filters, each of which is independently developed, tested, and maintained. Composition enables the creation of complex functionality without duplicating code, supports incremental updates, and facilitates parallel development across teams. Additionally, modular components allow organizations to adopt **feature-based development**, where features can be developed, deployed, or replaced independently, aligning with micro-frontend architectures and agile delivery practices.

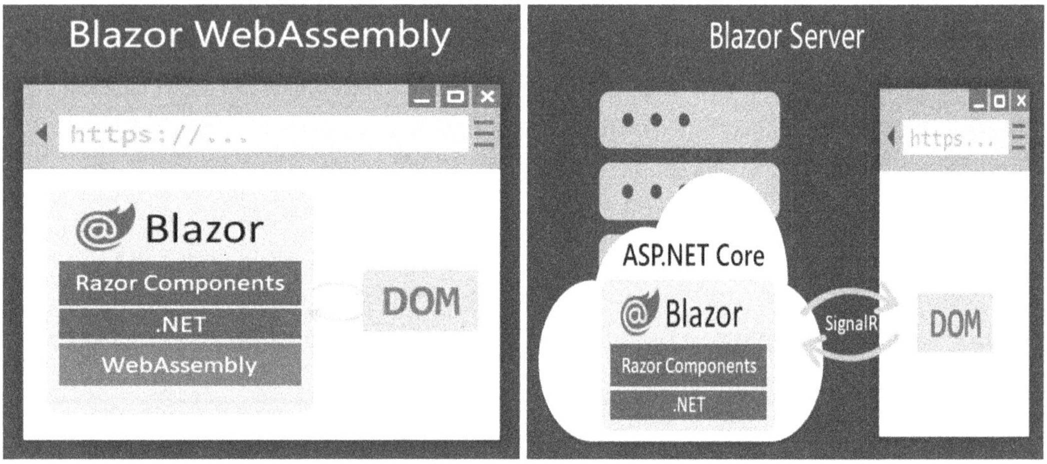

Figure 4-2. *Blazor WebAssembly vs. Blazor Server (Source: Microsoft)*

Versioning and lifecycle management are essential for reusable components that are shared across teams or projects. Components should be versioned using semantic versioning principles, allowing teams to track changes, introduce new features, and fix bugs without breaking dependent applications. Package managers such as **NuGet** or private artifact repositories can distribute reusable Blazor components, while CI/CD pipelines automate testing, packaging, and deployment. Proper versioning and lifecycle management reduce integration friction, ensure backward compatibility, and allow multiple applications to leverage the same component library safely.

Finally, the adoption of **advanced design patterns** enhances the scalability and maintainability of Blazor components. Patterns such as **MVVM (Model-View-ViewModel)**, **Mediator**, or **Decorator** can help organize component logic, manage dependencies, and extend functionality without violating encapsulation. For example, a form component could use the MVVM pattern to separate UI rendering from business rules, while a notification component could use the Mediator pattern to broadcast events to other components dynamically. Leveraging these patterns ensures that components remain flexible, extensible, and aligned with enterprise-grade architecture principles.

Facilitating Cross-Team Collaboration in UI Development

Building a sophisticated Blazor application that embraces micro-frontend principles and modular UI design requires more than technical expertise; it demands a deliberate approach to cross-team collaboration. Modern enterprise software seldom originates from a single developer or even a single department. Instead, large distributed teams of front-end engineers, back-end specialists, UX designers, QA testers, and DevOps practitioners must work in concert to deliver a cohesive user interface. Collaboration in this context extends beyond simply holding meetings or exchanging emails. It means creating processes, standards, and tools that allow many contributors to develop and evolve different parts of the application without introducing inconsistencies, performance bottlenecks, or duplicated effort.

A unified design language forms the first pillar of successful collaboration. When everyone adheres to a common set of visual and interaction patterns—typography, color palettes, spacing scales, and animation guidelines—the finished product feels seamless to the user even though dozens of people may have contributed to it. In a Blazor environment, this often takes the form of a shared component library that codifies the organization's design system into reusable Razor components. These components encapsulate markup, styling, and behavior so that teams across the company can pull from the same source of truth rather than re-implementing similar elements with small but noticeable differences. Design tools such as Figma or Adobe XD and development tools like Storybook can be linked into the workflow so that designers and developers iterate on the same living style guide. By eliminating ambiguity in look and feel, a design system prevents repetitive work and promotes consistency.

A central component library also accelerates development and fosters trust between teams. When a group publishes a button, modal, or data grid component to a private NuGet feed or an internal Git repository, other teams can immediately reuse it, confident that the package follows semantic versioning and has passed automated tests. Continuous integration pipelines can run unit tests with bUnit, static code analysis, and accessibility checks before new versions are distributed. This shared repository model encourages ownership of well-defined pieces of functionality and stops the endless cycle of “reinventing the wheel” that plagues large organizations. Teams can focus on higher-level problems knowing that the fundamental building blocks are stable and supported.

Of course, technology alone does not guarantee collaboration. Clear communication practices are equally important. Agile ceremonies such as sprint planning, backlog refinement, and daily stand-ups give teams visibility into each other’s progress and potential roadblocks. Architecture Decision Records capture the reasoning behind choices like API contracts or component boundaries so that future contributors understand why certain paths were taken. Tools such as Azure DevOps Boards, Jira, or GitHub Projects help manage stories and tasks across many squads. Pair programming sessions, design reviews, and asynchronous code reviews provide additional checkpoints where ideas can be shared and standards reinforced. When teams document and discuss their decisions openly, the project benefits from collective intelligence instead of isolated silos.

Defining the right team boundaries is another subtle but critical aspect of collaboration. Drawing inspiration from domain-driven design, organizations can align teams around specific business domains—billing, analytics, and user management—and let each group own the Blazor micro-frontends that implement their domain. These modules communicate with the rest of the system through well-defined APIs or message buses rather than by sharing tightly coupled code. Such autonomy enables each team to deploy, scale, and evolve its portion of the application independently while maintaining a unified end-user experience. This organizational structure mirrors the modular architecture of the software itself, reducing dependencies and coordination overhead.

Version control strategy also plays a decisive role. Whether the organization chooses a single mono repo or multiple repositories, branching patterns such as trunk-based development or GitFlow must be clearly defined to avoid integration headaches. Pull requests become the natural gate for peer review and automated testing, ensuring that new code meets agreed-upon standards before merging. Well-designed CI/CD pipelines can run bUnit component tests, Playwright or Selenium end-to-end tests, and static analysis so that regressions are caught early. Automated validation fosters confidence among teams that parallel development will not break the application.

Documentation serves as the connective tissue that keeps everyone aligned as the code base grows. Beyond a static wiki, living documentation generated from the code base using tools like DocFX or Markdown-based GitHub Pages ensures that API specifications, architectural diagrams, and component usage guides stay current.

Regular knowledge-sharing sessions, recorded demos, and internal conferences help spread insights from one module to the rest of the organization. When documentation and learning are treated as integral to the development process rather than afterthoughts, teams can onboard new members quickly and avoid repeating mistakes.

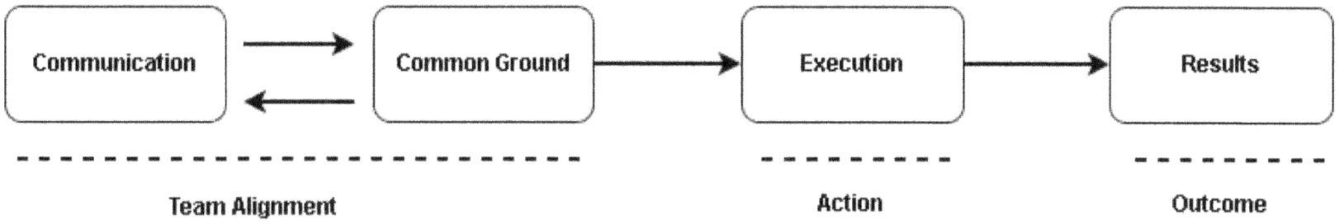

Figure 4-3. *Cross-Functional Team*

Many concerns in a large Blazor application cut across team boundaries and therefore demand coordinated solutions. Authentication, authorization, localization, telemetry, and performance monitoring should be implemented as shared services or middleware rather than duplicated in each micro-frontend. For example, a single authentication service can expose Razor components for login and token management so that all modules use the same secure flow. Centralized telemetry libraries and a unified observability stack with Azure Monitor or Application Insights make it possible to track performance and user behavior consistently across modules, simplifying troubleshooting and capacity planning.

Integrating Modular UI Components into Micro-Frontend Architecture

Integrating modular UI components within a micro-frontend architecture in a Blazor-based solution reflects a broader shift toward scalable and team-aligned front-end design. As applications grow in size and complexity, decomposing large monolithic front ends into independently developed units can improve maintainability and organizational agility. However, it is important to note that Blazor does not provide native micro-frontend isolation or orchestration out of the box. Implementing true micro-frontends requires additional architectural infrastructure, such as iframe-based isolation, reverse-proxy composition, backend-for-frontend (BFF) patterns, or other module composition strategies. These integration approaches are architectural decisions external to core Blazor and must be carefully designed to ensure consistent routing, authentication, shared design systems, and operational governance while still delivering a seamless user experience. The concept mirrors the microservices pattern on the back end but is applied to the user interface. The true art lies in bringing these independent pieces together into a coherent whole, and when combined with Blazor's component model, the process of integrating modular UI components requires careful planning, disciplined design, and the right supporting infrastructure.

At the heart of this approach is the idea of **modularity**. A modular UI component is self-contained, encapsulating its own markup, styling, behavior, and often its state management logic. In a Blazor application, components are naturally modular because each is defined in a Razor file with its own lifecycle methods and well-defined parameters for data exchange. However, when integrating such components into a micro-frontend ecosystem, the challenge shifts from simply reusing a component within a single project to enabling it to work across multiple independently deployed applications. This requires the component to be both technologically agnostic enough to survive different hosting environments and robust enough to handle various configurations and data contracts.

A critical step in integration is defining **clear contracts** between the micro-frontends and the components they consume. These contracts include data structures, events, and interaction patterns that must remain stable even as each micro-frontend evolves independently. In a Blazor context, this often involves strongly typed models shared through a versioned package, along with explicit component parameters and event callbacks. By clearly documenting these contracts and enforcing them through automated tests and continuous integration pipelines, teams can ensure that updates to a component do not inadvertently break the consuming micro-frontend or vice versa. Versioning becomes paramount: semantic versioning of component libraries allows multiple micro-frontends to depend on the same component while upgrading at their own pace, reducing the risk of regressions.

The deployment strategy also plays a pivotal role in integration. In a micro-frontend architecture, each team may deploy its piece of the UI independently, which means components must be packaged and delivered in a way that is discoverable and easy to integrate. For Blazor, reusable components are often published as NuGet packages or served as static assets via a content delivery network (CDN). Teams consuming these components must have pipelines capable of automatically retrieving the latest approved versions. This decoupled deployment empowers teams to innovate without waiting for a centralized release cycle, but it also demands strict quality controls, such as automated bUnit tests, static analysis, and security scanning before publishing a new component version.

Communication between micro-frontends and modular components requires thoughtful coordination. Because micro-frontends often operate in separate runtime contexts, sometimes even across different domains or servers, they cannot rely on direct in-memory method calls to share state. Instead, integration may occur through browser events, message buses, or shared services that expose APIs. For example, a global event dispatcher in JavaScript or a SignalR hub can broadcast events to which Blazor components subscribe, enabling them to react to changes elsewhere in the application. Components themselves can expose well-defined event callbacks, allowing parent micro-frontends to respond to user interactions without tightly coupling to the component's internal logic. This separation of concerns preserves independence while allowing seamless user flows.

Styling and theming present another dimension of integration. In a micro-frontend environment, different teams might adopt different CSS frameworks or naming conventions, leading to potential conflicts when components are composed together. Blazor's CSS isolation feature offers an elegant solution by scoping styles to the component's own markup, ensuring that styles do not leak across boundaries. At the same time, to maintain a unified brand identity, shared design tokens or CSS variables can be propagated across micro-frontends so that colors, typography, and spacing remain consistent. A global design system or style guide, ideally implemented as a shared Blazor component library, provides the foundation for visual coherence while allowing individual teams the flexibility to evolve their micro-frontends.

Performance optimization is essential when integrating modular UI components into a composite architecture. Each micro-frontend may load its own scripts, styles, and assets, and careless integration can result in redundant downloads, large bundle sizes, and slow initial page loads. To mitigate this, teams can adopt techniques such as code splitting, lazy loading, and asset deduplication. Blazor WebAssembly applications can optimize payload size and startup performance through multiple techniques, including static asset caching, publish-time trimming (PublishTrimmed) to remove unused IL code, and response compression such as Brotli. Where appropriate, optional Ahead-of-Time (AOT) compilation can further improve runtime performance, although it may increase the initial download size. These deployment time optimizations should be carefully evaluated based on application size, performance requirements, and hosting constraints. When components are delivered through a CDN, versioned caching policies ensure that browsers only download updated assets, improving both performance and scalability. Additionally, Blazor provides the <Virtualize> component to efficiently render large datasets by displaying only the items currently visible in the viewport. This can be used with an ItemsProvider delegate to support on-demand data loading or server-side paging. When implementing virtualization, developers should consider accurate item size estimation and measurement behavior, as incorrect sizing assumptions can affect scroll performance and user experience.

Security cannot be overlooked in a micro-frontend ecosystem, where multiple teams may contribute to code that runs within the same browser environment. Integrating modular components safely requires consistent authentication and authorization mechanisms across all micro-frontends. A shared identity provider, such as Microsoft Entra ID or another OpenID Connect–compliant service, enables centralized authentication so that users sign in once. Authentication and authorization context are then propagated across components through issued tokens and associated claims, rather than through direct credential sharing. Components themselves must implement robust input validation and adhere to best practices for preventing cross-site scripting (XSS) or injection attacks, especially when accepting data from external services. Secrets and API keys required by certain components, such as those integrating with Azure OpenAI services, must be securely managed through Azure Key Vault or similar services, never hard-coded in client-side code.

Testing and quality assurance become even more critical when multiple independent teams contribute modular components to a shared user interface. Automated testing frameworks such as bUnit for unit testing Blazor components, Playwright or Selenium for end-to-end testing, and load testing tools to simulate heavy traffic help ensure that integrated components behave as expected. Continuous integration pipelines should run these tests whenever a component or micro-frontend is updated, providing immediate feedback and preventing regressions. Consumer-driven contract testing can also verify that the contracts between components and micro-frontends remain intact, catching breaking changes early in the development cycle.

Effective observability is a natural extension of testing and monitoring. With many moving parts, identifying the source of a performance issue or bug can be challenging without centralized logging, tracing, and metrics. Integrating modular UI components into a micro-frontend architecture requires a unified observability strategy, typically leveraging Azure Monitor or Application Insights. Each component should emit structured logs and telemetry events with clear identifiers so that administrators can trace a user's journey across micro-frontends. Real-time dashboards and alerting systems provide insight into application health, helping teams detect and resolve issues quickly.

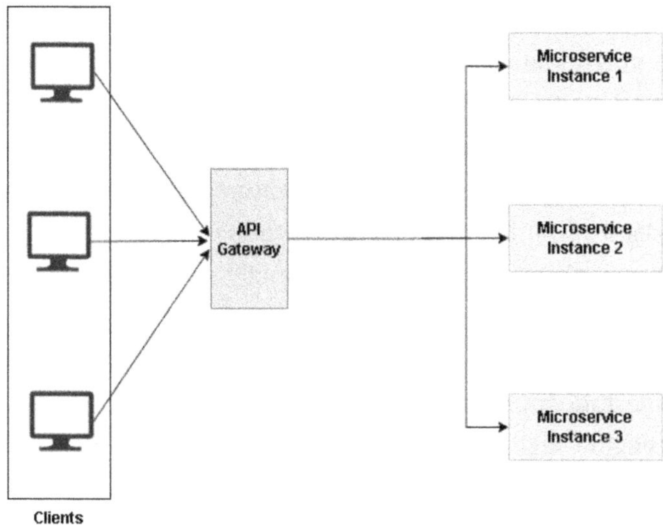

Figure 4-4. *Micro-Frontends: Reinventing UI in the Microservices World*

Cross-team collaboration is a cornerstone of successful integration. While each team may own its micro-frontend or component, they must all adhere to shared architectural guidelines and development practices to avoid chaos. This includes agreeing on coding standards, reviewing architecture decisions through documented records, and maintaining comprehensive documentation for every component's API and usage. A central governance group or architecture board can facilitate these discussions and enforce guidelines without stifling innovation. Teams should also hold regular knowledge-sharing sessions to surface lessons learned and align on upcoming changes, ensuring that everyone remains informed and engaged.

Deployment orchestration in production further illustrates the complexity of integrating modular UI components. Strategies such as blue-green deployments, canary releases, and feature flags allow individual components or micro-frontends to be updated independently without downtime. Infrastructure-as-code tools such as Bicep (preferred) or ARM templates, along with Terraform, can be used to provision and manage staging and production environments in a consistent and repeatable manner, while continuous deployment pipelines automatically promote approved builds. When executed properly, these practices enable rapid iteration and reduce the time from development to user feedback, a critical advantage in competitive markets.

The business benefits of integrating modular UI components into a micro-frontend architecture are substantial. Organizations gain the ability to scale development across multiple teams, accelerate delivery by allowing parallel workstreams, and enhance maintainability by isolating changes to specific domains. Teams can evolve their technology stacks and update frameworks semi-independently, provided they adhere to agreed integration contracts, shared interfaces, and architectural boundaries. For example, while one team builds a Blazor WebAssembly micro-frontend that interacts with Azure OpenAI services for intelligent chat features, another team can maintain a Blazor Server-based administrative dashboard, and both can integrate common components such as authentication controls or analytics widgets without conflict.

From a strategic perspective, the integration of modular UI components allows enterprises to future-proof their applications. As new technologies emerge or user expectations evolve, individual components can be replaced or upgraded without a full-scale rewrite. This agility aligns with modern DevOps practices and continuous delivery pipelines, enabling organizations to respond rapidly to market changes or regulatory requirements. Moreover, by embracing modularity, companies reduce technical debt, as components can be refactored or re-architected incrementally rather than in massive, risky overhauls.

In the end, integrating modular UI components into a micro-frontend architecture is both a technical and organizational challenge. It requires careful attention to component design, versioning, deployment, communication, styling, performance, security, testing, observability, and governance. Blazor's powerful component model provides a natural foundation for modular development, while Azure's cloud services supply the infrastructure to deploy and scale these components reliably. By embracing these practices, development teams can deliver rich, cohesive user experiences built from independently developed modules, striking the perfect balance between autonomy and consistency. The result is a Blazor application that not only meets current business needs but is also prepared to evolve gracefully as technology and requirements continue to advance.

CHAPTER 5

Event-Driven and Reactive Patterns

State Management Strategies

State management lies at the heart of any interactive web application, and in Blazor, it becomes even more critical because the framework blends the power of .NET with the dynamic requirements of modern single-page applications. "State" refers to any data that represents the current condition of an application: user preferences, session details, UI selections, cached API results, and more. Managing that state effectively is what ensures that a Blazor app remains responsive, predictable, and scalable, regardless of whether it runs on the server or directly in the browser through WebAssembly. Without a robust strategy, developers risk inconsistent UI updates, unnecessary re-renders, and hard-to-trace bugs as the application grows in complexity.

In .NET 10, Blazor applications are built using the Blazor Web App model, where components operate under configurable render modes: static server-side rendering (SSR), interactive server, interactive WebAssembly, or auto rather than separate hosting models [13]. Each render mode determines where components execute and where state is maintained, directly influencing lifecycle behavior, persistence strategy, scalability, and user experience. Consequently, state management in modern Blazor applications should be framed in terms of render modes instead of the earlier distinction between Blazor Server and Blazor WebAssembly. In Blazor Server, the state is maintained on the server and synchronized with the client through a persistent SignalR connection. This means the server memory footprint and the lifetime of the circuit directly affect how state is stored. Developers should carefully design state boundaries in interactive server scenarios. Transient UI state (such as view models or short-lived interaction

A. Prasad and H. Singh, *Advanced Blazor Architecture with .NET 10 and Azure OpenAI*,
https://doi.org/10.1007/979-8-8688-2518-7_5

data) can remain in memory for performance, whereas durable or cross-session state should be persisted in a distributed cache or database to ensure resilience and scalability. Reconnection scenarios should restore state from the authoritative store rather than relying solely on in-memory data. Implementing an idempotent restore pattern where state rehydration can safely occur multiple times without duplication or inconsistency further strengthens reliability and guards against partial failures or dropped connections. In contrast, Blazor WebAssembly executes entirely in the user's browser, so state typically resides in the client memory or is persisted to local browser storage. Here, strategies must consider bandwidth constraints, serialization formats, and offline support. Understanding these underlying mechanics is the first step in crafting an effective plan.

At the component level, Blazor naturally encourages encapsulation of local state. Each Razor component can maintain its own private fields and properties to track values like form inputs or UI toggle positions. This approach is ideal for simple, isolated interactions because the state lives only as long as the component instance does. For example, a counter component can store its count in a private integer field and update the UI instantly when a user clicks a button. Blazor's rendering engine automatically re-renders a component when its state changes within the normal UI event pipeline, removing the need for direct DOM manipulation. However, in event-driven or reactive scenarios, state changes often originate outside standard component callbacks such as from timers, background tasks, or external service events. In these cases, the renderer must be explicitly notified, typically by calling InvokeAsync(StateHasChanged) or by raising a change event from a shared state container. State changes triggered outside Blazor event callbacks therefore require deliberate notification to ensure the UI remains consistent and responsive. However, as soon as multiple components need to share or synchronize data, purely local state becomes inadequate.

When a state must be shared across components, developers often turn to cascading parameters. Cascading parameters allow a parent component to provide data to an entire subtree of child components without explicitly passing it through every intermediate level. This is perfect for cross-cutting concerns such as theming, localization, or user authentication context. For example, an application might define a CascadingAuthenticationState that provides the current user identity to every child component that needs it. Cascading parameters simplify data flow and reduce boilerplate code, but they still operate within the component hierarchy. They are not as effective when sibling components that are not in the same subtree need to communicate or when the state must survive page navigation.

For application-wide state, a more centralized approach is often necessary. A common pattern is to use state container services registered in the dependency injection (DI) container. A state container is simply a service class that holds data and exposes events to notify subscribers when the data changes. Components inject this service and update or read its properties as needed. For example, in a .NET 10 Blazor Web App, a ShoppingCartState service can encapsulate cart data and expose a change notification event that is raised whenever items are added or removed. Components that depend on this shared state can subscribe during OnInitialized and trigger a UI refresh when notified. To ensure correct lifecycle management, especially in interactive server render mode, where circuits are established and torn down dynamically, event subscriptions should be released in Dispose(). This pattern ensures components are always rendered consistently with the latest state while preventing memory leaks caused by lingering event handlers. Because the dependency injection (DI) container governs service lifetimes, developers must select lifetimes carefully based on the render mode and execution model in .NET 10 Blazor Web Apps. In interactive server scenarios, a Scoped service provides per-circuit (per-user session) state isolation, whereas a singleton service is shared across all connected users and must not store user-specific data to avoid leakage. In interactive WebAssembly, however, Scoped services effectively behave like singletons within the client application instance, since the entire app runs in the browser. Understanding these distinctions is essential to designing safe, predictable state management across render modes. This approach offers a clean separation of concerns and makes it easy to test or extend the state logic.

As Blazor applications scale further, especially when they adopt event-driven or reactive patterns, more advanced state management solutions become attractive. Flux-like architectures such as Fluxor or Redux-style stores provide a predictable, unidirectional data flow. In these systems, the application state is stored in a single immutable object tree, and changes occur through discrete actions that describe what happened rather than how to mutate the state. Reducer functions process these actions to produce a new state, which then triggers UI updates. This pattern makes complex state transitions easier to reason about, supports powerful debugging tools like time travel, and fits naturally with reactive programming. Fluxor, for example, integrates seamlessly with Blazor, enabling developers to define actions, reducers, and effects that handle asynchronous operations like API calls while keeping the state logic pure and testable.

Persistence is a fundamental aspect of state management in .NET 10 Blazor Web Apps, particularly when applications must retain user data across refreshes or sessions. In interactive WebAssembly scenarios, browser-based storage is commonly accessed through JavaScript interop or well-established community libraries rather than framework-provided wrappers. It is important to distinguish between simple key/value storage and structured client-side databases, as each serves different use cases.

localStorage and sessionStorage provide straightforward key/value persistence. Libraries such as Blazored.LocalStorage (which is limited to localStorage and sessionStorage patterns) simplify access, or developers can use direct JavaScript interop for finer control. localStorage persists across browser restarts and is appropriate for durable preferences or cached responses, while sessionStorage is cleared when the browser tab closes and is better suited for temporary state, such as in-progress form data.

IndexedDB, by contrast, is a client-side database designed for larger or structured datasets, offline capabilities, and more advanced caching strategies. Access typically requires JavaScript interop or specialized libraries built specifically for IndexedDB support, as it is not included in Blazored.LocalStorage.

Regardless of the storage mechanism, sensitive data should be encrypted before persisting to the client, and serialization should be handled carefully, commonly using System.Text.Json to maintain both security and performance.

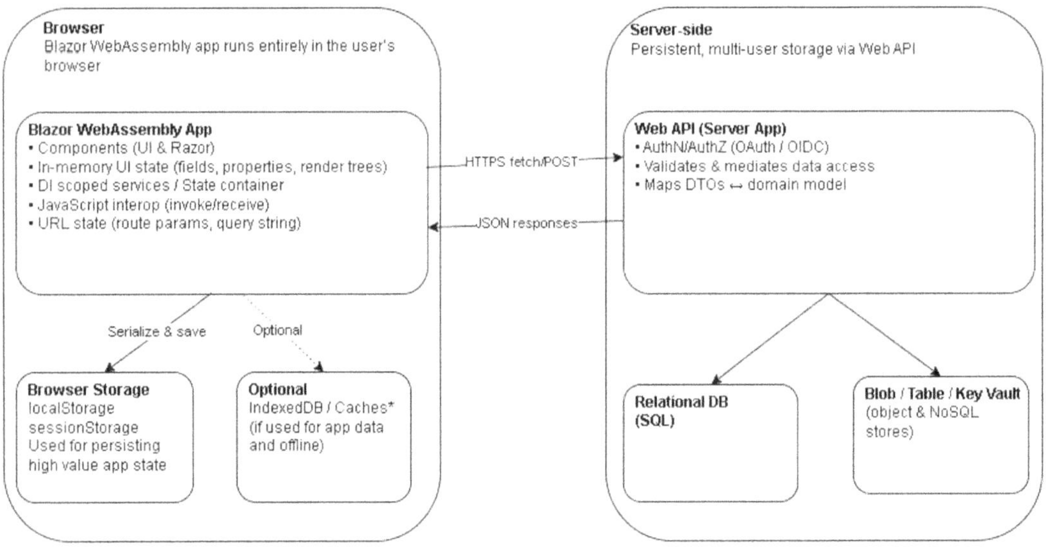

***Figure 5-1.** State Management in Blazor*

Blazor Server applications can also persist state using external stores such as distributed caches, SQL or NoSQL databases, or Azure services like Azure Cache for Redis [14]. Server-side state maintained within an interactive server circuit is transient and can be lost when a circuit terminates due to network interruptions or idle timeouts. For this reason, critical application data should be persisted outside the in-memory circuit, typically in a distributed cache or durable store. It is also important to distinguish between prerendering/hydration boundaries and circuit loss scenarios. During prerendering, components may execute on the server before becoming interactive, requiring explicit state restoration during hydration. Circuit termination, by contrast, represents a runtime disconnect that may require reloading state from an authoritative store. Treating these as separate recovery paths ensures consistent behavior and reliable state continuity across render modes. Developers might serialize session state to a database or a cache keyed by a session token so that a reconnecting client can seamlessly restore the user's context. This technique supports horizontal scaling across multiple server instances because state does not reside on a single machine.

Performance optimization plays a major role in successful state management. Every state change in Blazor can trigger a re-render of affected components. While the rendering system is efficient, unnecessary renders can hurt responsiveness. Developers can override the ShouldRender method to suppress unnecessary re-rendering when a state change does not impact the visible UI. This technique can improve performance in complex components; however, it should be used sparingly and with caution. Overuse or incorrect logic may lead to stale UI output or difficult-to-diagnose rendering issues. In most cases, Blazor's default rendering behavior is efficient, and manual intervention should be reserved for well-measured optimization scenarios. They can also break large pages into smaller components so that only minimal parts of the DOM update when data changes. Virtualization components, such as Virtualize, efficiently display long lists by rendering only visible items, reducing memory usage and improving scroll performance. Careful profiling using browser developer tools or Application Insights helps identify bottlenecks in real-time applications.

Effective state management must also consider real-time communication scenarios. Blazor integrates well with SignalR, allowing components to react instantly to server events such as chat messages, stock price updates, or IoT sensor readings. In these event-driven patterns, state changes originate on the server and must propagate to all connected clients. Components subscribe to SignalR events and update their state containers accordingly, ensuring that all users see up-to-date information. Combining

SignalR with Fluxor or similar reactive frameworks creates a powerful pipeline where external events trigger well-defined actions, maintain predictability, and keep the UI synchronized across distributed systems.

Security is inseparable from state management, particularly when dealing with authentication tokens, user roles, or sensitive business data. Developers must ensure that secrets or tokens are never exposed in client-side storage without encryption or proper expiration policies. Blazor provides data protection helpers such as ProtectedLocalStorage and ProtectedSessionStorage, which encrypt data before writing it to browser storage. These APIs are designed for server-interactive scenarios, where encryption and decryption occur on the server. However, their scope must be clearly understood; they help reduce the risk of casual inspection or tampering but do not make client-side storage inherently secure. Browser storage remains under user control, and sensitive or high-value data should not be relied upon solely because it is encrypted at rest. Proper threat modeling and server-side validation are still required when persisting data to the client. For server-hosted Blazor applications, integrating with ASP.NET Core Identity, Azure Active Directory, or OAuth providers ensures that stateful sessions align with robust authentication and authorization mechanisms. Additionally, components should always validate the state received from clients, as it may be tampered with in transit.

Testing and maintainability complete the picture of effective state management. Unit testing components and services ensures that state transitions behave as expected under various conditions. Frameworks like bUnit allow developers to render components in isolation, manipulate their state, and verify UI updates or event emissions. For complex state containers or Fluxor stores, developers can test reducer logic independently, ensuring that every action produces the correct new state. Automated testing integrated into continuous integration pipelines provides early detection of regressions as the application evolves.

As Blazor applications grow and teams adopt micro-frontend architectures or multi-team collaboration, state management also becomes an organizational concern. Clearly defined ownership of shared state services, consistent naming conventions, and thorough documentation prevent confusion when multiple teams work on different modules. Versioning shared state libraries and enforcing semantic contracts for state objects help maintain compatibility across evolving features.

In practice, effective state management in Blazor often involves combining several of these strategies rather than relying on a single technique. A small interactive widget might use only local component state. A user authentication context could flow through cascading parameters. A complex shopping cart might use a DI state container with persistence to local storage, while global application settings live in a Fluxor store. The key is to evaluate each scenario's requirements for scope, lifetime, performance, and security, then choose the simplest solution that satisfies those requirements.

Ultimately, state management is not an afterthought but a core architectural decision that shapes the reliability and responsiveness of a Blazor application. By understanding the strengths and trade-offs of component state, cascading parameters, DI services, Flux-like stores, and persistent storage options, developers can craft solutions that scale gracefully as features multiply and user expectations rise. Properly planned and well-tested state management leads to predictable data flow, easier debugging, and a seamless user experience. As event-driven and reactive patterns become increasingly central to modern web applications, mastering state management in Blazor is essential for building applications that remain robust, secure, and maintainable in the face of continuous change.

CQRS for Scalable Data Handling

Command Query Responsibility Segregation (CQRS) is a design pattern that separates write operations (commands), which modify application state, from read operations (queries), which retrieve data without changing it. By clearly distinguishing between these responsibilities, applications can optimize each path independently, improving clarity, scalability, and maintainability. While the idea may sound simple, the impact on scalability, maintainability, and performance in modern Blazor applications can be profound. By clearly distinguishing the pathways for reads and writes, developers can tune each side independently, leading to systems that handle high traffic loads, complex business logic, and ever-evolving user demands without sacrificing responsiveness.

In a traditional layered architecture, the same data model and service layer handle both queries and updates. For small applications, this shared model can work well, but as the system grows, it introduces friction. Read operations often require different optimizations than write operations. For example, a page displaying aggregated statistics might benefit from denormalized tables or precomputed views for speed, while write operations demand strict consistency and transactional guarantees. Coupling these concerns forces developers to make compromises, either slowing down reads to maintain consistency or relaxing integrity constraints to gain performance. CQRS resolves this tension by treating reads and writes as distinct concerns with their own models, storage patterns, and scaling strategies.

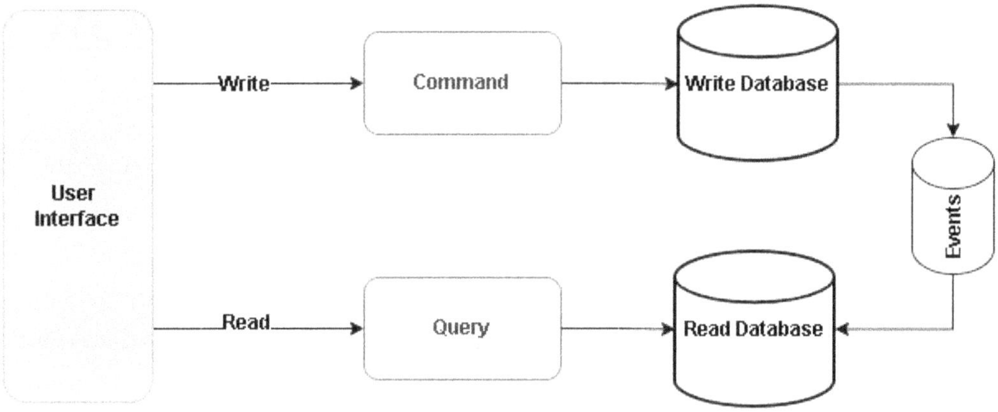

Figure 5-2. *CQRS Architecture*

In the context of a Blazor application, CQRS begins with how requests flow from the user interface. When a user interacts with the UI, perhaps submitting a form to create a new order, that action represents a command. Commands are intent-based; they specify *what* the user wants to do rather than dictating *how* the operation is performed. A command handler processes a command by enforcing business rules and coordinating the required state changes in the write model. In typical architectures, especially in WebAssembly-based applications, this logic resides behind a server-side API rather than in the client. The Blazor UI issues commands and queries through HTTP endpoints or service abstractions, keeping domain logic and persistence concerns on the server. When the UI needs to display data, for example, a customer's order history, it sends a query request to the read model, which returns data optimized for presentation without modifying application state. Queries are designed for efficient retrieval and can use read-optimized models, caching layers, or even entirely different database technologies to maximize speed. This separation allows each pathway to evolve according to its own performance and consistency needs.

Implementing CQRS typically involves defining distinct command and query objects, each with corresponding handlers. In .NET applications, one common option for implementing this pattern is the MediatR library, which acts as a mediator between Blazor components and the underlying application logic. MediatR helps decouple request dispatching from business logic execution, promoting separation of concerns and testability. However, it is not the only approach. Some teams prefer lightweight handler interfaces, vertical slice architectures, or alternative mediator libraries depending on application complexity, performance requirements, and dependency footprint. The choice should align with the overall architectural style rather than be treated as a default requirement. A Blazor component dispatches a command, MediatR routes it to the appropriate handler, and the handler executes the domain logic. For queries, the component issues a query object that retrieves the necessary data, again through a handler dedicated to read operations. This clear demarcation keeps the code base organized and easier to test: command handlers focus solely on side effects and state changes, while query handlers focus on fast, read-only data access.

A major advantage of CQRS is that it enables the use of different data stores for the read and write sides. The write model might use a normalized relational database to guarantee consistency and support complex transactions. Meanwhile, the read model can use a NoSQL store, a set of materialized views, or an in-memory cache like Azure Cache for Redis to deliver data quickly. Because the read side is decoupled from the write side, developers can precompute projections or join data from multiple sources without worrying about slowing down the transactional workload. In a high-traffic Blazor application, for example, a dashboard that must display real-time metrics to thousands of concurrent users, this flexibility can mean the difference between a sluggish user experience and a highly responsive one.

A more advanced evolution of CQRS is event sourcing, in which the state is derived from a sequence of immutable events rather than being stored solely as the current snapshot. Instead of updating records in place, each state transition is captured as an append-only event, allowing the system to reconstruct prior states and maintain a complete audit trail. While powerful, event sourcing introduces additional architectural complexity, storage considerations, and operational overhead. It should therefore be adopted deliberately, typically in domains that require strong auditability, temporal queries, or complex business workflows, rather than as a default extension of CQRS. Each command that modifies the system produces an event, which can be replayed to reconstruct the state at any point in time. In Blazor applications that require auditing, temporal queries, or complex business workflows, event sourcing provides a rich history of how the data evolved. The read side can subscribe to these events and update its projections accordingly, ensuring that queries always reflect the latest consistent view without tightly coupling to the write database.

Command Handling: Contains the command and handler responsible for processing requests that change application data

```
// Command representing a write request
public record BorrowBookCommand(string MemberId, string BookTitle);

// Contract for write-side persistence
public interface IBorrowingWriteRepository
{
    Task AddAsync(string memberId, string bookTitle, CancellationToken cancellationToken);
}

// Handles state-changing operations
public sealed class BorrowBookCommandHandler
{
    private readonly IBorrowingWriteRepository _repository;

    public BorrowBookCommandHandler(IBorrowingWriteRepository repository)
    {
        _repository = repository;
    }

    public Task HandleAsync(
        BorrowBookCommand command,
        CancellationToken cancellationToken)
    {
        return _repository.AddAsync(
            command.MemberId,
            command.BookTitle,
            cancellationToken);
    }
}
```

Query Handling: Contains the query and handler responsible for retrieving data without modifying application state

```
// Query representing a read request
1 reference
public record GetBorrowedBooksQuery(string MemberId);

// Contract for read-side data access
2 references
public interface IBorrowingReadRepository
{
    1 reference
    Task<IReadOnlyList<string>> GetByMemberAsync(
        string memberId,
        CancellationToken cancellationToken);
}

// Handles read-only operations
1 reference
public sealed class GetBorrowedBooksQueryHandler
{
    private readonly IBorrowingReadRepository _repository;

    0 references
    public GetBorrowedBooksQueryHandler(IBorrowingReadRepository repository)
    {
        _repository = repository;
    }

    0 references
    public Task<IReadOnlyList<string>> HandleAsync(
        GetBorrowedBooksQuery query,
        CancellationToken cancellationToken)
    {
        return _repository.GetByMemberAsync(
            query.MemberId,
            cancellationToken);
    }
}
```

Application Configuration and API Boundary: Configures dependency injection and exposes API endpoints that connect the Blazor UI to the server-side application logic

```
using Microsoft.AspNetCore.Builder;
using Microsoft.Extensions.DependencyInjection;
using Microsoft.Extensions.Hosting;

var builder = WebApplication.CreateBuilder(args);

// Register shared infrastructure store
builder.Services.AddSingleton<InMemoryBorrowingStore>();

// Bind store to read and write abstractions
builder.Services.AddSingleton<IBorrowingWriteRepository>(
    sp => sp.GetRequiredService<InMemoryBorrowingStore>());

builder.Services.AddSingleton<IBorrowingReadRepository>(
    sp => sp.GetRequiredService<InMemoryBorrowingStore>());

// Register application-layer handlers
builder.Services.AddScoped<BorrowBookCommandHandler>();
builder.Services.AddScoped<GetBorrowedBooksQueryHandler>();

var app = builder.Build();

// Write endpoint
app.MapPost("/api/borrowings",
    async (BorrowBookCommand command,
           BorrowBookCommandHandler handler,
           CancellationToken ct) =>
{
    await handler.HandleAsync(command, ct);
    return Results.Accepted();
});

// Read endpoint
app.MapGet("/api/borrowings/{memberId}",
    async (string memberId,
           GetBorrowedBooksQueryHandler handler,
           CancellationToken ct) =>
{
    var result = await handler.HandleAsync(
        new GetBorrowedBooksQuery(memberId), ct);

    return Results.Ok(result);
});

app.Run();
```

```
    // In-memory implementation for illustration
    3 references
    public sealed class InMemoryBorrowingStore :
        IBorrowingWriteRepository,
        IBorrowingReadRepository
    {
        private readonly List<(string MemberId, string BookTitle)> _borrowings = new();

        0 references
        public Task AddAsync(
            string memberId,
            string bookTitle,
            CancellationToken cancellationToken)
        {
            _borrowings.Add((memberId, bookTitle));
            return Task.CompletedTask;
        }

        0 references
        public Task<IReadOnlyList<string>> GetByMemberAsync(
            string memberId,
            CancellationToken cancellationToken)
        {
            IReadOnlyList<string> titles = _borrowings
                .Where(b => b.MemberId == memberId)
                .Select(b => b.BookTitle)
                .ToList();

            return Task.FromResult(titles);
        }
    }
```

In Blazor specifically, CQRS complements the framework's component-based design. Components can remain focused on rendering the UI and capturing user intent, delegating all business logic to the command and query handlers. This separation not only simplifies unit testing since handlers can be tested without rendering components but also enhances maintainability. Teams working on different parts of the application can evolve their command logic or query optimizations independently, reducing merge conflicts and enabling faster iteration.

Of course, adopting CQRS also introduces considerations that developers must manage carefully. Maintaining separate read and write models can increase complexity, particularly if the data schema changes frequently. Synchronizing the read model with the write model requires a reliable mechanism to propagate updates, whether through event handlers, message queues, or scheduled synchronization tasks. Inconsistent data between the two sides, even briefly, can lead to user confusion if not communicated properly. To mitigate these challenges, many systems adopt an event-driven messaging approach, using tools like Azure Service Bus or RabbitMQ to ensure that changes on the write side are promptly and reliably reflected in the read side. This pattern aligns naturally with Blazor's reactive capabilities, allowing components to subscribe to updates and refresh the UI when new events arrive.

Security is another essential factor. With commands and queries following distinct pipelines, developers must enforce authorization and validation rules on both sides. Commands require strict checks to ensure that only authorized users can modify data, while queries must guard against exposing sensitive information. Implementing role-based access control and ensuring encryption in transit are key steps when designing a secure CQRS architecture for applications that handle personal or financial data.

Despite these complexities, the benefits of CQRS for scalability and maintainability often outweigh the costs, especially as applications grow in size and traffic. By decoupling read and write concerns, teams can optimize performance, isolate failures, and scale each side independently. They can incorporate advanced patterns like event sourcing, caching, and asynchronous messaging without overhauling the core architecture. The result is a system that remains responsive and reliable under heavy load while still being flexible enough to evolve with changing business requirements.

In practice, applying CQRS in a Blazor application might start modestly. A team could begin by introducing separate command and query handlers without immediately splitting the database. Over time, as performance demands increase, they might introduce read replicas, caching layers, or specialized query stores. Because CQRS is a pattern rather than a rigid framework, it can be adopted incrementally, allowing developers to gain its advantages without a wholesale rewrite.

In summary, CQRS offers a robust blueprint for handling the competing demands of scalability, performance, and maintainability in modern Blazor applications. By segregating commands and queries, developers can tailor each side to its unique requirements, leverage specialized data stores, and integrate event-driven messaging for near-real-time updates. While it adds architectural complexity, the pattern rewards teams with clearer code organization, improved testing capabilities, and the flexibility to handle large-scale, data-intensive workloads with confidence. For Blazor projects that aspire to grow in features and traffic while maintaining a responsive user experience, CQRS is a powerful ally in building scalable, future-ready data handling.

Messaging in Blazor Apps

Messaging and reactive event patterns form the communication backbone of modern distributed applications, and their relevance becomes even more pronounced when you build interactive client experiences with Blazor. In a traditional monolithic web application, components usually communicate through direct method calls or tightly coupled services. While this can suffice for smaller applications, it quickly becomes unwieldy when the system must scale, handle real-time updates, or integrate with microservices, cloud-based resources, or Internet-of-Things (IoT) endpoints. Messaging decouples components by introducing an intermediary message that represents data or instructions passed between independent parts of the system. Reactive event patterns, in turn, allow those components to respond to events asynchronously, often in real time, producing a user experience that feels immediate and dynamic. In a Blazor application that needs to operate seamlessly across clients and services, these two concepts work hand in hand to create responsive, maintainable, and scalable architectures.

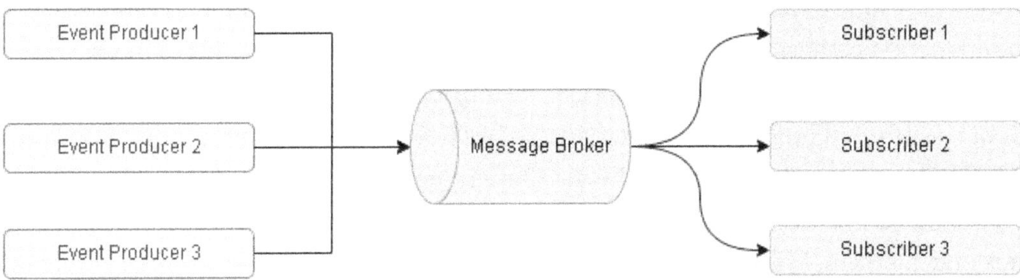

Figure 5-3. *Event-Driven Architecture*

In a Blazor context, messaging can occur within the application itself between Razor components or extend to external services and APIs. Within the app, developers often use a lightweight event bus or mediator pattern to avoid tight coupling. Instead of a parent component directly invoking methods on a child component, it can publish a message to a central bus, and any component interested in that message can subscribe and react. This is particularly powerful in larger projects where different sections of the UI may need to update in response to a shared change in application state, such as a user login, a theme switch, or a notification of new data. This approach simplifies code maintenance: when new features require reacting to those events, developers can simply subscribe new components without altering existing ones, preserving the Open/Closed Principle and facilitating parallel team development.

When applications extend beyond the client boundary, messaging is typically handled by back-end services that integrate with brokers such as Azure Service Bus, Azure Event Hubs, RabbitMQ, or Apache Kafka. The Blazor UI does not communicate directly with these messaging systems. Instead, server-side components process brokered messages and propagate relevant updates to the client using mechanisms such as SignalR, gRPC streaming, or, where necessary, HTTP-based polling. This separation preserves architectural boundaries while enabling reactive, real-time user experiences. Blazor applications can integrate with messaging infrastructure through asynchronous communication patterns implemented in back-end services. Rather than connecting directly to message brokers, the application typically relies on server-side components to publish and consume messages, then relay relevant updates to the UI. This approach preserves clear architectural boundaries while enabling responsive, event-driven user experiences. A server-side Blazor app might listen to a Service Bus topic for notifications about inventory changes, while a WebAssembly Blazor app could rely on SignalR to receive real-time push updates from a server that itself subscribes to an Event Hub stream. This separation ensures that the Blazor front end is not tightly bound to the business logic or data sources; instead, it merely responds to messages describing changes. Such decoupling greatly improves scalability. For example, imagine a retail dashboard built with Blazor that displays live order information from thousands of customers. Instead of querying the database repeatedly or polling endpoints, the dashboard can subscribe to a stream of order events. Whenever new orders arrive in the back end, an event is published to an Azure Event Grid topic, the server picks it up, and SignalR pushes a message to all active Blazor clients. Users see updates almost instantly, and system resources are used efficiently.

Reactive event patterns complement this messaging architecture by defining how the application responds to those messages. The term "reactive" refers to a programming style where data flows as streams of events, and the system reacts to changes rather than polling for them. In the .NET ecosystem, libraries like Reactive Extensions (Rx.NET) or built-in IAsyncEnumerable constructs provide powerful tools for composing asynchronous event streams. In a Blazor application, you might create observables that represent sequences of user interactions, API responses, or sensor data. Components can subscribe to these observables and update the UI when new values are emitted. This allows for complex interactions like combining multiple event sources, filtering data, buffering bursts of events, or throttling updates without resorting to intricate callback chains.

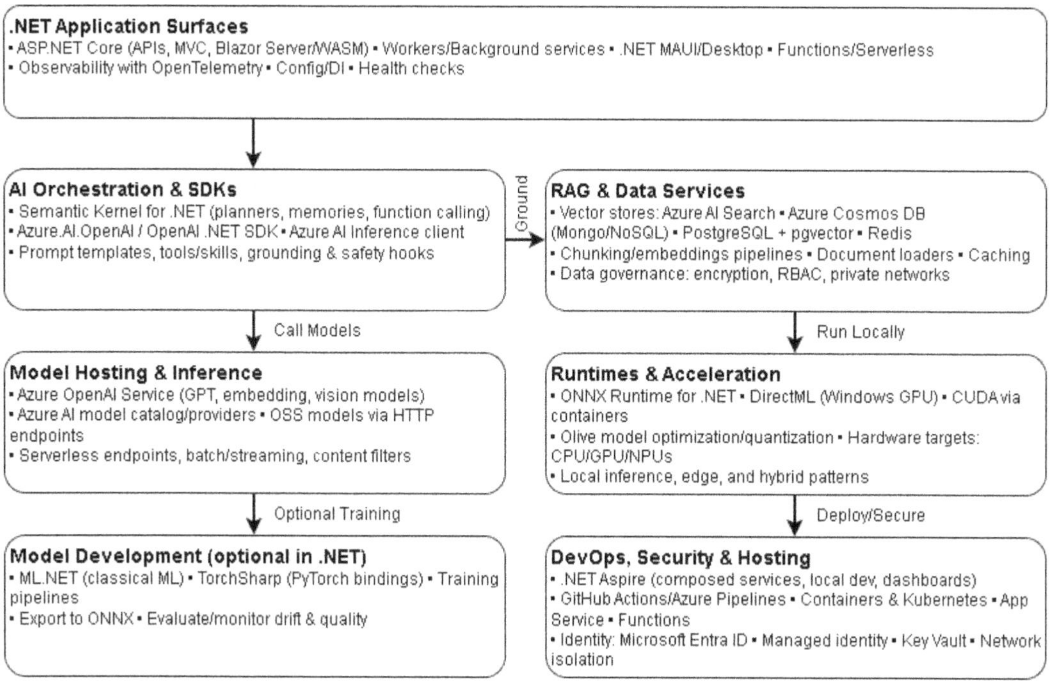

Figure 5-4. *.NET AI Ecosystem*

Consider a real-time stock trading dashboard built with Blazor WebAssembly. Market price updates arrive through a WebSocket connection as a continuous event stream. With a reactive pattern, you can represent those updates as an observable sequence and declaratively define how the UI should respond. You might buffer updates to avoid overwhelming the user, display average price changes over a sliding window, or trigger alerts when certain thresholds are crossed. All of this happens without writing imperative loops or manual timers. The system merely reacts to data as it flows in, yielding a responsive and maintainable code base. The same principles apply to sensor data from IoT devices, chat messages in collaboration tools, or telemetry events from a gaming platform.

A critical advantage of messaging and reactive event patterns is their impact on performance and scalability. Because messages are asynchronous, producers and consumers are decoupled in time as well as in structure. A producer, such as an order-processing microservice, can publish messages to a queue or topic without waiting for consumers to process them. This means that sudden spikes in demand, say, a flash sale generating a surge of orders, do not overload downstream services or the Blazor front end. Consumers process messages at their own pace, and if they need to scale horizontally, additional consumers can be added to share the load. This elasticity is a key design goal for modern cloud-native applications, and Azure services provide built-in features like autoscaling and dead-letter queues to ensure reliability and fault tolerance.

Implementing messaging and reactive patterns in a Blazor application built on .NET 10 often begins with selecting the right infrastructure. Azure Service Bus is a fully managed message broker that supports queues for point-to-point messaging and topics for publish-subscribe scenarios. When a Blazor app needs to receive notifications of new orders, for example, a back-end worker service can subscribe to a topic and then relay updates to connected clients using SignalR. Azure Event Grid, designed for high-scale event routing, can deliver events from many sources including Azure Blob Storage, IoT devices, or custom applications to endpoints like Azure Functions or webhooks. If you need near-real-time event ingestion from a vast number of producers, Azure Event Hubs offers a high-throughput solution ideal for telemetry or analytics pipelines. Integrating these services with Blazor typically involves creating a back-end API or worker service that listens to the message broker and uses SignalR hubs or gRPC streams to communicate with the Blazor front end. This hybrid approach balances scalability with the interactive requirements of modern web UIs.

Inside the Blazor application itself, developers can employ an internal event bus pattern to propagate state changes among components. This is often implemented using a simple singleton service that holds event delegates or, for a more sophisticated approach, a mediator library like MediatR. When a component publishes an event, the bus notifies all subscribers asynchronously. This reduces the need for parent–child component hierarchies to pass state through cascading parameters or direct references. For example, a shopping cart component could broadcast a "CartUpdated" event whenever items change, and other parts of the UI such as a mini-cart in the header or a checkout summary will automatically refresh without direct coupling. This internal messaging keeps components reusable and focused on their own responsibilities.

Security is another crucial consideration when applying messaging and reactive event patterns. Because messages can contain sensitive data and may traverse networks or multiple services, encryption and authentication are essential. Azure Service Bus supports Shared Access Signatures (SAS) and Azure Active Directory integration to ensure that only authorized producers and consumers can access queues and topics. For Blazor applications that use SignalR to receive real-time messages, authentication tokens must be properly validated on the server side, and connections should use HTTPS/WSS to protect data in transit [15]. Likewise, when using Rx.NET or other reactive libraries, developers must ensure that subscriptions are properly disposed of to avoid memory leaks and that error handling is in place to prevent unhandled exceptions from destabilizing the app.

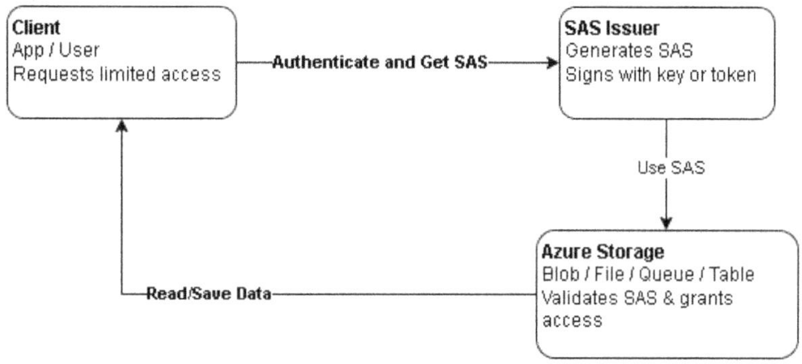

Figure 5-5. *Shared Access Signatures*

From a development workflow perspective, adopting messaging and reactive patterns encourages a mindset shift. Instead of focusing on direct function calls and immediate responses, teams think in terms of event contracts and asynchronous flows. Documentation must clearly define the schema of messages, including their payload and metadata, because producers and consumers may be developed by different teams or even different organizations. Versioning of message formats becomes important to avoid breaking changes. Testing also changes: rather than relying solely on traditional unit tests, developers use integration tests that simulate message publishing and verify that consumers respond appropriately. Tools like Azure Service Bus Explorer, Kafka console utilities, or custom in-memory event bus fakes help replicate real conditions for test automation.

In addition to system-level benefits, messaging and reactive event patterns enhance the user experience of Blazor applications. Real-time updates mean users don't need to refresh pages or manually request new data. For collaborative applications such as project management tools, live dashboards, or multiplayer games, this responsiveness is essential. When combined with Blazor's component model and .NET 10's performance improvements, developers can build highly interactive applications that rival native desktop or mobile apps. Features like Hot Reload and better asynchronous streaming in .NET 10 further simplify the development of reactive interfaces, allowing developers to preview and adjust UI changes in real time while data continues to flow.

Ultimately, messaging and reactive event patterns provide the foundation for building modern, cloud-ready Blazor applications that are both resilient and responsive. They enable decoupled architectures where services communicate through well-defined messages, ensuring that the system can scale horizontally, evolve over time, and handle bursts of activity gracefully. By leveraging Azure services such as Service Bus, Event Hubs, and SignalR, developers can implement these patterns without managing complex infrastructure. At the same time, using reactive programming techniques with tools like Rx.NET allows the Blazor client to respond to data streams intuitively and efficiently. As organizations continue to demand richer, real-time web experiences and as distributed systems grow in complexity, mastering these patterns is essential for any team that aims to deliver enterprise-grade solutions on the Microsoft stack.

The exploration of event-driven and reactive patterns in Blazor applications reveals that these approaches are more than just architectural preferences; they are essential strategies for building scalable, responsive, and future-proof web solutions. Throughout the chapter, we examined three key pillars: effective state management, the Command Query Responsibility Segregation (CQRS) pattern for scalable data handling, and the adoption of messaging with reactive event flows. Together, these practices enable a Blazor application to remain highly interactive while coping gracefully with complex, distributed workloads.

State management sits at the heart of every Blazor project. Without a solid plan for handling and synchronizing application state, even the most elegant user interface becomes brittle. By using techniques such as cascading parameters, scoped services, and centralized stores, developers can ensure that components remain cohesive yet loosely coupled. This allows UI elements to respond to user interactions or back-end changes without redundant rendering or excessive data transfers. The result is a seamless user experience and a code base that remains maintainable as the project grows.

CQRS builds on that foundation by separating the concerns of reading and writing data. Instead of relying on a single model for both tasks, commands handle mutations while queries focus on optimized reads. This division not only improves clarity and maintainability but also makes it far easier to scale specific parts of the system independently. High-volume reads can be routed to specialized read stores or caches, while critical writes remain consistent and secure. In a Blazor environment, CQRS empowers developers to handle heavy traffic or real-time updates such as dashboards, ecommerce inventory, or live analytics without sacrificing performance or correctness.

Messaging and reactive event patterns complete the picture by allowing the application to embrace true asynchronicity. Whether through internal event buses for component communication or cloud-level services like Azure Service Bus and Event Hubs, messages decouple producers and consumers. Components no longer wait for one another; they publish or subscribe, letting the system scale and evolve dynamically. Reactive programming with observables or streams amplifies this effect on the client side, enabling Blazor apps to process continuous flows of data, be it IoT sensor updates, stock market feeds, or collaborative editing events in real time. This responsiveness delivers the kind of modern, instantaneous user experience that today's audiences expect.

Taken together, these patterns transform Blazor from a straightforward .NET web framework into a platform capable of supporting complex, distributed, enterprise-grade applications. By adopting event-driven design, developers gain resilience and flexibility; by leveraging CQRS, they achieve scalability and clarity; and by embracing messaging with reactive programming, they unlock real-time interactivity. This chapter underscores that these techniques are not isolated tactics but complementary elements of a cohesive architectural approach. Teams that internalize these principles will be well prepared to build applications that remain maintainable, secure, and responsive even as user demands, data volumes, and infrastructure complexity continue to grow.

CHAPTER 6

Introducing Azure OpenAI in Blazor

Fundamentals of Integrating AI APIs

In recent years, artificial intelligence (AI) has become a transformative force across industries, reshaping how applications interact with users, analyze data, and automate complex processes. Microsoft's Azure OpenAI Services represents a significant advancement in this evolution, offering developers powerful AI models through a secure, scalable cloud platform. Understanding the core capabilities of Azure OpenAI and how it integrates within modern frameworks like Blazor is essential for building next-generation applications that are both intelligent and efficient.

Azure OpenAI Services brings the power of OpenAI's advanced language models, including GPT (Generative Pre-trained Transformer) variants, to the Azure cloud environment [16]. These models are designed to understand and generate human-like text, offering developers the ability to build conversational agents, automated content generators, summarization tools, and more. Unlike traditional AI APIs that rely on rigid rules or limited datasets, OpenAI models leverage deep learning on vast amounts of internet text to generate contextually rich and coherent responses, making them uniquely suited for complex natural language tasks.

The integration of Azure OpenAI within the .NET ecosystem, particularly with Blazor applications, opens new opportunities for building intelligent web applications and hybrid desktop experiences, such as those developed with Blazor Hybrid using .NET MAUI or WPF, where AI-powered capabilities can be integrated into both browser-based and native client interfaces. Blazor, a modern framework for building

A. Prasad and H. Singh, *Advanced Blazor Architecture with .NET 10 and Azure OpenAI*,
https://doi.org/10.1007/979-8-8688-2518-7_6

interactive web UIs with .NET, supports multiple execution models including Blazor Server, Blazor WebAssembly, and hybrid hosting. Across these models, AI integration enables developers to embed intelligent, data-driven features into user interfaces while leveraging the broader .NET ecosystem for secure and scalable back-end orchestration. This could range from chatbot assistants responding in real time to user queries to advanced recommendation systems, content generation, or automated code completion within developer tools. The capability to call Azure OpenAI APIs asynchronously from Blazor components allows seamless user experiences without sacrificing performance or responsiveness.

Azure OpenAI Services provide multiple models optimized for different tasks. The GPT family of models (e.g., GPT-3.5 and GPT-4) is accessed in Azure OpenAI Service via deployed model IDs, with versioning and availability managed at the service level rather than referenced solely by model name. Models can perform a variety of tasks such as text completion, translation, summarization, question answering, and conversational dialogue. Developers can control model behavior through prompt engineering, crafting structured prompts and system instructions to guide the model's responses. This differs from fine-tuning, which involves training a custom model on labeled examples to adapt it to specific tasks or domain requirements. This flexibility makes the Azure OpenAI platform highly adaptable, able to serve a broad spectrum of use cases from creative writing assistants to technical document summarizers.

Another crucial aspect of Azure OpenAI Services is the robust infrastructure supporting these models. Hosted on Microsoft's secure Azure cloud, the service ensures high availability, scalability, and compliance with enterprise-grade security standards. This makes it ideal for applications with demanding workloads or those requiring strict data governance. Enterprises benefit from Microsoft's broad compliance portfolio and regulatory commitments, including support for GDPR obligations and HIPAA-aligned safeguards through appropriate service configurations and agreements (such as a Business Associate Agreement where applicable). This helps organizations integrate AI capabilities while maintaining privacy, security, and regulatory alignment.

The service architecture itself revolves around RESTful APIs, which makes integration language-agnostic and accessible to any platform capable of making HTTP requests. However, when working within the .NET ecosystem and Blazor specifically, developers can utilize SDKs and libraries such as the Azure.AI.OpenAI client library (or Microsoft.Extensions.AI abstractions) to integrate AI capabilities into their applications that abstract much of the low-level API interaction, simplifying authentication, request formatting, and response parsing. This enhances developer productivity and reduces the likelihood of integration errors.

Key capabilities of Azure OpenAI Service include embeddings, fine-tuning, and support for Retrieval-Augmented Generation (RAG) patterns. Embeddings enable semantic search and similarity comparison by converting text into vector representations, while RAG combines model prompting with external knowledge retrieval to ground responses in enterprise data sources. Fine-tuning, by contrast, involves training a custom model variant on labeled examples to adapt behavior more deeply.

Prompting vs. RAG vs. Fine-Tuning

- **Prompting** is suitable when behavior can be guided through structured instructions or system messages without modifying the underlying model.
- **RAG** is appropriate when responses must incorporate up-to-date or domain-specific knowledge stored in external systems (e.g., documents, databases, vector stores).
- **Fine-tuning** is recommended when consistent behavioral adaptation or specialized domain output is required beyond what prompting alone can achieve.

For example, a legal firm might fine-tune a model on case law texts to improve its ability to generate summarize legal documents.

Embeddings enable semantic search and similarity comparisons by converting text into high-dimensional vector representations, empowering applications with enhanced search capabilities beyond simple keyword matching.

Within Blazor applications, leveraging these capabilities enables innovative user experiences. Imagine an interactive document editor powered by AI that suggests improvements or generates content on the fly. Or a customer support portal where AI-driven chatbots assist users 24/7, handling complex queries with natural language understanding and escalating issues only when necessary. The seamless integration within Blazor's component model means AI features can be encapsulated and reused across the application, maintaining clean architecture and modularity.

Performance considerations are also paramount when understanding Azure OpenAI services. While the models are powerful, invoking them involves network latency and processing time in the cloud. Developers must design Blazor applications to handle these asynchronous calls gracefully, using techniques such as optimistic UI updates, loading indicators, and caching results where appropriate. Microsoft provides usage guidelines and best practices for managing request rates and handling throttling, ensuring that applications remain responsive even under heavy load.

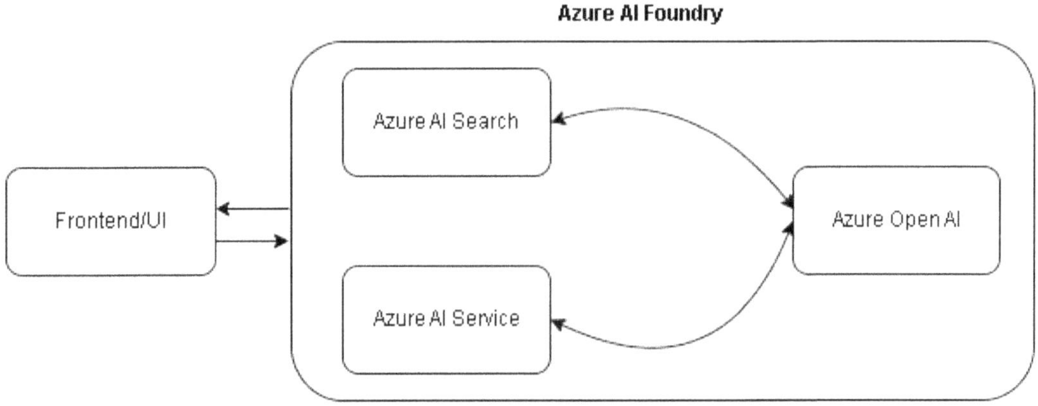

Figure 6-1. *Azure OpenAI Integration Options*

From a cost perspective, Azure OpenAI operates on a pay-as-you-go model where charges depend on the number of tokens processed, both input and output. This requires developers to be mindful of prompt length and model complexity to balance performance and expense. Fortunately, the Azure portal offers detailed monitoring and analytics, enabling teams to track usage patterns and optimize their applications accordingly.

The introduction of Azure OpenAI also raises important ethical considerations. The models generate content based on patterns learned from vast datasets that include publicly available internet data, which may contain biases or inappropriate content. Microsoft actively works to mitigate these issues by incorporating content filters, usage policies, and continuous model improvements.

Developers integrating these services must remain vigilant, implementing safeguards such as content moderation, user disclaimers, and transparency about AI involvement in their applications.

Limitations of Azure OpenAI Services and Their Capabilities

While Azure OpenAI services provide advanced natural language processing and generation capabilities, they also have inherent limitations that developers must understand. These models are trained on large datasets but lack true understanding or common-sense reasoning, which can lead to generating plausible-sounding but factually incorrect or misleading outputs. Their responses can sometimes be inconsistent or sensitive to slight changes in input phrasing, affecting reliability in critical applications. Additionally, these AI services operate as black boxes, offering limited transparency into how decisions or outputs are derived, which complicates debugging and explainability. There are also usage constraints such as rate limits, latency issues, and potential downtime, which may impact application responsiveness. Furthermore, AI models may inadvertently produce biased or harmful content, reflecting biases present in their training data, requiring ongoing monitoring and filtering. Lastly, integrating Azure OpenAI Service requires careful attention to data privacy and security. While Microsoft provides enterprise-grade safeguards including data isolation, encryption in transit and at rest, and contractual commitments that customer data is not used to retrain foundation models, organizations remain responsible for proper handling of sensitive information. This includes implementing PII redaction where appropriate, configuring data retention policies, managing logging hygiene to avoid unintended exposure of prompts or responses, and enforcing role-based access controls. Effective AI integration therefore combines Azure's platform-level protections with disciplined application-level governance to ensure compliance, confidentiality, and regulatory alignment.

Ethical and Responsible Use of AI in Blazor

As AI technologies like Azure OpenAI become deeply integrated into Blazor applications, it is essential to prioritize ethical and responsible use to maintain user trust and comply with regulatory standards. One of the foremost considerations is data privacy and user consent. Since AI models process user data to generate intelligent responses, developers must ensure that sensitive information is protected through secure communication protocols such as HTTPS, encryption, and limited data collection. Additionally, applications must adhere to data privacy regulations like GDPR and CCPA by clearly communicating how user data is used, offering transparency through privacy policies, and allowing users to opt out of AI-based processing if they choose.

Another critical challenge is addressing bias and fairness in AI outputs. AI models, including those offered by Azure OpenAI, are trained on large datasets that may contain inherent biases, which can unintentionally lead to unfair or discriminatory results. To mitigate these risks, developers should regularly test AI components for biased behavior, especially in applications influencing decisions with significant social impact, such as hiring or lending. Employing diverse training data, applying content filters, and incorporating human oversight can help reduce biased or harmful outputs and promote fairness.

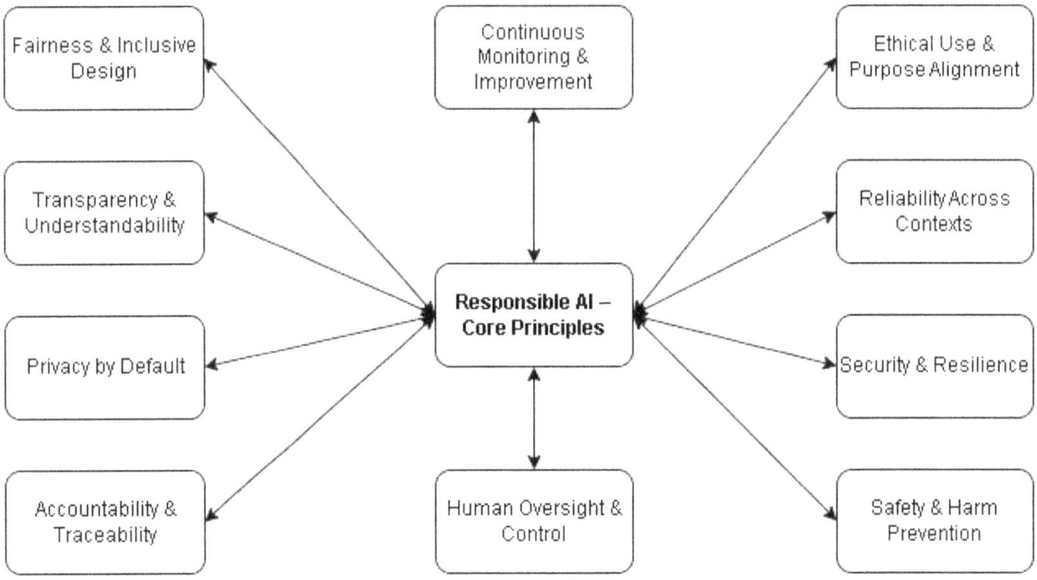

Figure 6-2. *Ethical and Responsible Use of AI in Blazor*

Transparency and explainability also play vital roles in responsible AI use. Users should be clearly informed when AI is generating content or providing recommendations, ideally through visible labeling or disclaimers within the UI. Providing explanations or contextual information about AI decisions enhances user understanding and trust, fostering a more informed interaction with the application.

Security considerations must not be overlooked. Protecting Azure OpenAI API keys and endpoints is crucial to prevent unauthorized access. Best practices include securely managing credentials and avoiding exposure on the client side, especially in Blazor WebAssembly applications, where code executes in the browser [17]. Secrets should never be embedded in client-side code. Instead, use secure storage mechanisms such as Azure Key Vault, environment variables, or managed configuration providers.

In production environments, prefer role-based authentication using Microsoft Entra ID and Managed Identities, allowing back-end services to authenticate without storing static keys. For server-side components (e.g., Blazor Server or API layers), secrets can be injected via secure configuration providers.

Preferred Authentication Hierarchy

1. Managed identity (recommended for Azure-hosted services)
2. Microsoft Entra ID with OAuth 2.0/OpenID Connect
3. Azure Key Vault–backed secret injection
4. Environment variables (for controlled environments)
5. Static API keys (last resort, server-side only)

In all cases, client-side applications such as Blazor WebAssembly should call back-end APIs rather than directly invoking external AI services, ensuring that secrets remain protected.

Moreover, it is important to apply defensive design patterns to mitigate prompt injection and related risks. Simple input sanitization alone is not sufficient. Instead, applications should combine structured system prompts, strict separation between user input and control instructions, output validation, allow-list or policy enforcement mechanisms, and, where appropriate, content filtering and human-in-the-loop review. For higher-assurance scenarios, retrieval sources should be constrained and validated, and sensitive operations should require explicit authorization checks outside the model's response. Monitoring API usage and implementing rate limits further help defend against abuse and maintain application stability.

Designing AI interactions with user control and continuous feedback mechanisms ensures a more responsible AI experience. Users should have the option to edit AI-generated content, request human review, or disable AI assistance altogether. Incorporating logging and feedback tools allows developers to monitor AI outputs and address issues promptly. Establishing ethical AI policies within your development team or organization helps maintain alignment with community standards and promotes a culture of responsible innovation.

Limitations in Ethical and Responsible Use of AI in Blazor

Despite best efforts to implement ethical AI practices in Blazor applications, several limitations persist. AI models can unintentionally perpetuate biases present in their training data, making it challenging to fully eliminate unfair or discriminatory outputs. Ensuring complete transparency and explainability of AI decisions is difficult due to the complex, often opaque nature of machine learning models, which can hinder user trust. Protecting user privacy is also limited by the need to send data to cloud-based AI services, exposing potential risks related to data leaks or non-compliance with evolving privacy regulations. Furthermore, it is challenging to guarantee that all AI-generated content is free from harmful or misleading information, requiring constant monitoring and manual intervention.

Architectural Best Practices for AI-Driven Blazor Applications

Integrating AI services such as Azure OpenAI into Blazor applications opens up exciting possibilities to create intelligent, personalized, and highly interactive user experiences. However, embedding AI functionality into Blazor apps also introduces architectural complexities that developers must carefully address to ensure the resulting applications are scalable, secure, maintainable, and performant. One of the fundamental considerations when building AI-driven Blazor applications is understanding the differences between Blazor's hosting models, Blazor Server and Blazor WebAssembly, and how these affect AI integration. Blazor Server applications run UI components on the server and communicate with the client over SignalR connections, allowing sensitive AI service credentials, such as API keys, to remain securely on the server. This simplifies securing the integration but requires a well-designed back-end infrastructure to handle potentially large volumes of AI calls without degrading performance. On the other hand, Blazor WebAssembly runs entirely in the browser, which poses a security challenge since embedding AI API keys in client-side code risks exposure. To mitigate this, Blazor WebAssembly applications often implement a Backend-for-Frontend (BFF) pattern, a dedicated back-end API that acts as a proxy between the client and AI services. The BFF securely manages credentials, handles validation and sanitization of inputs, enforces rate limiting, and can apply caching strategies to optimize performance. This layered approach helps maintain security and scalability while keeping the client application lightweight and focused on rendering the UI.

Selecting the right architectural pattern is critical for efficient AI integration. Besides the BFF pattern for Blazor WASM apps, event-driven architectures can greatly enhance responsiveness and fault tolerance in AI-driven workflows. Because AI processing especially natural language tasks can take several seconds or longer, decoupling user actions from AI responses by leveraging messaging systems such as Azure Service Bus, Storage Queues, and Event Hubs for async processing pipelines. Using SignalR to push completion/progress updates back to clients allows the UI to remain responsive. User inputs can be published as events, processed asynchronously, and the results delivered to the client once ready. This approach prevents the application from blocking while awaiting AI responses and supports scalable processing pipelines that can handle fluctuating workloads gracefully. Moreover, applications must be designed with performance in mind, as AI service calls inherently introduce latency. Using asynchronous programming patterns in Blazor is essential to prevent UI freezes and improve the user experience. Providing users with clear feedback during AI processing, such as loading spinners or progress indicators, helps set appropriate expectations.

Caching strategies further improve responsiveness and reduce operational costs. Because AI-generated results may be costly to compute and often repetitive for common inputs, caching at multiple levels of server memory, distributed caches like Azure Redis, or even client-side caching can drastically reduce the number of API calls. Careful cache invalidation policies are necessary to ensure data freshness without compromising performance. Additionally, scalability considerations require applications to be prepared for high concurrency, particularly in Blazor Server apps where AI calls originate from the server. Horizontal scaling with load balancers can improve throughput and availability, but in Blazor Server applications, this requires careful consideration of circuit affinity. Because each user maintains a persistent SignalR connection (circuit) tied to server-side state, load balancers should be configured with session affinity (sticky sessions) or backed by a distributed state store to ensure connection consistency. Without proper affinity or state externalization, users may experience dropped circuits or inconsistent UI state when requests are routed to different instances. At scale, architects should plan for connection routing, distributed caching (e.g., Redis), and resilient reconnection strategies to maintain a seamless user experience.

Security remains a paramount concern throughout the architecture. Protecting Azure OpenAI API keys requires never exposing them in client code, securely storing them using services like Azure Key Vault, and rotating keys regularly. Input validation and sanitization are vital to prevent injection attacks or attempts to manipulate AI prompts in harmful ways. Leveraging AI content moderation tools to filter outputs for offensive or inappropriate content further strengthens security and ethical compliance. All communications should be encrypted with HTTPS to protect data in transit, and back-end endpoints must enforce robust authentication and authorization to ensure only authorized users access AI capabilities.

The rapid evolution of AI models demands a flexible and maintainable architecture. Abstracting AI interactions behind interfaces or services allows applications to swap out or upgrade AI models with minimal disruption to the UI or business logic layers. Versioning AI model usage enables developers to track which versions are in production and conduct regression testing to verify output quality. Because AI outputs can sometimes be unpredictable, implementing comprehensive error handling is critical. Retry policies with exponential backoff handle transient failures, while circuit breakers prevent cascading issues during service outages. Fallback mechanisms provide default content or disable AI features gracefully to maintain core application functionality. Logging and telemetry are indispensable for diagnosing issues, auditing AI usage, and monitoring abnormal behavior or potential abuse.

User experience considerations must also guide architectural choices. Transparency about AI involvement builds user trust; clear UI indicators that show when AI is generating content or assisting decisions inform users about the source of information. Allowing users to provide feedback, edit AI-generated content, or opt out of AI features empowers users and improves system quality over time. Designing for graceful degradation ensures the app remains usable even if AI services are slow or unavailable. Finally, monitoring and analytics play an essential role in managing AI-driven applications. Integrating services such as Azure Application Insights provides real-time metrics on API usage, performance, and errors. Monitoring costs, usage patterns, and anomalies helps manage operational budgets and optimize AI service utilization. Compliance with data privacy laws like GDPR and CCPA requires secure logging of AI interactions, anonymization of user data, and transparent management of user consent regarding AI data processing.

A typical AI-driven Blazor application architecture might consist of a Blazor WebAssembly client that sends user prompts to a secure back-end API. This back-end API handles all AI requests, safely stores credentials, enforces security policies, applies caching, and calls Azure OpenAI. The results are then returned to the client with a clear indication that AI generated the content. Telemetry and monitoring services track system health, usage patterns, and costs, while authentication systems like Azure Active Directory secure user access. This layered architecture separates concerns, enhances security, supports scalability, and simplifies maintenance.

To future-proof your AI-driven Blazor application, design components to be loosely coupled and modular, enabling easy updates or swapping of AI services without major refactoring. Stay informed of advances in AI capabilities and evolving best practices to continuously improve your system. Emphasize ethical AI usage, transparency, and user empowerment throughout the application lifecycle to build trust and deliver responsible, effective AI-powered experiences.

While integrating AI services like Azure OpenAI into Blazor applications offers powerful capabilities, it is important to recognize several inherent limitations that impact architectural decisions and user experience. First, the latency associated with AI API calls, especially large language models, can range from hundreds of milliseconds to several seconds, which may affect the responsiveness of Blazor applications, particularly those running in Blazor Server mode, where server-side processing latency directly impacts UI updates. This requires careful design to prevent UI blocking and maintain user engagement through asynchronous programming and effective loading states. Second, security challenges arise primarily in Blazor WebAssembly applications, where client-side execution exposes application code and potentially sensitive information, necessitating back-end proxies or BFF (Backend-for-Frontend) layers to protect API keys and enforce validation. Third, the costs associated with AI API usage can be significant, especially when handling high volumes of requests or complex prompts, requiring architectural patterns that optimize calls through caching and rate limiting to manage operational expenses. Fourth, AI models themselves have limitations including unpredictability in outputs, potential biases, and ethical concerns that must be addressed through prompt engineering, output filtering, and user feedback mechanisms. Additionally, dependency on external AI services introduces potential availability risks; outages or service degradation can disrupt application functionality if fallback strategies are not well-implemented. Lastly, compliance with data privacy regulations demands robust handling of user data when interacting with AI APIs, adding complexity to logging, auditing, and consent management.

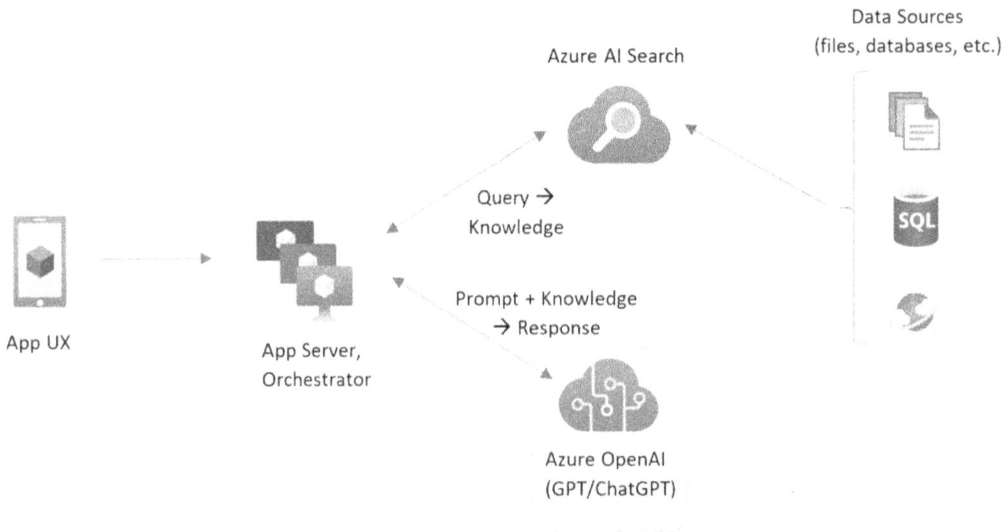

Figure 6-3. *Azure OpenAI with Azure API Management*

Another important architectural consideration is modularity and abstraction. AI technologies and APIs evolve rapidly, with new models and features constantly emerging. Designing AI interactions behind well-defined interfaces or service abstractions decouples the rest of the application from specific AI providers or versions. This modularity facilitates easy replacement, upgrade, or parallel usage of multiple AI models without significant changes to UI components or business logic. Dependency injection frameworks in .NET and Blazor encourage this pattern by allowing AI services to be injected into components or services based on configuration or runtime conditions. Such flexibility supports continuous improvement and experimentation with AI capabilities, enabling developers to quickly adopt advances in language understanding, image generation, or other AI domains while maintaining application stability.

Security is a central concern in any AI integration architecture. The handling of API keys, user data, and AI-generated content must adhere to best practices and compliance requirements. For Blazor WebAssembly applications, where client code is fully visible to end users, all calls to AI services must be routed through secure back-end APIs to prevent key leakage. On the server side, keys should be stored securely using Azure Key Vault or environment variables, with regular rotation and strict access controls. Furthermore, user inputs destined for AI prompts must be validated and sanitized to protect against injection attacks or prompt manipulation. Output moderation and filtering can help prevent the AI from generating harmful or inappropriate content, enhancing the ethical use of AI. All data exchanged between clients, back ends, and AI services should be encrypted in transit using HTTPS/TLS. Additionally, authentication and authorization mechanisms must protect AI endpoints, ensuring only authorized users can invoke AI features.

In contrast, Blazor Server applications inherently run on the server, with UI components rendered server-side and communicated to the client via SignalR connections. This hosting model simplifies some security aspects because AI API calls can be executed safely on the server without exposing keys to clients. However, direct integration of AI services within the Blazor Server code requires attention to scalability and performance. AI calls often introduce latency ranging from hundreds of milliseconds to several seconds, depending on the model and request complexity. To prevent the UI from freezing or becoming unresponsive, it is critical to implement asynchronous programming patterns. Blazor Server's real-time SignalR communication can be leveraged to update the UI dynamically once AI processing completes. Nevertheless, if AI calls are made synchronously during page rendering or event handling, the request pipeline or component render cycle can be delayed, leading to increased latency and a degraded user experience. In Blazor Server, this may block the active circuit while awaiting the response, and in Blazor WebAssembly, it can delay client-side execution. To avoid this, AI calls should be performed asynchronously with proper cancellation, timeout handling, and UI feedback mechanisms. To alleviate this, many architectures incorporate background processing mechanisms. For instance, Blazor Server apps may enqueue AI requests to Azure Service Bus or use Azure Functions as worker processes that execute AI calls asynchronously. Once results are ready, these background components can notify the client via SignalR or update shared state accessed by the Blazor components. This approach decouples AI workloads from UI responsiveness and enables better horizontal scalability by distributing processing across multiple workers or serverless instances.

Handling failures and errors gracefully is another critical architectural concern. AI service calls may fail due to network issues, rate limits, or service outages. Implementing retry policies with exponential backoff reduces transient failure impacts, while circuit breakers prevent cascading failures by temporarily halting AI calls during extended downtime. Applications should provide fallback behaviors, such as default content or disabling AI features with user-friendly messages, to maintain usability when AI services are unavailable. Comprehensive logging and telemetry enable monitoring of AI usage patterns, performance, and errors, facilitating proactive maintenance and troubleshooting.

.NET 10 Implementation Note

In .NET applications, resilience patterns can be implemented using **HttpClientFactory** in combination with **Microsoft.Extensions.Http.Resilience** (built on Polly). Retry, timeout, and circuit breaker policies can be configured during service registration:

```
builder.Services.AddHttpClient("AzureOpenAI")
    .AddStandardResilienceHandler();
```

Structured logging can be implemented using ILogger<T>, and distributed tracing can be enabled via OpenTelemetry for end-to-end observability. These built-in resilience and telemetry features allow AI integrations to remain robust without introducing excessive custom infrastructure.

From a user experience perspective, architectural decisions influence how AI-powered features are presented and controlled. Transparency about AI involvement is essential to build trust; interfaces should clearly indicate when content or suggestions are AI-generated. Providing users the ability to edit or reject AI outputs empowers them and improves overall satisfaction. Applications should be designed to degrade gracefully if AI functionality is slow or inaccessible, maintaining core usability. Furthermore, gathering user feedback on AI results can be incorporated into the architecture to refine prompts or train custom models over time.

A modular and loosely coupled architecture significantly benefits AI-driven Blazor applications. AI technologies and APIs are evolving rapidly; models improve, new capabilities emerge, and service providers release updates frequently. Designing the system with abstraction layers such as interfaces or service wrappers between the Blazor front end and AI integration logic decouples AI provider-specific code from the application's core. Dependency injection frameworks available in .NET and Blazor support this approach, enabling developers to swap AI implementations or upgrade models with minimal changes to UI components or business rules. Modular architecture facilitates unit and integration testing of AI interaction layers, helping maintain code quality and reliability. Moreover, it enables parallel experimentation with different AI services, supporting a continuous improvement mindset where applications evolve alongside advancements in AI technology.

From a user experience perspective, architectural patterns influence how AI-powered features are presented and controlled within Blazor applications. Transparency is essential to build user trust. UI elements should clearly indicate when content is AI-generated or assisted, avoiding confusion or misleading users. Providing users with controls to accept, edit, or reject AI outputs fosters engagement and improves the quality of results over time. Designing applications to degrade gracefully if AI services are slow or offline maintains usability and prevents frustration. Gathering user feedback on AI results and incorporating this data into AI prompt refinement or custom model training can be architected as a continuous feedback loop, enhancing personalization and accuracy.

CHAPTER 7

Practical AI Features in Blazor

Integrating Azure OpenAI APIs into a Blazor application typically begins by establishing secure and reliable communication between the application's back-end layer and Azure OpenAI Service. In Blazor Server, calls to Azure OpenAI can be made directly from the server-side application layer. In contrast, Blazor WebAssembly applications should route requests through a secure back end or Backend-for-Frontend (BFF) API, which then communicates with Azure OpenAI to ensure secrets and tokens are not exposed to the browser. Developers install the official Azure OpenAI SDK by adding the Azure.AI.OpenAI NuGet package to the project, which provides a strongly typed client for interacting with the API. Configuration values such as the Azure OpenAI endpoint and credentials should be stored using configuration providers appropriate to the deployment environment, rather than hard-coded in application source code. In production scenarios, this typically involves secure secret stores or managed identity–based authentication to prevent accidental exposure and ensure proper access control.

Using dependency injection, an application service is defined to encapsulate all interactions with the Azure OpenAI API. The service creates an instance of AzureOpenAIClient using the configured endpoint and an appropriate credential (such as one constructed from an API key or a managed identity). It then obtains a chat client via GetChatClient (deploymentName) and invokes chat completion operations through that client to process requests against the specified model deployment. A core method within the service accepts a collection of chat messages representing the conversation context, constructs a ChatCompletionsOptions instance, and asynchronously invokes GetChatCompletionsAsync, specifying the target deployment name (e.g., gpt-35-turbo). The method then returns the AI-generated response from the first completion choice in the result set.

A. Prasad and H. Singh, *Advanced Blazor Architecture with .NET 10 and Azure OpenAI*, https://doi.org/10.1007/979-8-8688-2518-7_7

On the UI side, a Blazor component injects this service to manage user interaction and conversation flow. The component maintains a collection of chat messages to preserve the conversation history, typically beginning with a system message that defines the assistant's behavior. When a user submits input, the component appends the message to the conversation and invokes the OpenAI service to retrieve a response. While awaiting the AI-generated result, during request processing, the UI can disable the send button and display a loading indicator to provide immediate feedback. It should also offer a cancel option, present user-friendly error messages when failures occur, and include a clear "Try Again" action. At the service layer, optional resilience patterns such as exponential backoff and retry policies can be implemented to handle transient errors gracefully. Once the response is received, it is added to the conversation, and the input field is cleared in preparation for the next message.

This approach allows the Blazor application to maintain conversational context, enabling coherent and context-aware AI interactions. Throughout the integration, asynchronous operations must be handled carefully, with Use StateHasChanged() when updates occur outside the normal UI event flow to reflect message updates or loading-state transitions. By isolating OpenAI interactions within a dedicated service and limiting UI components to conversation management, the architecture remains clean, maintainable, and testable, supporting production-ready applications.

Designing AI-Driven UI Components in Blazor

Designing AI-driven UI components in Blazor involves combining interactive web UI capabilities with intelligent back-end services to build responsive and context-aware applications. Blazor's component-based architecture supports the creation of modular, reusable UI elements that interact with AI models, such as those provided by Azure OpenAI, enabling scenarios including conversational assistants, content generation, sentiment analysis, and summarization within applications.

Central to this design are state management, user interaction handling, and asynchronous communication with AI services, which must be coordinated to provide a consistent user experience. The first step in designing AI-driven components is understanding how user input flows through the system. Typically, a Blazor component that integrates AI typically includes input controls such as text fields and buttons to capture user queries. Where voice interaction is required, it can be supported via browser APIs or platform services integrated into the component. This input is then forwarded to an AI service through an injected application service responsible for API communication, for example, an OpenAI client wrapper.

To maintain responsiveness, calls to AI APIs are performed asynchronously, requiring the UI to provide feedback such as loading indicators or progress notifications while requests are processed. Blazor's event-driven programming model supports these interactions by allowing component state to be updated and relevant UI fragments to be re-rendered efficiently without full page reloads.

A key design consideration is managing conversational or interaction state within the component. Many AI-driven scenarios involve multi-turn conversations or context-aware queries, making it necessary to maintain a history of exchanged messages. This is commonly achieved by storing a collection of messages, each annotated with a role (e.g., user, assistant, or system), which is included with each API request to preserve context.

The component is responsible for appending new user messages, incorporating AI-generated responses, and rendering them appropriately in the UI, often through a scrollable chat interface or structured dialogue view. User experience can be further improved by supporting features such as message editing, retrying failed requests, or clearing conversation history, all of which require careful state synchronization and event handling within the Blazor component lifecycle.

Beyond basic input and output, AI-driven components can benefit from advanced UI elements that improve usability. For example, implementing streaming responses—where the AI output is rendered incrementally as it is generated—can make interactions more responsive. In Blazor Server, UI updates are already delivered over SignalR as part of the framework's circuit model. To enable streaming AI responses, a component can consume an asynchronous stream such as incremental response chunks and progressively append content while triggering controlled re-renders.

In Blazor WebAssembly, similar behavior can be achieved through progressive UI updates driven by asynchronous processing on the client. In both hosting models, developers must carefully manage partial responses, cancellation tokens, and state transitions to ensure consistency and avoid rendering anomalies.

Additionally, components may incorporate interactive controls such as suggestion buttons, selectable completions, or context menus to guide user input and reduce friction. Custom styling, animations, and accessibility considerations are also important to ensure that AI features are effective, usable, and inclusive.

Integration with other Blazor features such as form validation, dependency injection, and component parameters further enhances AI-driven components. For example,

AI-generated content can be validated or sanitized before rendering to mitigate security risks such as cross-site scripting (XSS). Dependency injection can be used to supply AI services or configuration options, allowing components to be configured for different models or languages. Passing parameters between parent and child components supports more complex UI compositions in which AI-driven elements coexist with traditional UI functionality, promoting modularity, reuse, and maintainability.

Security and privacy considerations must also be incorporated into component design. While communication with Azure endpoints is secured by default using HTTPS/TLS, architectural considerations should focus more on data minimization, sensitive data redaction, and disciplined logging policies. Designing AI integrations with least-privilege data exposure and controlled telemetry practices is more impactful than simply relying on transport-level encryption and adhering to applicable data protection regulations such as GDPR or CCPA. The UI can be designed to obtain explicit user consent for AI data processing, present transparency notices, and allow users to review or delete interaction history. Content moderation mechanisms may also be integrated to filter or flag inappropriate AI-generated responses before display, helping to protect users and maintain platform integrity.

Designing AI-driven UI components in Blazor is an iterative process informed by user feedback and ongoing refinement. Components should be designed with extensibility in mind, enabling updates as AI models evolve or new capabilities become available. Incorporating analytics on user interactions with AI features can help identify usage patterns and usability issues, guiding UI improvements and prompt adjustments. By combining Blazor's web UI capabilities with Azure OpenAI services, developers can build AI-powered applications that are usable, maintainable, and aligned with responsible design principles.

In summary, AI-driven UI components in Blazor combine interactive web technologies with AI services through asynchronous, stateful, and modular design. Managing user input, conversational context, and API communication within components enables dynamic and personalized experiences. Advanced UI techniques such as streaming responses, interactive suggestions, and structured error handling improve usability, while performance, security, and privacy remain foundational concerns. Adhering to these principles enables the development of AI-enabled Blazor applications that are both effective and reliable.

When incorporating AI capabilities into Blazor applications, it is also important to acknowledge ethical and practical limitations related to responsible AI use. AI models may exhibit bias and potentially produce unfair or unintended outcomes if not carefully monitored. Because Blazor applications often surface AI-generated content directly to end users, mitigating bias requires ongoing evaluation, prompt refinement, and post-processing controls, which add complexity and may not fully eliminate bias. Transparency presents another challenge, as AI-generated outputs can be difficult to explain or justify, potentially reducing user trust. In addition, AI systems may generate inaccurate or inappropriate content, necessitating moderation layers that increase development and runtime overhead. Privacy considerations further constrain design choices, as transmitting user data to external AI services requires strict compliance with data protection regulations, secure handling, and explicit consent management. Finally, the variability and occasional failure of AI responses complicate the delivery of consistent user experiences, particularly in interactive Blazor interfaces where latency and errors must be handled gracefully.

Ethical Considerations in AI Integration and Usage

Integrating artificial intelligence (AI) into Blazor applications, particularly through services such as Azure OpenAI, introduces significant opportunities to enhance user experiences and automate complex tasks. At the same time, it introduces important ethical considerations that must be addressed when deploying AI-driven functionality. These considerations include fairness, privacy, transparency, accountability, and harm prevention, all of which should be incorporated into the design, development, and deployment lifecycle to ensure that AI systems are used responsibly and safely.

One of the primary ethical concerns in AI integration is bias. AI models, including large language models, are trained on extensive datasets that may contain historical and societal biases. When reflected in AI outputs, these biases can unintentionally reinforce stereotypes, misinformation, or discriminatory language. In Blazor applications, AI-powered chat interfaces, content generators, or assistants may therefore produce responses that negatively affect certain user groups or introduce inaccuracies. Mitigating these risks requires deliberate design choices, including careful prompt construction, output filtering, and ongoing monitoring of AI behavior. Techniques such as prompt engineering, human-in-the-loop review, and the use of content moderation tools are commonly employed to support fairness and inclusivity.

Figure 7-1. *Ethical Principles Influencing the Design of AI-Enabled Blazor User Interfaces*

Privacy is another critical ethical dimension when integrating AI into Blazor applications. AI-driven features often require collecting and processing user data to generate relevant or personalized responses. This data may include sensitive information, preferences, or behavioral patterns. Developers are responsible for minimizing data collection, securing data in transit and at rest, and complying with applicable regulations such as GDPR, CCPA, or HIPAA, depending on the application domain. Transparency regarding data usage, access, and retention should be clearly communicated to users, with appropriate consent mechanisms integrated into the UI. Users should also be provided with control over their data, including options to review, export, or delete AI interaction history.

Transparency and explainability are additional ethical considerations. Because AI models can be opaque in their operation, users may find it difficult to understand how responses or decisions are generated. In Blazor applications, this can reduce trust if AI-generated outputs are presented without context. To support responsible AI use, UI components can provide contextual information, such as confidence indicators, summaries of reasoning, or references to source material where appropriate. Applications should clearly indicate when content is AI-generated to set accurate user expectations. For example, responses can include an "AI-generated" badge, brief microcopy such as "AI responses may be incorrect," or a contextual link labeled "How this feature works" that explains data sources and limitations.

Accountability is also essential when deploying AI-enabled Blazor applications. Since AI systems may produce unexpected or incorrect outputs, organizations must establish mechanisms for monitoring, auditing, and correcting AI behavior. This typically includes implementing logging and telemetry for AI interactions to monitor usage, performance, and errors. However, teams must exercise caution, as prompts and model responses may contain sensitive or personally identifiable information (PII), escalation processes for handling inappropriate outputs, and iterative updates to models or prompts based on observed issues. Accountability spans multiple roles, including developers, product owners, and governance teams, who must ensure that AI usage aligns with organizational policies and ethical standards.

Ensuring accessibility and inclusiveness represents another ethical responsibility. AI-driven components in Blazor applications should be designed to be accessible and inclusive for users with diverse abilities, languages, and cultural backgrounds. In practice, this means building AI chat interfaces with proper ARIA roles, screen reader support, keyboard navigation, and sufficient color contrast. Dynamic responses should announce updates appropriately (e.g., using aria-live regions), and controls should remain usable without a mouse. Localization support, clear language, and culturally neutral design patterns further improve usability across global audiences [18]. This includes compliance with accessibility standards such as WCAG, support for multilingual interactions, and careful evaluation of AI outputs to avoid exclusionary or harmful language. Inclusive design practices help ensure that the benefits of AI are broadly accessible and do not reinforce existing inequities.

Preventing harm is a foundational requirement of responsible AI use, but this also means planning for how the system behaves when things go wrong. Applications should anticipate common failure modes such as the model refusing a request, generating unsafe or inappropriate content, or timing out due to service issues. In these cases, the UI should handle responses gracefully with clear messaging, safe fallbacks, and controlled feature behavior. Designing for refusal handling, content moderation checks, and timeout recovery ensures that AI features remain predictable, trustworthy, and aligned with user safety expectations. AI systems may generate content that is misleading, inappropriate, or unsafe if left unchecked. In Blazor applications, safeguards such as content filtering, moderation layers, and fallback handling should be implemented to prevent harmful outputs from reaching users. Defining acceptable use guidelines and educating users about the limitations of AI-generated content further reduces the risk of misuse or misinterpretation.

Ethical AI integration also requires consideration of broader societal impacts. While AI-enabled features can improve efficiency and engagement, they may also alter workflows or reduce opportunities for human interaction. Developers and organizations should aim to design AI systems that augment human capabilities rather than replace them and clearly communicate the role and limitations of AI within the application.

Finally, fostering an organizational culture that prioritizes ethical AI is critical. This includes providing education on AI ethics, incorporating diverse perspectives into design decisions, and establishing review processes that assess ethical, legal, and social implications. Ethical considerations should be addressed early in the development process rather than retrofitted later. Blazor developers integrating Azure OpenAI should apply principles of fairness, transparency, privacy, and accountability to build AI-enabled applications that are trustworthy and responsible.

CHAPTER 8

Secure AI Prompt Handling

Safe AI Usage in Enterprise Apps

As enterprises increasingly adopt AI technologies, particularly in advanced frameworks like Blazor with .NET 10 and integrations such as Azure OpenAI, establishing a robust data governance framework becomes essential to harness AI's power while managing risks. Data governance refers to the set of policies, standards, and processes that ensure the effective and secure management of data assets throughout their lifecycle. For AI integration, especially in prompt handling and model training, data governance assumes a critical role not only to comply with legal and ethical standards but also to maintain trust, data quality, and operational excellence.

AI-driven systems depend on data across different stages of their lifecycle. During training or fine-tuning, curated datasets shape and improve model behavior under controlled governance. During inference, the trained model processes live application data to generate real-time predictions or responses. Because these stages serve different purposes, they introduce distinct operational and data governance considerations. In prompt-driven AI systems, such as models hosted via Azure OpenAI (Azure AI Foundry), the structure and handling of prompt data play a decisive role in output quality. Well-designed prompts, combined with secure data handling and clear governance, directly influence the accuracy, consistency, and reliability of the model's responses. Poor governance can lead to compromised data quality, breaches of sensitive information, biased AI outcomes, and regulatory penalties. Therefore, establishing a structured framework to govern AI-related data is a foundational step toward safe, compliant, and efficient AI integration.

A. Prasad and H. Singh, *Advanced Blazor Architecture with .NET 10 and Azure OpenAI*,
https://doi.org/10.1007/979-8-8688-2518-7_8

The first pillar of a robust data governance framework for AI integration is the definition of clear policies and roles. This involves identifying data stewards, owners, custodians, and users within the enterprise, clarifying responsibilities for managing AI prompt data and training datasets. Data policies must explicitly define what constitutes acceptable data sources, permissible data types, retention periods, and access protocols. For instance, enterprises should mandate that any data used by organizations should establish clear policies governing how data is used in AI prompts and model development, ensuring that sensitive information such as personally identifiable data is handled in accordance with applicable legal and regulatory frameworks. Lawful processing may depend on consent, contractual necessity, legitimate interest, or other recognized bases, depending on jurisdiction. Clear role definitions further strengthen governance; data stewards are responsible for data quality and compliance oversight, while data custodians implement and maintain the necessary technical safeguards.

Closely tied to roles and policies is the classification and cataloging of data. Not all data carry the same sensitivity or importance. AI prompt data should be classified based on confidentiality, regulatory requirements, and business impact. For example, data containing health information or financial details would be classified as highly sensitive, demanding stringent controls. Implementing a metadata-driven catalog helps maintain visibility into what data is ingested by AI systems, where it originates, and how it flows through the AI pipeline. This transparency is vital for auditing and troubleshooting.

Data quality management is another core aspect of governance. AI models are only as good as the data they are trained and prompted with. Poor-quality data containing errors, inconsistencies, or biases can degrade AI performance and propagate harmful outputs. Enterprises must institute processes for validating, cleansing, and enriching prompt data before feeding it into AI models. Techniques such as automated data validation rules, anomaly detection, and manual review checkpoints help maintain data integrity. Additionally, monitoring ongoing data quality ensures that evolving inputs continue to meet established standards, preventing model drift or unexpected behavior.

Data governance frameworks extend beyond policy and include security controls designed specifically for AI workloads. Because prompts may contain business-sensitive information or user data, they should be protected accordingly. This means enforcing strong access controls, applying encryption both at rest and in transit, and using secure communication channels to reduce the risk of unauthorized access or data exposure. Role-based access control (RBAC) ensures that only authorized personnel or systems can access or modify AI prompt data. Encryption at rest and in transit protects against unauthorized interception or breaches. Additionally, logging and monitoring all access and changes to AI datasets and prompt repositories provide an audit trail for compliance and forensic analysis.

Beyond internal controls, enterprises must ensure compliance with regulatory and ethical standards governing data usage in AI. Regulations such as GDPR [19], CCPA, HIPAA, and industry-specific mandates impose strict requirements on data privacy, consent, and usage transparency. A governance framework should incorporate compliance checks, ensuring AI prompt data collection and processing adhere to these laws. For example, GDPR mandates data minimization and the right to erasure, requiring prompt data to be handled accordingly. Moreover, organizations should adopt ethical AI principles, promoting fairness, transparency, and accountability in AI outputs, thereby avoiding discriminatory or harmful results.

Another important element is risk management and mitigation related to AI prompt data. AI systems are vulnerable to various threats, including prompt injection attacks, data poisoning, and exposure of sensitive information through model outputs. A governance framework should include proactive risk assessments, threat modeling, and mitigation strategies. For example, prompt sanitization filters can reduce the risk of prompt injection of malicious commands, while anomaly detection can identify unusual data patterns indicating poisoning attempts. Regular security audits and penetration testing enhance resilience. Additionally, incident response plans tailored for AI-specific data breaches ensure quick containment and remediation.

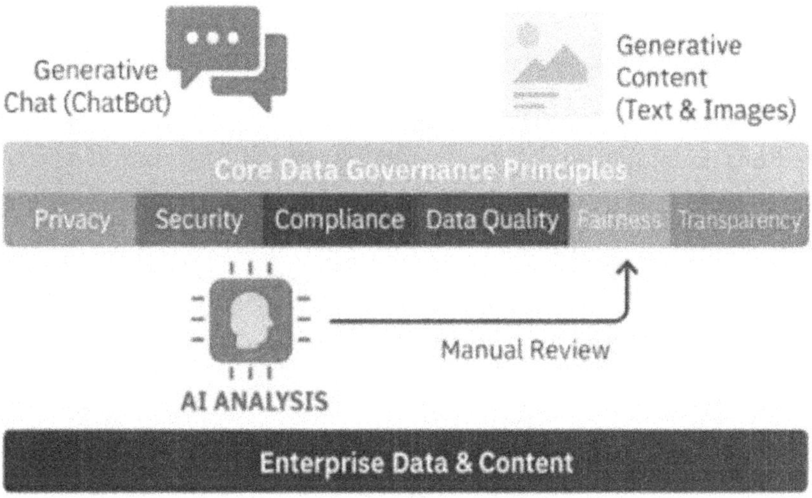

Figure 8-1. *Data Governance in the Age of Generative AI*

A robust governance framework also supports data lifecycle management, defining how prompt data is collected, stored, used, archived, and ultimately disposed of. Effective lifecycle management ensures that data is not kept longer than necessary, reducing exposure to risks. Automated policies can enforce data retention schedules and secure deletion protocols. Furthermore, version control of prompt datasets helps track changes over time, facilitating rollback in case of errors or compliance queries.

Integral to successful governance is cross-functional collaboration. AI integration involves diverse stakeholders including data scientists, developers, security teams, legal experts, and business leaders. Establishing governance committees or councils fosters communication, aligning data governance goals with business objectives and technical realities. Regular training and awareness programs educate teams on governance policies, ethical AI practices, and security responsibilities.

Technological solutions underpin many governance activities. Enterprises should leverage data governance platforms and tools that offer data cataloging, lineage tracking, policy enforcement, and auditing capabilities. Integration with AI development pipelines ensures real-time governance checks without impeding agility. Additionally, adopting standards like the FAIR principles (Findable, Accessible, Interoperable, Reusable) enhances data usability and governance maturity.

In summary, establishing robust data governance frameworks for AI integration requires a holistic approach combining clear policies, role definitions, data classification, quality assurance, security controls, compliance adherence, risk mitigation, lifecycle management, collaboration, and enabling technologies. This framework ensures that AI prompt data is managed responsibly, securely, and efficiently, unlocking the transformative potential of AI while safeguarding enterprise interests and user trust.

As AI continues to evolve and permeate enterprise applications, governance frameworks must adapt to new challenges and opportunities. Continuous monitoring, feedback loops, and governance maturity assessments help organizations refine their frameworks over time. Ultimately, a strong data governance foundation is a key enabler of secure, ethical, and high-performing AI solutions that drive innovation and competitive advantage in the digital age.

Compliance with Regulatory Standards in AI-Driven Applications

As artificial intelligence (AI) technologies rapidly become integral to enterprise applications, ensuring compliance with regulatory standards has emerged as a critical challenge and priority. AI-driven applications ranging from automated decision-making systems to AI-powered chatbots and predictive analytics handle vast amounts of data, often including sensitive personal and business information. Consequently, organizations must navigate a complex landscape of data protection laws, industry regulations, and emerging AI-specific guidelines to ensure legal compliance, protect user privacy, and maintain public trust.

At the core of regulatory compliance in AI applications is the protection of personal data. Globally recognized data privacy regulations such as the European Union's General Data Protection Regulation (GDPR), the California Consumer Privacy Act (CCPA), and sector-specific laws like the Health Insurance Portability and Accountability Act (HIPAA) in the United States impose stringent requirements on how organizations collect, process, store, and share personal information. AI applications frequently process personal data to deliver personalized experiences or automated decisions, which means compliance with these regulations is non-negotiable.

The GDPR, widely regarded as the most comprehensive data privacy regulation, mandates principles such as lawfulness, fairness, transparency, purpose limitation, and data minimization. For AI-driven applications, this means that organizations must clearly inform individuals about how their data will be used by AI systems, obtain explicit consent where necessary, and limit data processing to what is strictly necessary for the AI's purpose. The regulation also grants individuals rights such as data access, correction, deletion (the right to be forgotten), and objection to automated decision-making, requiring enterprises to build mechanisms within their AI applications to honor these rights. Failure to comply with GDPR can lead to hefty fines and reputational damage.

Similarly, the CCPA enhances consumer privacy rights in California by allowing residents to know what personal data is collected, request deletion, and opt out of data sales. AI applications that serve or collect data from California residents must incorporate processes to respect these rights. For example, an AI-driven recommendation engine must be capable of excluding users who opt out of data collection or personalized advertising. The increasing adoption of CCPA-like laws in other US states underscores the growing regulatory momentum around AI and data privacy.

Industry-specific regulations introduce further compliance complexities. For example, HIPAA regulates the handling of protected health information (PHI) in healthcare applications. AI solutions used in healthcare, such as diagnostic tools or patient management systems, must implement safeguards to ensure PHI confidentiality, integrity, and availability. This includes encryption, access controls, audit logging, and breach notification procedures. Non-compliance can result in severe penalties and loss of trust in AI technologies deployed in sensitive domains.

Beyond data privacy, regulatory compliance in AI applications also involves addressing algorithmic transparency, fairness, and accountability. Many jurisdictions are introducing or considering laws that require organizations to demonstrate that AI decisions are explainable and free from bias. For example, the European Union's Artificial Intelligence Act, which entered into force in August 2024, establishes requirements for risk management, documentation, and transparency, particularly for high-risk AI systems that may affect fundamental rights. Organizations must be prepared to document AI model design, data sources, and decision-making logic to comply with these evolving standards.

Explainability in AI is crucial not only for regulatory reasons but also to build user trust. If an AI system denies a loan application or recommends medical treatment, users and regulators demand clear explanations on how these decisions were reached. Compliance frameworks increasingly require organizations to integrate explainability tools and conduct fairness assessments, identifying and mitigating biases that could lead to discriminatory outcomes. For example, if an AI recruiting tool disproportionately filters out candidates from certain demographics, compliance audits should detect and correct this bias.

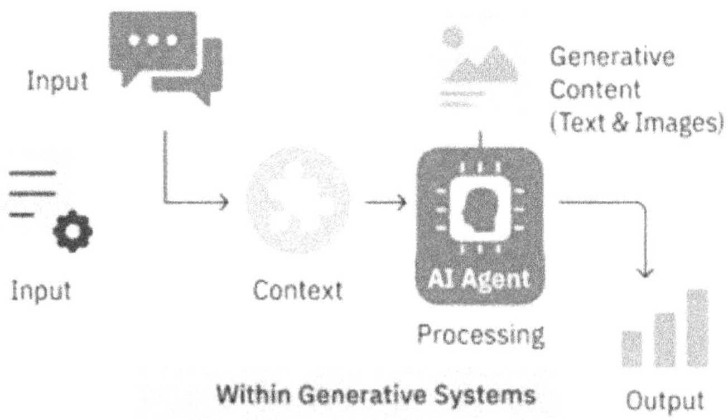

Figure 8-2. *AI Agents Work*

Risk management and impact assessments are integral to regulatory compliance strategies for AI. Many regulations, including GDPR, require organizations to conduct Data Protection Impact Assessments (DPIAs) when processing operations pose high risks to individuals' rights and freedoms. Similarly, AI-specific regulations advocate for AI Risk Assessments to evaluate potential harms, biases, and ethical concerns. These assessments guide the implementation of mitigation measures such as data anonymization, bias correction, robust testing, and continuous monitoring to ensure ongoing compliance.

Data governance frameworks closely tie into compliance efforts by enforcing policies around data quality, access control, and lifecycle management. Ensuring that AI prompt data and training datasets meet regulatory standards minimizes risks associated with improper data usage. Secure storage, encryption, and controlled data sharing are vital to comply with confidentiality requirements. Moreover, audit trails and logging mechanisms provide evidence of compliance, enabling organizations to demonstrate adherence to regulators during inspections or investigations.

Compliance also extends to vendor and third-party management, as many enterprises rely on cloud providers, AI service platforms, and data suppliers. Contractual agreements should include clauses addressing regulatory responsibilities, data protection measures, and incident notification processes. Organizations must verify that vendors comply with relevant laws and standards, as liability for data breaches or non-compliance can extend to the enterprise using the AI solutions.

Automation plays a significant role in supporting regulatory compliance in AI-driven applications. Automated workflows can enforce consent management, data subject rights fulfillment, and policy enforcement in real time. For example, when a user requests data deletion, automated processes can propagate this request across AI datasets and prompt repositories. Similarly, automated monitoring tools can detect anomalies or suspicious activities indicating compliance risks, triggering alerts or remediation actions.

Training and awareness programs are equally essential to maintain a compliance culture around AI. Employees across technical, legal, and business functions must understand the regulatory landscape and their role in ensuring compliance. Regular updates on new laws, best practices, and ethical AI principles empower teams to proactively address compliance challenges and avoid inadvertent violations.

Despite these efforts, regulatory compliance in AI remains a dynamic and complex domain. The rapid pace of AI innovation often outstrips regulatory development, leading to uncertainty and diverse interpretations of compliance requirements. Emerging frameworks like the EU's AI Act, the OECD AI Principles, and various national AI strategies emphasize responsible AI development, but harmonized global standards are still evolving. Organizations must stay informed of legal developments, participate in industry forums, and engage with regulators to shape and anticipate compliance expectations.

Compliance with regulatory standards in AI-driven applications is multifaceted, encompassing data privacy, transparency, fairness, accountability, risk management, and governance. Enterprises deploying AI must implement comprehensive compliance programs that integrate legal requirements into the entire AI lifecycle from data collection and model training to deployment and ongoing monitoring. Such programs not only mitigate legal risks but also foster ethical AI use, build user confidence, and sustain competitive advantage in an increasingly AI-powered world. By proactively aligning AI initiatives with regulatory frameworks, organizations can responsibly unlock AI's transformative potential while safeguarding individual rights and societal values.

Techniques for Ensuring Privacy and Data Protection in AI Prompts

In the rapidly evolving domain of AI-driven applications, safeguarding privacy and data protection within AI prompts has become paramount. AI prompt data often contains sensitive, personally identifiable, or proprietary information, and its exposure or misuse can lead to severe consequences including regulatory violations, reputational harm, and loss of user trust. As enterprises increasingly integrate AI capabilities through platforms like Azure OpenAI, establishing robust techniques to ensure privacy and data protection during prompt creation, transmission, storage, and processing is essential.

A foundational technique for privacy assurance in AI prompts is data minimization. This principle, central to many data protection regulations such as GDPR [20], mandates that only the minimal necessary data be collected and used for a specific purpose. When designing AI prompts, organizations should carefully evaluate the type and amount of data included, avoiding any unnecessary or excessive sensitive information. For instance, instead of embedding full user profiles in prompts, only anonymized or aggregated data points relevant to the AI task should be used. This reduces the risk surface and limits potential data exposure.

Security considerations must also extend to how model responses are handled. AI-generated output should be treated as untrusted input. When rendering responses in the UI, proper output encoding is essential to mitigate cross-site scripting (XSS) and injection risks. By combining data minimization with secure transmission, access controls, and safe output rendering practices, organizations can significantly strengthen privacy and protection in AI-enabled applications.

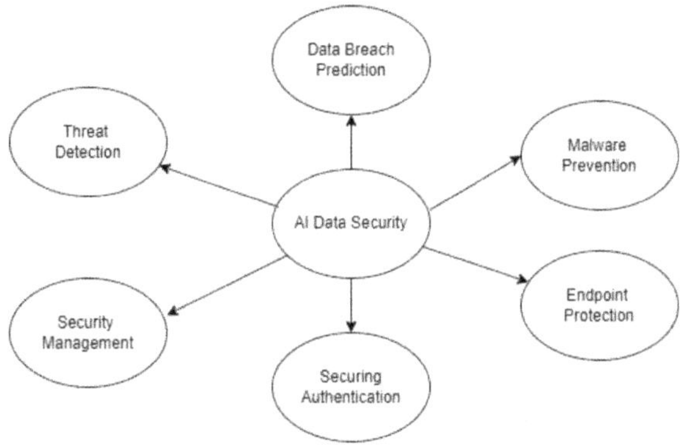

Figure 8-3. *AI in Data Security*

Closely linked to data minimization is the practice of data anonymization and pseudonymization. Anonymization involves irreversibly removing or masking personally identifiable information (PII) so that individuals cannot be re-identified, whereas pseudonymization replaces identifiers with pseudonyms that can only be resolved with additional information stored separately. In AI prompts, this means removing names, addresses, or other sensitive attributes before feeding data into the AI system. Techniques such as tokenization, hashing, or generalization (e.g., replacing exact ages with age ranges) help achieve this. However, it is crucial to balance anonymization with data utility, ensuring that the AI can still perform effectively while safeguarding privacy.

Encryption plays a critical role in protecting AI prompt data both at rest and in transit. Data encryption ensures that even if prompt data is intercepted or accessed without authorization, it remains unreadable without the appropriate decryption keys. Transport Layer Security (TLS) protocols secure prompt data during transmission between client applications and AI services. Similarly, encryption of stored prompt datasets and logs prevents unauthorized access within enterprise environments or cloud platforms. Employing strong encryption standards such as AES-256 and maintaining rigorous key management practices are industry best practices.

Another vital technique is access control and authentication. Limiting access to AI prompts to authorized users and systems reduces the risk of data leaks or misuse. Role-based access control (RBAC) frameworks assign permissions based on job roles, ensuring that individuals only access prompt data necessary for their functions. Multi-factor authentication (MFA) adds a layer of security, requiring multiple proofs of identity before granting access. In enterprise AI pipelines, integrating identity and access management (IAM) tools helps enforce these controls systematically.

Secure coding and input validation are indispensable to prevent vulnerabilities in AI prompt handling. Poorly validated prompt inputs can be exploited through injection attacks, where malicious data is crafted to manipulate AI behavior or access unauthorized information. Implementing strong input validation and enforcing well-defined data schemas can help reduce misuse and ensure prompt data aligns with expected formats. However, traditional techniques such as character escaping, effective in SQL or HTML contexts, do not reliably mitigate prompt injection risks in large language models. Prompt handling should therefore focus on contextual validation, constrained input patterns, and clear separation of trusted and untrusted data rather than relying solely on escaping mechanisms. Regular security code reviews and penetration testing further reduce the attack surface.

Privacy-preserving computation techniques have emerged as advanced methods to enhance data protection in AI prompts. Federated learning, for example, enables AI models to be trained across multiple decentralized devices or servers holding local data samples, without exchanging the data itself. Federated learning primarily applies to distributed training scenarios rather than runtime inference. While its principles—such as keeping sensitive data local and sharing only aggregated updates—are valuable in broader AI architecture discussions, they fall outside the scope of prompt-handling patterns in Application-layer design and are better treated separately in training-focused contexts. Similarly, homomorphic encryption allows computations on encrypted data without decryption, enabling AI models to process prompts while preserving privacy. Though computationally intensive, these techniques represent the frontier of privacy assurance in AI.

Differential privacy is another sophisticated approach that introduces controlled noise into data or AI outputs to prevent the identification of individuals from aggregate information. By applying differential privacy to AI prompts and responses, organizations can mitigate risks of data leakage, even if prompt data contains sensitive elements. For example, when AI models generate text completions or predictions based on prompts with personal data, differential privacy mechanisms help obscure individual contributions, ensuring compliance with privacy mandates.

Regular monitoring and auditing of AI prompt data access and usage form a key component of privacy enforcement. Implementing detailed logging of who accessed prompt data, when, and for what purpose provides accountability and traceability. Automated monitoring tools can detect unusual access patterns or data exfiltration attempts, triggering alerts for investigation. Audits, both internal and external, verify compliance with privacy policies and regulatory requirements, fostering a culture of responsibility.

The human factor remains critical in ensuring privacy in AI prompts. Training and awareness programs educate developers, data scientists, and operational staff on best practices for handling sensitive prompt data. Clear guidelines on prompt content, data sharing, and incident reporting reduce inadvertent privacy breaches. Organizations should establish a culture where privacy is a shared responsibility, reinforced by policies and ongoing communication.

Legal and contractual safeguards complement technical measures. Enterprises should incorporate data processing agreements and privacy clauses with AI vendors, cloud providers, and third-party partners to delineate responsibilities and obligations related to prompt data privacy. Such agreements often include requirements for data handling, breach notification, and compliance with relevant laws, mitigating risks in multi-party AI ecosystems.

Finally, privacy by design and by default principles mandate embedding privacy considerations into AI prompt systems from inception. This proactive approach involves threat modeling, privacy impact assessments, and iterative design reviews to identify and address privacy risks early. Incorporating privacy features into AI development workflows ensures that data protection is not an afterthought but a foundational aspect of AI prompt handling.

Ensuring privacy and data protection in AI prompts requires a multi-layered approach combining data minimization, anonymization, encryption, access controls, secure coding, advanced privacy-preserving computations, monitoring, training, legal safeguards, and privacy-centric design. As AI continues to permeate enterprise applications, adopting these techniques not only protects sensitive information and meets regulatory requirements but also builds user trust and sustainable AI ecosystems. Organizations that prioritize privacy in AI prompt handling will be better positioned to leverage AI's transformative potential responsibly and securely.

Limitations

Despite the wide range of techniques available to ensure privacy and data protection in AI prompts, several limitations persist that impact their effectiveness and practicality in enterprise environments. One of the foremost limitations is the incomplete effectiveness of anonymization and pseudonymization. While these techniques reduce the risk of re-identification, advances in data correlation, AI inference, and pattern matching can still enable attackers or unintended recipients to re-identify individuals from de-identified data, especially when combined with auxiliary datasets. This undermines the guarantees of anonymity, particularly in high-risk or high-volume applications where data diversity is low.

Data minimization, though fundamental to privacy, also introduces trade-offs in AI prompt performance. Reducing input data can lead to less contextual richness, potentially degrading model accuracy or limiting its utility. Striking the right balance between privacy and functionality is challenging, especially in natural language models where subtle context changes can affect outputs significantly. In some cases, overly minimal prompts may render the AI less useful or even unfit for purpose, creating friction between privacy and performance objectives.

Encryption technologies, while essential, bring limitations related to performance and operational complexity. Encrypting prompt data at rest and in transit ensures confidentiality, but it does not prevent misuse once the data is decrypted for processing. Moreover, advanced encryption methods like homomorphic encryption or secure multi-party computation, while promising in theory, remain computationally intensive and not yet viable for real-time prompt processing at scale. As a result, their adoption in live AI applications is limited, restricting privacy gains to research or specialized use cases.

Similarly, federated learning, though privacy-enhancing, has limited applicability in the context of prompt handling, where inference, not training, is the dominant concern. Implementing federated mechanisms for prompt transmission or processing is technically complex, especially when relying on third-party APIs like Azure OpenAI, which centralize inference workloads. This limits enterprise control over the underlying infrastructure and restricts the use of federated or on-device privacy-preserving methods.

Access control systems also face practical limitations, particularly in dynamic or distributed environments. While RBAC and IAM frameworks help restrict access, they are only as effective as their configuration and oversight. Misconfigured access rules, privilege creep, or insider threats can still expose sensitive prompt data, especially in organizations with poor access hygiene or lacking centralized identity governance. Additionally, enforcing granular controls across heterogeneous cloud, hybrid, and vendor environments is a persistent challenge.

Secure coding and input validation, while helpful in minimizing injection attacks and data leakage, cannot eliminate risks arising from the AI model's inherent openness to manipulation. For instance, prompt injection remains an evolving attack surface, particularly in large language models that interpret and generate responses based on flexible, human-readable inputs. Attackers can craft sophisticated inputs that bypass traditional input sanitization, highlighting the need for ongoing adaptation and defense-in-depth strategies.

Advanced privacy techniques like differential privacy also face practical barriers. Adding noise to data or outputs can impair model accuracy or usability, especially when dealing with small datasets or requiring high precision. Furthermore, implementing differential privacy effectively requires deep mathematical expertise and a strong understanding of the trade-offs between utility and privacy, which may be lacking in many enterprise AI teams.

Monitoring and auditing systems, while essential for accountability, come with limitations in detection capabilities and response speed. Sophisticated data exfiltration or misuse patterns may evade traditional logging systems, and anomalies may be difficult to distinguish from legitimate usage in high-volume environments. Additionally, audits often occur after privacy violations have occurred, making them more reactive than preventative. Automating audits and integrating them with real-time alerting can improve visibility but requires significant investment and operational maturity.

Mitigating Risks and Ensuring Safe AI Usage in Enterprise Contexts

In the contemporary enterprise landscape, the adoption of artificial intelligence (AI) technologies has transformed the way organizations operate, innovate, and compete. However, alongside the immense benefits of AI such as increased efficiency, enhanced decision-making, and new business models come significant risks that require careful mitigation to ensure safe and responsible AI usage. These risks arise from the inherent complexities of AI systems, including their reliance on large datasets, opaque decision-making processes, susceptibility to bias, and novel cybersecurity vulnerabilities. Enterprises must establish comprehensive frameworks that address these multifaceted risks to safeguard their operations, maintain regulatory compliance, and uphold public trust.

Understanding AI risks is the foundational step in mitigation. AI systems are heavily dependent on data, which, if incomplete, biased, or of poor quality, can lead to inaccurate or unfair outcomes. For example, biased training data can perpetuate discrimination in AI-powered hiring systems or lending decisions, exposing enterprises to ethical and legal challenges. Additionally, AI's black-box nature, where even developers may not fully comprehend how a model reaches certain conclusions, complicates transparency and accountability, making risk detection and correction difficult. Enterprises also face cybersecurity risks unique to AI, such as adversarial attacks where malicious actors subtly manipulate input data to deceive AI models or data poisoning attacks that corrupt training datasets. Furthermore, operational risks including system outages, failures in AI integration, or misaligned objectives can disrupt critical business functions and degrade user experience.

To effectively mitigate these risks, enterprises must implement robust AI governance frameworks that bring together cross-disciplinary expertise from legal, compliance, security, data science, and business units. Such governance bodies oversee AI risk assessments, policy development, and continuous monitoring throughout the AI lifecycle. Regular impact assessments evaluate potential harms and guide mitigation strategies before deployment, while iterative audits ensure ongoing compliance with evolving standards. A key aspect of governance involves defining risk tolerance and prioritizing AI applications based on their potential impact on privacy, fairness, security, and operational stability. High-risk systems, such as those used in healthcare, finance, or legal decision-making, demand especially stringent controls and oversight.

Data management is central to mitigating AI risks. Enterprises must enforce rigorous data quality assurance to eliminate errors, inconsistencies, and biases in datasets. Techniques such as data cleaning, normalization, and bias detection algorithms help maintain dataset integrity. Tracking data provenance and lineage ensures transparency, allowing enterprises to trace data origins and transformations, which is essential for audits and accountability. Protecting sensitive data through encryption, anonymization, and strict access controls mitigates privacy risks and aligns with data protection regulations such as GDPR and CCPA. Furthermore, ongoing data monitoring is necessary to detect shifts in data distributions known as data drift that could degrade AI model performance or introduce new biases over time.

Addressing bias and ethical concerns in AI is not only a legal imperative but a moral one. Enterprises should adopt fairness frameworks that guide data collection, model development, and evaluation to prevent discriminatory outcomes. This involves assembling diverse datasets, applying fairness constraints during model training, and conducting adversarial testing to expose potential biases. Transparency and explainability techniques are also vital; explainable AI models enable stakeholders to understand AI decision rationale, fostering trust and facilitating regulatory compliance. Human oversight remains indispensable; embedding humans in decision loops helps ensure that AI recommendations or actions are reviewed and validated, reducing the risk of errors or unethical consequences.

Security measures tailored to AI systems are critical to safeguarding enterprise assets. Protecting training data from poisoning attacks requires secure data pipelines and validation protocols. Model security includes measures to prevent unauthorized extraction or reverse engineering that could reveal sensitive information or intellectual property. Input validation and sanitization defend against prompt injection attacks or adversarial inputs designed to manipulate AI outputs maliciously. Employing multi-factor authentication, role-based access controls, and encrypted communication channels fortifies the perimeter around AI systems. Adversarial training where models are exposed to deliberately crafted malicious examples during development can improve resilience against certain classes of attacks. This approach is relevant when an organization controls model training or fine-tuning. For hosted model APIs, however, teams typically focus instead on runtime defenses, structured evaluation, and red-teaming practices to identify and mitigate emerging risks.

Continuous monitoring of AI systems is essential for early detection of anomalies, performance degradation, or emerging risks. Automated monitoring tools analyze AI behavior in production environments, tracking metrics such as accuracy, fairness, and response times. Alerts triggered by unusual patterns enable rapid intervention. Incident response plans tailored to AI environments outline steps for containment, root cause analysis, and remediation in case of failures or breaches. Lessons learned from incidents feed back into governance processes, fostering a culture of continuous improvement. This proactive approach ensures that AI systems remain robust, reliable, and aligned with enterprise risk management goals.

Human-in-the-loop approaches blend AI automation with human judgment to enhance safety and accountability. In high-stakes applications, AI-generated outputs should be reviewed by domain experts before final decisions are made. This hybrid model helps catch errors, biases, or ethical issues that automated systems might overlook. Moreover, combining rule-based systems with AI allows enterprises to retain greater control and interpretability, which is critical when regulatory compliance or user trust depends on explainability. By integrating human insight into AI workflows, enterprises mitigate risks while benefiting from AI efficiency.

Third-party and vendor management is another dimension of risk mitigation, as many enterprises leverage external AI platforms or data providers. Establishing rigorous due diligence procedures, contractual obligations, and service-level agreements ensures that partners adhere to security, privacy, and ethical standards. Regular audits and transparent communication channels help maintain alignment and quickly address emerging concerns. Shared responsibility models clarify liabilities and reinforce collaborative risk management across the AI supply chain.

Cultivating an organizational culture that prioritizes AI risk awareness and ethical usage is fundamental. Leadership must champion responsible AI initiatives and allocate resources toward training employees on privacy, security, bias mitigation, and compliance. Creating open channels for reporting AI-related concerns without fear of retaliation encourages transparency and timely issue resolution. Embedding AI risk considerations into strategic planning and innovation pipelines ensures that responsible AI practices become a core organizational competency rather than an afterthought.

Regulatory compliance is a dynamic and evolving challenge in AI risk mitigation. Enterprises must navigate a growing body of laws and guidelines, including the GDPR's data protection mandates, the California Consumer Privacy Act's consumer rights, and emerging frameworks like the European Union's proposed Artificial Intelligence Act. Proactively interpreting and integrating these requirements into AI development, deployment, and monitoring processes mitigates legal risks and reinforces stakeholder confidence. Maintaining thorough documentation, audit trails, and impact assessments supports regulatory reporting and demonstrates due diligence.

Looking ahead, enterprises must future-proof their AI risk mitigation strategies by investing in research, participating in standard-setting initiatives, and embracing emerging technologies. Innovations such as privacy-enhancing computation, including federated learning and homomorphic encryption, offer promising avenues for balancing data utility and privacy. Advances in explainability, adversarial robustness, and bias detection tools will further strengthen safe AI deployments. Flexible, modular AI architectures allow rapid adaptation to new threats or regulatory changes, maintaining resilience in a shifting landscape.

Mitigating risks and ensuring safe AI usage in enterprise contexts demands a comprehensive, multi-layered approach. By understanding AI-specific risks, implementing governance frameworks, maintaining rigorous data quality and security, addressing bias and ethics, incorporating human oversight, managing third-party relationships, fostering a risk-aware culture, and staying abreast of regulatory developments, enterprises can responsibly harness AI's transformative potential. This holistic strategy not only protects against operational, legal, and reputational harm but also builds enduring trust with customers, partners, and regulators, an essential foundation for sustainable AI-driven growth.

Limitations

While the strategies and frameworks discussed offer a strong foundation for mitigating AI risks in enterprise environments, several inherent limitations persist that challenge their full effectiveness. One of the most significant limitations is the complexity and opacity of advanced AI models, particularly those built using deep learning techniques. These models often function as "black boxes," making it difficult for even experienced engineers to fully explain or trace their decision-making processes. This lack of transparency hampers efforts to implement explainability and accountability, especially in regulated industries where justification of automated decisions is essential. Furthermore, while fairness and bias mitigation tools have evolved, they remain limited in their ability to detect subtle, context-specific biases that may only become apparent under real-world usage conditions.

Another major limitation lies in data dependency and quality control. Even with rigorous data governance practices, enterprise datasets may still contain historical biases, missing values, or labeling inconsistencies. This makes the risk of unintentionally encoding discriminatory patterns into AI models a persistent concern. Additionally, maintaining data quality over time is difficult; as environments and behaviors shift, data drift can reduce model reliability and increase operational risks, requiring constant retraining and recalibration that many organizations are not equipped to perform at scale.

CHAPTER 9

Deploying Blazor at Scale

Deploying Blazor with Azure App Services

Deploying Blazor with Azure App Services is one of the most practical and streamlined approaches for organizations that want to leverage the benefits of cloud hosting without being overwhelmed by the complexities of managing infrastructure. Azure App Services is a fully managed Platform-as-a-Service (PaaS) [21] offering from Microsoft that enables developers to deploy, scale, and monitor their applications, APIs, and background services with minimal operational overhead. It provides native support for .NET applications, making it an ideal fit for Blazor, which is built on top of the .NET ecosystem. The primary advantage of App Services lies in its ability to abstract away server management and configuration tasks, allowing developers and DevOps engineers to focus on writing code, optimizing user experiences, and implementing business logic. This approach reduces time-to-market significantly, which is often critical in fast-moving enterprise environments. By using Azure App Service, teams gain access to built-in platform capabilities such as automatic scaling, high availability, and integrated monitoring. In addition, security-related controls can be configured directly within the service, including managed identities for secure service-to-service authentication, TLS configuration for encrypted traffic, App Service Authentication (Easy Auth) for identity integration, private endpoints and VNet integration for network isolation, and Key Vault references for secure secret management. These features allow teams to implement enterprise-grade security practices without managing the underlying infrastructure.

The deployment process itself is straightforward. Developers can publish their Blazor applications directly from Visual Studio, Visual Studio Code, or command-line interfaces. Alternatively, integration with Azure DevOps or GitHub Actions enables continuous integration and continuous delivery (CI/CD) pipelines that automate builds, testing, and deployments. This automation ensures that new features and bug fixes

A. Prasad and H. Singh, *Advanced Blazor Architecture with .NET 10 and Azure OpenAI*,
https://doi.org/10.1007/979-8-8688-2518-7_9

are delivered quickly and consistently, eliminating the risks associated with manual deployment processes. Azure App Services also provides staging slots, which allow organizations to test new versions of Blazor applications in isolated environments before swapping them into production with support for near-zero downtime for stateless workloads. This capability supports safe rollouts, rollback mechanisms, and smooth user experiences even during frequent updates.

From a scaling perspective, Azure App Services offers both manual and automatic scaling. Organizations can configure scaling rules based on CPU utilization, memory usage, request counts, or even time-based schedules. This elasticity ensures that Blazor applications can handle varying workloads from predictable business traffic during office hours to unexpected surges during promotions or product launches without compromising performance. In high-demand scenarios, the service automatically provisions additional instances to maintain responsiveness, and during periods of low demand, it scales down to save costs. This dynamic resource allocation is especially valuable for applications that need to balance cost-efficiency with user experience.

Security is another cornerstone of deploying Blazor on Azure App Services. The platform offers built-in integration with Microsoft Entra ID (formerly Azure AD) for centralized authentication and authorization and supports identity providers such as Microsoft, Google, Facebook, and enterprise SAML-based systems. This makes it simple to secure Blazor applications with single sign-on (SSO), multi-factor authentication (MFA), and authorization happens at two different levels. Inside the application, authorization is handled using ASP.NET Core policies, roles, and claims to determine what a signed-in user is allowed to see or do. Separately, Azure role-based access control (Azure RBAC) governs who can manage or access Azure resources such as App Service, Key Vault, or Azure Container Registry. In simple terms, application authorization controls user behavior within the app, while Azure RBAC controls access to the underlying cloud infrastructure. Both are essential, but they serve distinct purposes in a secure architecture. SSL/TLS certificates can be easily configured to encrypt traffic, ensuring secure communication between users and the application. Additionally, Azure App Service integrates with Azure Key Vault to securely manage application secrets. In practice, this is commonly implemented using Key Vault references together with a managed identity. The App Service is assigned a managed identity, granted access to the required secrets in Key Vault, and the application configuration references those secrets without storing them directly in code or configuration files. This approach allows secrets to be resolved securely at runtime while avoiding hardcoded credentials. These security features reduce the risk of vulnerabilities and align deployments with enterprise compliance requirements such as GDPR, HIPAA, or ISO certifications.

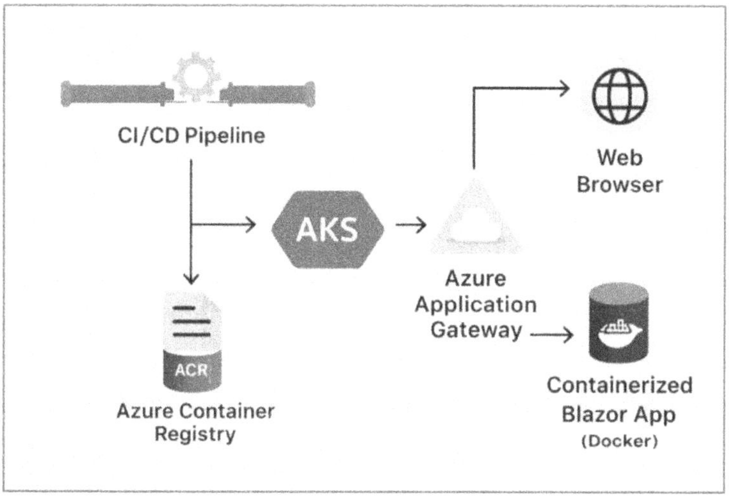

Figure 9-1. *Container Deployment*

Monitoring and diagnostics are also first-class capabilities within App Services.

Application Insights, part of Azure Monitor, provides real-time telemetry such as request duration, dependency calls, exceptions, and availability metrics by default when properly configured. In Blazor applications, server-side request telemetry and dependency tracking are collected automatically, but user behavior tracking (such as custom events, page interactions, or feature usage) requires explicit instrumentation within the application. Developers must intentionally log custom events using the telemetry SDK rather than assuming behavioral data is captured automatically.

When enabling telemetry, it is also important to apply data minimization principles. Avoid logging personally identifiable information (PII) in request payloads or custom events, configure appropriate sampling to control data volume, and align retention settings with organizational compliance policies such as GDPR.

With Application Insights integrated into a Blazor application, developers can detect bottlenecks, identify unresponsive pages, and even trace requests end-to-end across distributed services. The ability to analyze logs, metrics, and alerts within a unified dashboard helps organizations adopt a proactive approach to application management. Instead of reacting to outages or complaints, teams can predict issues and resolve them before they impact users. This observability is crucial for maintaining reliability in production environments where downtime can directly affect revenue and customer satisfaction.

One of the most valuable features of Azure App Services is its global reach. Microsoft maintains data centers in multiple regions around the world, enabling organizations to deploy Blazor applications close to their users. This reduces latency and improves performance for geographically distributed audiences. Deployment slots in Azure App Service enable staged rollouts such as staging and production within the same region and App Service instance. They are not used for multi-region deployments. Achieving regional redundancy requires deploying separate App Service instances in each target region, typically coordinated using Azure Front Door or Azure Traffic Manager to route traffic and provide failover capabilities. Blazor applications hosted on App Services can deliver fast, secure, and highly available experiences across the globe.

Cost management is another important aspect of deploying Blazor with App Services. Because Azure App Service follows a PaaS model, organizations manage applications without maintaining the underlying infrastructure. Billing is typically based on the provisioned App Service plan (instance size and scale configuration), rather than per-request consumption. The flexible pricing tiers allow businesses to start with minimal resources for small-scale applications and then scale up as usage grows. Developers can begin with free or shared tiers during development and testing phases, then move to higher tiers with more powerful compute options, custom domains, and scaling capabilities when moving to production. By monitoring resource consumption and setting alerts for budget thresholds, organizations can avoid unnecessary spending while ensuring that their applications remain performant.

Despite its advantages, it is important to acknowledge some limitations of using Azure App Services for Blazor. Because it is a managed platform, developers have less control over the underlying infrastructure compared to containerized or Kubernetes-based deployments. For example, scenarios that require OS-level customization such as installing native dependencies, modifying low-level system configurations, or implementing highly specialized networking setups can be more restrictive in a managed PaaS environment like Azure App Service. Standard application middleware integration within ASP.NET Core is fully supported, but deeper infrastructure-level control may require containerization or an IaaS-based deployment model. For many enterprise applications, however, these trade-offs are acceptable, as the productivity and simplicity of App Services outweigh the need for granular control. Moreover, when organizations eventually outgrow App Services, they can easily transition to containerized workflows or Azure Kubernetes Service (AKS) while retaining the same CI/CD pipelines and Azure ecosystem integrations.

Real-world case studies demonstrate the power of this model. Small startups often choose Azure App Services to quickly launch minimum viable products (MVPs) without investing heavily in infrastructure expertise. Larger enterprises leverage App Services for internal business applications where security, compliance, and ease of maintenance are more important than infrastructure customization. For example, an enterprise could deploy a Blazor-based employee portal on App Services with integration to Azure AD for authentication, use Application Insights to monitor employee engagement, and rely on automatic scaling to support thousands of concurrent users during peak times such as performance reviews or corporate announcements.

Containerized Workflows for Blazor Applications

Containerized workflows for Blazor applications represent a modern, flexible, and highly portable deployment strategy that has become essential for organizations seeking agility, consistency, and scalability in cloud-native environments. Unlike traditional deployment approaches that rely on installing applications directly onto servers or even managed platforms, containerization packages a Blazor application along with its dependencies, runtime, libraries, and configuration into a lightweight, portable unit called a container. This packaging ensures that the application behaves consistently across development, testing, and production environments, eliminating the classic "it works on my machine" problem. Docker is the most widely used containerization technology, and when combined with Azure services such as Azure Container Registry (ACR), Azure Container Instances (ACI), or Azure Container Apps, it enables a smooth end-to-end workflow for building, deploying, and scaling Blazor applications. The adoption of containerized workflows fits naturally with DevOps practices, as it allows continuous integration, automated testing, and rapid deployments across multiple environments, while also opening the door to microservices architectures where Blazor can function as a standalone UI component or as part of a larger ecosystem of distributed services.

The process of containerizing a Blazor application typically begins with defining a multi-stage Dockerfile. Multi-stage builds reduce image size by separating the build environment from the final runtime image. This file defines the base image (often a .NET runtime image), copies the Blazor application into the container, restores dependencies, builds the project, and configures the environment for execution. The result is a Docker image that encapsulates the Blazor application in a fully reproducible way. This image is then pushed to a container registry such as Azure Container Registry (ACR), which acts as a secure and centralized repository for storing and distributing container images. With ACR, enterprises can manage access controls, automate vulnerability scanning, and integrate with Azure DevOps or GitHub Actions to streamline build pipelines. Once stored in the registry, these images can be deployed across multiple environments, ensuring that the exact same image tested in staging is the one running in production, thereby eliminating inconsistencies that can lead to bugs or downtime.

Deploying Blazor containers in Azure can take several forms depending on the scale and complexity of the application. For lightweight workloads or proof-of-concept deployments, Azure Container Instances (ACI) provides a serverless container hosting platform where developers can quickly run a Blazor application without worrying about virtual machines or orchestration. This is particularly useful for short-lived applications, batch processing tasks, or testing environments. For more advanced scenarios, Azure Container Apps provides a managed platform for running containers with built-in support for scaling, networking, and observability. Azure Container Apps can scale Blazor applications dynamically based on HTTP traffic and configurable scaling rules. However, scaling behavior depends on defined minimum and maximum replica settings, concurrency limits, and revision configuration. Cold starts, resource limits, and state management considerations must also be evaluated, particularly for stateful workloads such as Blazor Server applications that maintain active connections, events, or custom metrics, making them suitable for production workloads that require elasticity. They also integrate seamlessly with Azure Functions, Azure Logic Apps, and Event Grid, enabling developers to build event-driven applications where Blazor serves as the front-end experience while back-end processing is handled by serverless components.

The flexibility of containerized workflows becomes even more evident when Blazor is part of a microservices ecosystem. Instead of deploying a monolithic application that handles all user interactions, data access, and business logic, teams can break down functionality into smaller, independent services. For example, a Blazor WebAssembly front end can be deployed as one container, while APIs for authentication, order management, or reporting are deployed as separate containers. This separation allows each service to evolve independently, scale based on demand, and be maintained by different teams without interfering with one another. Containers provide a natural boundary for microservices, isolating dependencies and ensuring version compatibility. This architecture not only enhances scalability but also improves resilience, as failures in one service do not necessarily bring down the entire system.

Security is another key benefit of containerized workflows for Blazor. By isolating applications within containers, organizations reduce the attack surface and minimize the risk of vulnerabilities spreading across environments. Azure enhances this security posture with features like Microsoft Defender for Cloud, which can scan container images in ACR for known vulnerabilities, misconfigurations, or outdated dependencies. Additionally, secrets and sensitive configuration values, such as API keys or database connection strings, can be managed through Azure Key Vault and injected into containers at runtime. This ensures that sensitive data is not hard-coded into container images or source code. Role-based access control (RBAC) within Azure allows organizations to tightly manage who can build, push, or deploy container images, further strengthening security.

From an operational standpoint, containerized workflows bring consistency and predictability to Blazor deployments. Developers, testers, and the operations team all work with the same container image, which reduces friction and misalignment between environments. CI/CD pipelines play a central role in this model. With Azure DevOps or GitHub Actions, pipelines can be configured to automatically build new Docker images when code changes are pushed, run automated tests against those images, and then publish them to ACR. From there, deployment pipelines can roll out these updated images to Azure Container Apps or Kubernetes clusters, ensuring a smooth and automated flow from code commit to production release. This automation accelerates delivery cycles while maintaining high quality, reliability, and traceability of changes.

Monitoring and observability are equally important in containerized Blazor workflows. Azure Monitor and Application Insights integrate with containerized applications to provide telemetry on performance, error rates, and user interactions. Developers can view real-time dashboards showing request response times, CPU utilization, memory usage, and scaling events. These insights are invaluable for diagnosing issues quickly, understanding user behavior, and ensuring that containerized Blazor applications remain responsive under varying loads. The ability to set up alerts and automated remediation actions ensures that potential problems are addressed before they impact end users, aligning containerized workflows with the principles of Site Reliability Engineering (SRE).

Another advantage of containerized workflows is portability across cloud and on-premises environments. Because containers are self-contained, a Blazor application packaged into a Docker image can run not only on Azure but also on other clouds such as AWS, Google Cloud, or on-premises Kubernetes clusters. This multi-cloud flexibility reduces vendor lock-in and enables organizations to adopt hybrid deployment strategies. For example, sensitive workloads could remain on-premises for compliance reasons, while public-facing Blazor applications are deployed on Azure for scalability and global reach. This level of portability and flexibility is difficult to achieve with traditional deployment models, making containerization a powerful option for enterprises with diverse infrastructure needs.

Despite its many benefits, containerized workflows also introduce challenges that organizations must address. Building and maintaining Docker files requires careful attention to security, performance, and size optimization. Large or poorly optimized images can slow down deployments and increase storage costs. Teams must also invest in container lifecycle management practices, such as regularly updating base images, applying security patches, and cleaning up unused images. Furthermore, as the number of containers grows, orchestration becomes a necessity, which leads many organizations to adopt Kubernetes through Azure Kubernetes Service (AKS). While this adds complexity, it also unlocks advanced scaling, networking, and resiliency features that are not available in simpler container hosting models.

In real-world scenarios, containerized workflows have proven invaluable for organizations modernizing their .NET applications. For instance, an ecommerce company could deploy a Blazor storefront as a containerized application, with separate microservices handling product catalogs, user authentication, and payment processing. During high-traffic events such as holiday sales, each container can scale independently based on demand, ensuring that the checkout process remains smooth even if product browsing sees an enormous surge in traffic. Similarly, enterprises building internal dashboards with Blazor can use containerized deployments to ensure consistent environments across development, testing, and production, minimizing the risk of discrepancies and maximizing developer productivity.

Scaling Blazor applications with Kubernetes, particularly through Azure Kubernetes Service (AKS), represents the most advanced and enterprise-ready approach to deploying modern web applications in the cloud. Kubernetes has emerged as the de facto standard for orchestrating containerized workloads, and its power lies in automating deployment, scaling, networking, and resilience for distributed applications. While deploying a Blazor application on Azure App Services provides simplicity and containerized workflows deliver flexibility, Kubernetes offers the ultimate balance of scalability, control, and reliability needed for mission-critical systems. Azure Kubernetes Service builds on the open source Kubernetes platform but integrates it deeply with

Azure's ecosystem, reducing the management burden while enabling organizations to harness enterprise-grade security, observability, and operational automation. Deploying Blazor on AKS allows development teams to deliver applications that can handle millions of users, withstand infrastructure failures, and support complex deployment strategies without downtime. This makes AKS a natural choice for organizations that have already adopted microservices, require high availability, or operate in industries where resilience and compliance are non-negotiable.

The process of scaling Blazor with AKS begins with containerization, since Kubernetes operates entirely around containers. Developers first package the Blazor application into a Docker image and publish it to a container registry such as Azure Container Registry (ACR). From there, Kubernetes manifests or Helm charts are used to define how the Blazor application should run in the cluster. These configuration files specify deployment details such as the number of replicas, resource allocations (CPU and memory), networking policies, and scaling rules. When applied to AKS, Kubernetes ensures that the desired state is always maintained if a Blazor container crashes, Kubernetes automatically restarts it, and if a node fails, the workload is rescheduled on another node in the cluster. This self-healing capability is one of the defining features of Kubernetes, providing resilience without manual intervention.

In Azure Kubernetes Service (AKS), scaling is primarily achieved horizontally by increasing or decreasing the number of pod replicas. Horizontal Pod Autoscaling (HPA) is particularly powerful for Blazor applications, as it allows the system to automatically add or remove instances of the Blazor container based on real-time metrics such as CPU usage, memory utilization, or even custom metrics like request latency or active user sessions. For example, if a Blazor web application suddenly experiences a surge of traffic during a product launch or promotional event, HPA ensures that additional replicas are created automatically to maintain responsiveness. When the traffic subsides, the system scales back down to save costs. Vertical scaling is also supported, allowing administrators to allocate more resources to existing containers when workloads require more processing power or memory. The elasticity provided by these scaling models ensures that Blazor applications remain performant under dynamic workloads while optimizing resource usage.

One of the most advanced capabilities AKS enables for Blazor deployments is sophisticated release management through deployment strategies such as rolling updates, blue-green deployments, and canary releases. In rolling updates, Kubernetes gradually replaces old versions of the Blazor container with new ones, ensuring minimal downtime. In blue-green deployments, two environments (blue and green) are maintained simultaneously, with traffic routed to the new version only when it is fully validated. This approach allows immediate rollback in case of issues. Canary releases take this concept further by exposing a new version of the Blazor application to a small subset of users before rolling it out to everyone. These strategies allow organizations to release updates frequently while minimizing risk, which is especially valuable for Blazor applications that serve large and diverse user bases.

Networking and service discovery are also key strengths of Kubernetes. In AKS, services act as stable endpoints for accessing Blazor applications, even as pods (the smallest deployable units in Kubernetes) are created or destroyed dynamically. For public-facing Blazor applications deployed to AKS, ingress controllers such as NGINX Ingress or Azure Application Gateway handle HTTP routing, load balancing, and TLS termination and can integrate with Azure Front Door for global traffic distribution. However, production readiness requires more than basic ingress configuration. Readiness and liveness probes should be defined to ensure traffic is directed only to healthy pods. Timeout settings must be tuned appropriately for WebSockets or other long-lived connections (particularly important for Blazor Server). Graceful shutdown should be implemented using preStop hooks and appropriate terminationGracePeriodSeconds to enable connection draining. Pod Disruption Budgets (PDBs) should also be configured to maintain availability during maintenance or scaling events.

Within the cluster, Kubernetes networking enables communication between Blazor services and dependent microservices, databases, or APIs. Network policies can be applied to enforce controlled east–west traffic, limiting communication paths and strengthening the overall security posture.

Security in AKS is multi-layered and deeply integrated with Azure's identity and compliance ecosystem. Azure Active Directory (Azure AD) can be used for authenticating and authorizing access to the Kubernetes cluster, ensuring that only approved personnel can perform administrative actions. Role-based access control (RBAC) within Kubernetes allows fine-grained control over who can deploy, manage, or scale Blazor applications. Secrets management is also streamlined by integrating Kubernetes secrets with Azure Key Vault, providing a secure and centralized way to manage sensitive information such as API keys or certificates. Additionally, Microsoft Defender for Cloud continuously monitors AKS clusters for vulnerabilities, compliance violations, and runtime threats, giving organizations confidence that their Blazor deployments are protected against modern attack vectors.

Observability is another area where AKS excels, especially for large-scale Blazor applications. By integrating with Azure Monitor, Log Analytics, and Application Insights, teams can gain end-to-end visibility into application performance, cluster health, and user behavior. Metrics such as response times, error rates, and pod-level resource consumption can be visualized in real-time dashboards, while distributed tracing allows developers to follow requests across multiple services and pinpoint bottlenecks. Alerts can be configured to notify teams of anomalies, and automated remediation workflows can resolve issues without human intervention. This level of observability is critical in complex environments where a Blazor front end interacts with dozens of back-end services, databases, and third-party APIs.

Another key advantage of scaling Blazor with AKS is multi-region and hybrid deployment support. Global enterprises often need to serve users across continents while ensuring compliance with regional data residency laws. With AKS, Blazor applications can be deployed to multiple clusters in different Azure regions, and traffic can be intelligently routed using Azure Front Door or Traffic Manager. This not only reduces latency for end users but also provides geo-redundancy, ensuring continuity even if an entire region goes offline. Furthermore, AKS supports hybrid scenarios, allowing Blazor applications to run seamlessly across on-premises Kubernetes clusters and Azure cloud infrastructure, giving organizations flexibility in adopting cloud-native strategies without abandoning existing investments.

While AKS provides unparalleled scalability and control, it also introduces operational complexity compared to simpler deployment models like App Services or Container Apps. Teams need expertise in Kubernetes concepts such as pods, deployments, services, ingress, ConfigMaps, and Helm charts. They must also manage cluster upgrades, node scaling, and cost optimization. To address this, Azure simplifies many aspects of Kubernetes management through automated upgrades, integrated security patches, and managed node pools. Nonetheless, adopting AKS requires organizations to invest in training, governance frameworks, and DevOps practices to fully realize its potential. The complexity, however, is justified for enterprises that require global scalability, high availability, and deep customization for their Blazor applications.

Real-world use cases highlight the transformative impact of AKS for Blazor deployments. Consider a global financial services firm deploying a Blazor-based trading platform that must handle millions of concurrent users with near-zero downtime. AKS provides the resilience, autoscaling, and global distribution required to meet such demands. Similarly, a healthcare provider can use Blazor with AKS to deliver secure patient portals, ensuring compliance with HIPAA regulations while scaling effortlessly during peak times such as health crises. These scenarios underscore the strategic advantage of using Kubernetes to elevate Blazor applications from departmental tools to mission-critical systems serving diverse, global audiences.

Scaling Blazor with Kubernetes and Azure Kubernetes Service (AKS)

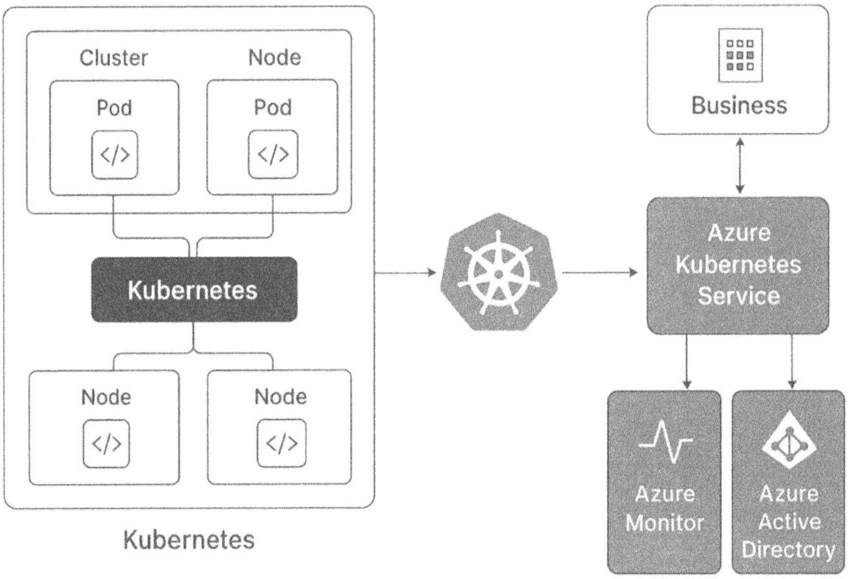

Figure 9-2. Kubernetes and Azure Kubernetes Service

Scaling Blazor applications with Kubernetes particularly through Azure Kubernetes Service (AKS) is a natural progression for organizations that require advanced orchestration, resilience, and elastic scalability. While Azure App Service handles many scaling scenarios effectively, enterprise environments with fluctuating workloads, long-lived connections (such as Blazor Server circuits), and distributed architectures often require more granular control over scaling behavior and infrastructure management.

Kubernetes addresses these needs by enabling horizontal scaling, distributing workloads across multiple pods and nodes to handle increased concurrency. Rather than relying solely on vertical scaling, adding more resources to a single instance, Kubernetes allows applications to scale out dynamically based on demand. This model improves fault tolerance and resource efficiency, ensuring that Blazor applications remain responsive during traffic spikes while reducing resource consumption during quieter periods.

Azure Kubernetes Service simplifies Kubernetes adoption by managing the control plane, handling upgrades, and integrating with Azure-native services. This reduces operational overhead while still providing the flexibility of a full Kubernetes environment. For Blazor teams, this means maintaining control over containerized deployments without managing cluster internals from scratch. AKS also integrates with Azure Monitor for observability, Microsoft Entra ID for identity management, and Azure DevOps or GitHub Actions for CI/CD workflows.

In practice, a Blazor application is packaged into a Docker container, pushed to Azure Container Registry (ACR), and deployed as pods within an AKS cluster. These pods are exposed through Kubernetes services and ingress controllers such as NGINX or Azure Application Gateway. Each layer—front end, back-end APIs, and data services—can scale independently, enabling a modular and resilient architecture suited for enterprise-grade workloads.

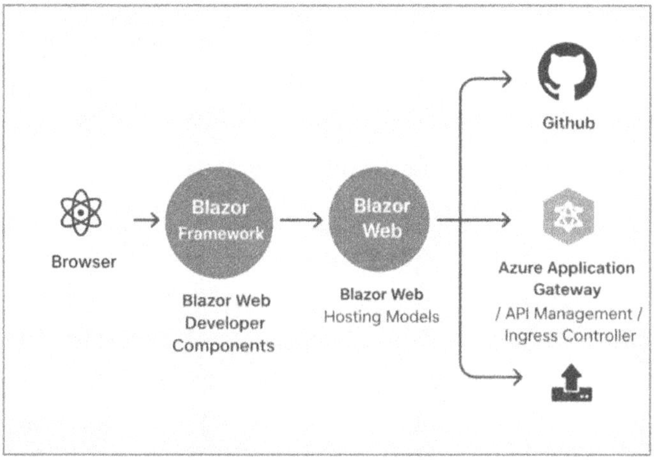

Figure 9-3. *Scale a Blazor Framework*

The deployment workflow for Blazor on AKS is streamlined through CI/CD pipelines. Developers typically containerize the application using Docker, store the images in Azure Container Registry, and define the deployment configuration with Kubernetes manifests written in YAML. These manifests specify how many replicas of a Blazor pod should run, what resources they require, and how they connect with other services. For more complex deployments, Helm charts are often used to simplify and standardize configurations across environments. Continuous deployment is then automated using Azure DevOps or GitHub Actions, ensuring that every code commit is built, tested, and deployed into AKS in a consistent manner. This reduces manual intervention, speeds up delivery cycles, and guarantees reliable rollouts.

Scaling strategies for Blazor in AKS go beyond simply adding more pods. Kubernetes provides multiple mechanisms for intelligent scaling, such as the Horizontal Pod Autoscaler (HPA), which increases or decreases the number of Blazor pods based on CPU, memory, or custom performance metrics. The Cluster Autoscaler further extends this by adding or removing underlying virtual machine nodes in the AKS cluster when resource demand changes. For event-driven workloads, Kubernetes Event-Driven Autoscaling (KEDA) can dynamically adjust Blazor pods based on queue length in Azure Service Bus or Kafka event streams, ensuring that the application remains responsive even when workloads spike unpredictably. In global deployments, multiple AKS clusters can be deployed across Azure regions, with Azure Front Door providing intelligent traffic distribution, latency optimization, and geo-failover. Together, these strategies allow Blazor applications to meet demanding performance and availability requirements while optimizing resource consumption.

Security is another cornerstone of running Blazor applications at scale on AKS. Container images must be scanned for vulnerabilities before deployment, and organizations should adopt a practice of building from minimal base images to reduce attack surfaces. Secrets such as API keys and database credentials should never be stored in plain YAML files; instead, they should be managed securely through Azure Key Vault and injected into Kubernetes pods at runtime. Role-based access control ensures that only authorized users and services can access cluster resources, while network policies enforce boundaries between services to prevent lateral attacks within the cluster. All communication, from ingress traffic to internal pod-to-pod requests, should be encrypted with TLS to maintain confidentiality and integrity. By following these practices, enterprises can reduce the risks of breaches, comply with regulatory standards, and instill confidence in their users.

Monitoring and observability are critical once Blazor is deployed on AKS, as scaling decisions and performance optimizations rely heavily on insights from telemetry. Azure Monitor for Containers provides an integrated solution to track CPU and memory utilization, pod health, and node performance, while Prometheus and Grafana can offer more customizable, real-time dashboards. Distributed tracing plays a critical role in modern Blazor applications, especially those built on microservices. By instrumenting services with

OpenTelemetry and exporting traces and metrics to Azure Monitor or Application Insights, teams gain end-to-end visibility into how requests move through the system. Maintaining consistent correlation IDs across services allows a single user request to be tracked from the Blazor UI through back-end APIs, databases, and external dependencies.

This level of visibility makes it much easier to diagnose performance bottlenecks, identify failing components, and understand system behavior under load. When combined with alerts and automated remediation workflows, observability becomes proactive rather than reactive, helping teams detect and resolve issues before they significantly impact end users.

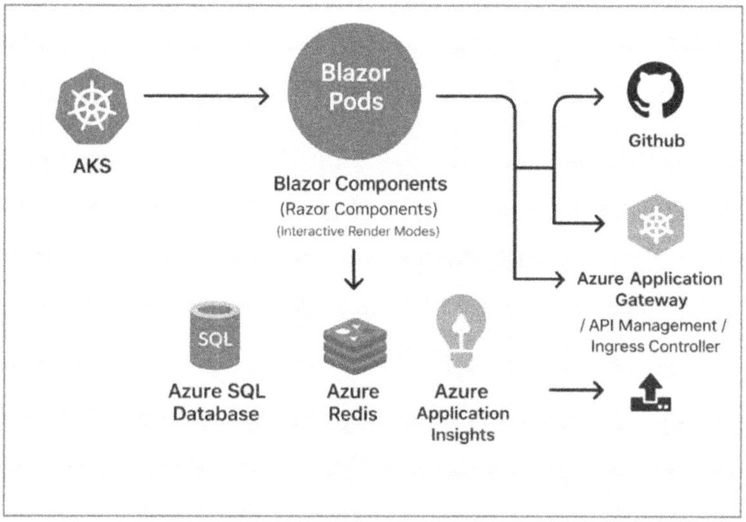

Figure 9-4. *Scalable Application*

A real-world example of these principles can be seen in a large-scale ecommerce platform built with Blazor WebAssembly. During peak shopping seasons, user traffic surges from a few thousand concurrent connections to hundreds of thousands within hours. By deploying the application to AKS, the platform can automatically scale its Blazor front end to dozens of pods, while back-end APIs scale based on service bus queue length using KEDA. Azure Front Door distributes traffic globally, ensuring customers from Asia, Europe, and North America experience consistent, low-latency performance. The system is continuously monitored through Azure Monitor and Grafana dashboards, while Key Vault ensures that sensitive credentials remain protected. This architecture not only prevents downtime during critical revenue-generating events but also ensures that the platform avoids unnecessary costs by scaling down during quieter periods.

Looking ahead, the future of scaling Blazor with AKS will become even more sophisticated as Kubernetes evolves. Features like virtual nodes with Azure Container Instances allow for burst scaling without managing extra VMs, GitOps approaches simplify and standardize deployments using tools like Flux or ArgoCD, and while most production environments today rely on reactive autoscaling based on metrics such as CPU, memory, or request count, emerging patterns are exploring predictive scaling models that anticipate workload changes before they occur. These approaches typically combine historical telemetry with machine learning techniques to forecast demand and adjust capacity proactively. Although predictive autoscaling is not yet a mainstream default capability across all platforms, it represents an evolving area of research and innovation in cloud-native operations. As enterprises continue to adopt Blazor for building interactive, real-time web applications, leveraging AKS as the scaling backbone will become increasingly standard practice. This combination not only addresses today's challenges of high availability, performance, and security but also lays the groundwork for innovation and resilience in the years to come.

While Kubernetes and Azure Kubernetes Service (AKS) provide powerful mechanisms for scaling Blazor applications, there are several limitations and challenges that organizations need to recognize before adopting them at enterprise scale. One of the most prominent limitations is the complexity of Kubernetes itself. Even though AKS abstracts away much of the control plane management, developers and DevOps engineers must still understand concepts such as pods, deployments, services, ingress controllers, persistent volumes, and network policies. For teams without strong containerization and Kubernetes expertise, this learning curve can significantly slow down adoption and introduce errors in deployment or scaling configurations. Another limitation relates to cost and resource overhead. Running AKS clusters incurs not only compute and storage expenses but also costs associated with monitoring, logging, ingress controllers, and backup solutions. In many cases, the operational overhead of managing an AKS cluster can outweigh the benefits, especially for smaller Blazor applications that could have been adequately served by simpler solutions such as Azure App Services.

From a performance perspective, latency and connection management can pose limitations for Blazor Server applications. Because Blazor Server relies on maintaining persistent SignalR connections between clients and servers, deploying across multiple pods in Kubernetes introduces complexities around session affinity, sticky connections, and scaling SignalR hubs. Load balancers and ingress controllers may not always handle these long-lived connections optimally, leading to connection drops or degraded user experience. While workarounds exist, such as using Azure SignalR Service, they introduce additional cost and architectural complexity. Similarly, scaling Blazor WebAssembly back ends on AKS may face limitations in handling stateful interactions, since Kubernetes is primarily designed for stateless microservices. Any session state or caching must be offloaded to external services like Redis or Azure SQL, which adds dependencies and potential bottlenecks.

Another limitation is the operational overhead of monitoring and troubleshooting. While tools like Azure Monitor, Prometheus, and Grafana provide observability, setting them up and maintaining accurate dashboards can be challenging. Debugging issues in a distributed Blazor deployment on AKS is inherently more complex than on a single-node Azure App Service. Logs and traces are spread across multiple pods, and pinpointing issues such as memory leaks, failed deployments, or configuration mismatches requires advanced DevOps practices. Additionally, the deployment pipeline complexity can be a limitation. A proper CI/CD workflow for AKS typically involves containerization, Helm charts, YAML manifests, secret management, and automated rollouts with rollback strategies. This complexity introduces additional points of failure compared to simpler deployment models, and small misconfigurations in manifests can result in downtime or scaling failures.

Security, while generally strong in AKS, also brings its own limitations. Enterprises must implement strict role-based access control, manage secrets securely, and define network policies to prevent lateral movement of attacks. However, these configurations are non-trivial, and missteps can create vulnerabilities rather than preventing them. Furthermore, managing multi-region deployments of Blazor on AKS introduces challenges with data consistency and replication latency, particularly if the application depends heavily on real-time updates or tightly coupled stateful services.

Lastly, there is the question of vendor lock-in and operational sustainability. While Kubernetes is technically cloud-agnostic, AKS integrates deeply with Azure services such as ACR, Azure Monitor, and Azure Active Directory. This makes migration to another cloud provider difficult, potentially locking organizations into the Azure ecosystem. Additionally, because AKS evolves rapidly, keeping up with frequent updates, deprecated APIs, and changes in best practices can place continuous pressure on DevOps teams.

CHAPTER 10

CI/CD for Blazor and AI Apps

Planning a CI/CD Workflow for Blazor and AI Projects

Planning a CI/CD workflow for a solution that combines Blazor front-end components with AI-powered services introduces additional considerations beyond a typical web application pipeline. In addition to standard build and deployment steps, teams must account for model integration, prompt/configuration management, secure handling of API credentials, and environment-specific configuration of AI services. A well-designed pipeline does more than automate builds and deployments; it enforces code quality, secures sensitive assets, and creates the repeatable processes that let teams move quickly without sacrificing reliability. The planning phase is therefore critical because the decisions you make here shape how the pipeline scales, how easily it adapts to new features, and how confidently you can ship updates to production.

The first consideration is understanding the unique nature of a Blazor and AI application. Blazor brings the modern .NET ecosystem to the browser, supporting both WebAssembly (WASM) and server-side hosting models. AI capabilities might come from custom machine learning models packaged as .NET services or from cloud offerings such as Azure OpenAI Service, Azure Cognitive Services, or custom Python microservices exposed through REST or gRPC. These two domains—the rich interactive front end and the compute-intensive AI back end—mean that your CI/CD pipeline must handle a diverse set of components, including C# Razor code, .NET APIs, potentially containerized Python services, and configuration for external Azure resources. Early in planning, it helps to create a clear inventory of every artifact the pipeline will manage:

A. Prasad and H. Singh, *Advanced Blazor Architecture with .NET 10 and Azure OpenAI*,
https://doi.org/10.1007/979-8-8688-2518-7_10

Blazor client projects, server APIs, shared class libraries, AI model files, infrastructure templates, and environment-specific configuration such as connection strings and API keys.

The below diagram illustrates a typical end-to-end CI/CD workflow, starting from development activities such as branching and defining changes, followed by planning and code review through pull requests and validation pipelines. Once approved, changes are merged, versioned, and deployed, ensuring a structured and repeatable process from development to delivery. It highlights how automation and review checkpoints work together to maintain quality and reliability throughout the software lifecycle.

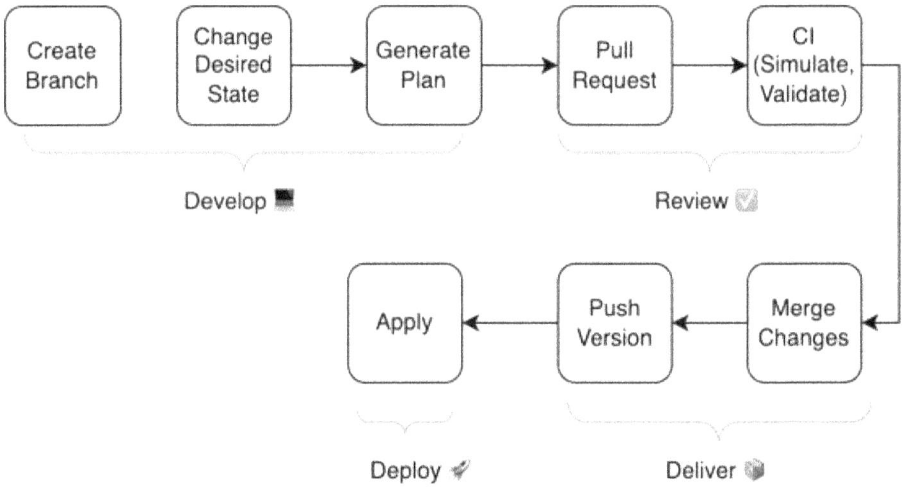

Figure 10-1. *CI/CD Workflow*

```yaml
name: blazor-ai-ci-cd

on:
  push:
    branches: [ main ]
  pull_request:

env:
  DOTNET_VERSION: '10.0.x'
  ACR_NAME: myregistry.azurecr.io
  IMAGE_NAME: blazor-ai-app

jobs:
  build:
    runs-on: ubuntu-latest
    steps:
      - uses: actions/checkout@v4  # Get code

      - uses: actions/setup-dotnet@v4
        with:
          dotnet-version: ${{ env.DOTNET_VERSION }}  # Setup .NET

      - run: dotnet restore  # Restore deps
      - run: dotnet build --no-restore -c Release  # Build
      - run: dotnet test --no-build -c Release  # Unit + integration tests

      - run: |
          python ai-tests/prompt_test.py  # Basic AI validation

  container:
    needs: build
    runs-on: ubuntu-latest
    if: github.event_name != 'pull_request'
    steps:
      - uses: actions/checkout@v4

      - uses: azure/login@v2  # Auth via OIDC
        with:
          client-id: ${{ secrets.AZURE_CLIENT_ID }}
          tenant-id: ${{ secrets.AZURE_TENANT_ID }}
          subscription-id: ${{ secrets.AZURE_SUBSCRIPTION_ID }}

      - run: az acr login --name $(echo $ACR_NAME | cut -d'.' -f1)  # ACR login

      - run: |
          docker build -t $ACR_NAME/$IMAGE_NAME:${{ github.sha }} .
          docker push $ACR_NAME/$IMAGE_NAME:${{ github.sha }}  # Build + push image

  deploy:
    needs: container
    runs-on: ubuntu-latest
    if: github.ref == 'refs/heads/main'
    steps:
      - uses: azure/login@v2
        with:
          client-id: ${{ secrets.AZURE_CLIENT_ID }}
          tenant-id: ${{ secrets.AZURE_TENANT_ID }}
          subscription-id: ${{ secrets.AZURE_SUBSCRIPTION_ID }}

      - run: |
          az containerapp update \
            --name my-app \
            --resource-group my-rg \
            --image $ACR_NAME/$IMAGE_NAME:${{ github.sha }}  # Deploy latest image
```

Sample YAML CI/CD Template

Once the scope is defined, you can outline the stages of the workflow. A typical high-level flow begins when a developer pushes changes to a source control repository such as GitHub or Azure Repos. The continuous integration portion runs automated builds and tests on each commit or pull request, generating build artifacts and verifying that code meets quality standards. Continuous delivery then takes over, promoting validated artifacts to staging and eventually to production environments using controlled, auditable steps. This overarching pattern applies to any modern web application, but planning for a Blazor-plus-AI solution requires some specific refinements.

One refinement is parallelism. Because Blazor and AI components may have different build requirements, it is wise to design the pipeline to build them in parallel rather than sequentially. For example, the Blazor WebAssembly front end might be compiled and optimized with the latest .NET SDK; in cases where you are self-hosting inference or training-related services, the AI microservice may require Docker image builds that include GPU-enabled dependencies or specialized Python packages. By defining separate build jobs in your pipeline configuration, say, one job for the Blazor client and another for the AI service, you reduce overall pipeline time and isolate failures. Parallel builds also make it easier to scale teams: front-end developers can iterate on UI changes while data science engineers update model serving code without stepping on each other's toes.

Testing is the next major planning focus. Automated testing should cover unit tests for C# components and integration tests for APIs, along with AI-specific validation. This may include prompt tests, schema validation of responses, safety and content filtering checks, regression datasets to ensure consistent model behavior, and where relevant latency and cost validations to monitor performance and usage characteristics. Because AI components can produce nondeterministic results, your pipeline may include statistical checks, threshold validations, or comparison against known baselines to ensure that a model update does not degrade accuracy. For Blazor applications, testing should be layered. Component-level or unit testing (e.g., using bUnit) can validate rendering logic and component behavior in isolation, while UI testing frameworks such as Playwright or Selenium can be used for end-to-end browser interactions to confirm that pages render correctly after a change. This approach avoids over-reliance on browser automation while improving test reliability and execution speed. Deciding which tests run on every commit vs. which run only on nightly builds is part of balancing speed and coverage. Lightweight unit tests might run on every pull request, while heavier model evaluation or full browser tests can run in scheduled builds or on a staging branch.

Security planning must permeate the CI/CD workflow from the start. Secrets such as database passwords, Azure Service Bus keys, or OpenAI credentials must never be hard-coded or stored in plain text. Modern pipeline tools such as GitHub Actions, Azure Pipelines, or GitLab CI integrate with secure secret stores rather than acting as the primary source of truth for sensitive data. In practice, secrets are managed in services like Azure Key Vault or similar vault solutions, and pipelines are configured to retrieve them securely at runtime, allowing the pipeline to access them as environment variables or injected configuration at runtime. Incorporating static code analysis and dependency scanning also protects against vulnerabilities. For .NET projects, tools like SonarCloud or GitHub's Dependabot can be wired into the CI stage to block merges if known vulnerabilities exist. When working with AI models, it is important to include explicit data governance and validation steps in the pipeline. This may involve PII scanning on training and evaluation datasets, checks for unintended data leakage in model outputs, and enforcement of policies around approved and compliant data sources. Ensuring that datasets and model behavior align with privacy regulations should be a required gate before deployment.

Infrastructure as code (IaC) is another key planning decision. Blazor and AI solutions typically involve multiple Azure resources working together in a cohesive architecture. For example:

- **Front-End Hosting:** Azure App Service or Azure Static Web Apps (for Blazor WebAssembly)
- **Back-End APIs/BFF Layer:** ASP.NET Core services hosted on App Service, AKS, or Container Apps
- **AI Services:** Azure OpenAI Service or other Azure AI offerings
- **Data Layer:** Azure SQL Database, Cosmos DB, or Blob Storage
- **Secrets and Configuration:** Azure Key Vault with managed identity
- **Observability:** Azure Monitor and Application Insights

This layered approach helps separate concerns, improves scalability, and enables independent deployment and governance of each component. Azure Container Apps or Kubernetes for model serving, Key Vault for secrets, and Azure Cognitive or OpenAI services for AI APIs. Managing these manually invites drift and errors. Instead, plan to represent your infrastructure in declarative templates using Bicep, ARM, or Terraform. The CI/CD pipeline can then provision or update resources automatically during deployment, ensuring that development, staging, and production remain consistent. Version-controlling these templates also makes environment changes auditable and repeatable.

Choosing the right branching and promotion strategy is equally important. A common pattern is GitFlow or a simplified trunk-based development approach with feature branches. In a GitFlow-like setup, developers create feature branches, merge into a develop branch for integration, and promote to main or release branches when ready for production. The pipeline can be configured so that commits to develop trigger deployments to a staging environment, while tagged releases trigger production deployments. For AI components, you might introduce additional gating: for example, require that a model pass an A/B test in a staging environment before promotion. These branching policies, when enforced by the CI/CD system, give teams confidence that only well-tested, well-reviewed code reaches customers.

Deployment strategies for Blazor apps vary depending on the hosting model. For Blazor WebAssembly, a static site deployment to Azure Static Web Apps or an Azure Blob Storage container is often sufficient. Server-side Blazor apps or APIs for AI services may be packaged as Docker containers and deployed to Azure App Service, Azure Container Apps, or Azure Kubernetes Service. Your pipeline should accommodate these targets by producing the appropriate artifacts: a zipped build for static hosting or a container image pushed to Azure Container Registry. If zero-downtime upgrades are important, plan for blue-green or canary deployments, where new instances are warmed up before traffic is switched over. Azure Pipelines and GitHub Actions both support these strategies with built-in tasks.

Monitoring and feedback loops round out the planning process. A CI/CD pipeline is not just about pushing code; it is also about continuously learning from the system's behavior in production. Plan to integrate telemetry from Application Insights or Azure Monitor so that each deployment automatically updates dashboards and alerts. When anomalies occur, whether an AI model's accuracy drops or a Blazor page load time spikes, your team should receive notifications and have the option to roll back or deploy a hotfix quickly. Automating rollback steps in the pipeline, such as redeploying a previous container image or restoring an earlier static build, adds resilience.

Equally critical is team culture and communication. CI/CD succeeds only when all contributors—front-end developers, back-end engineers, data scientists, and DevOps specialists—embrace shared ownership of the pipeline. Early planning sessions should include representatives from each group to define requirements, agree on test coverage, and set performance expectations. Documentation of the pipeline's stages, environment variables, and approval gates helps new team members onboard quickly and reduces the risk of accidental misconfigurations. Because AI projects often involve experimentation, the pipeline should also support controlled experimentation, such as branching strategies or shadow deployments, where new models can be evaluated without impacting end users. These experiments should follow defined governance practices, including clear lifecycle management, approval checkpoints before promotion to production, and cleanup processes to retire unused models, datasets, and infrastructure. This ensures that experimentation remains traceable, cost-efficient, and aligned with organizational policies.

Selecting the tooling to implement this plan comes near the end of the planning stage. Azure DevOps and GitHub Actions are natural fits for .NET 10 and Azure OpenAI integrations, offering first-class support for building .NET projects, running container jobs, and deploying to Azure resources. However, the principles remain consistent across platforms: define your pipeline as code, keep configuration version-controlled, and aim for repeatability. Start simple with a single YAML pipeline that builds, tests, and deploys a proof of concept [22]. Gradually layer in parallel jobs, caching strategies, and environment promotions as the project grows.

Finally, planning must also address cost management and sustainability. CI/CD pipelines consume compute resources for builds, tests, and deployments. By measuring build times, caching dependencies, and pruning unused environments, you can reduce both expense and environmental impact. For AI workloads, where training or inference can be resource-intensive, you might schedule certain heavy jobs during off-peak hours, or Azure Spot instances can be used to reduce costs for noncritical or interruptible workloads, such as batch processing or experimental tasks. However, because Spot capacity can be reclaimed at any time, these instances should not be used for critical release gates or production workflows unless interruptions are explicitly acceptable and properly handled.

In summary, designing a CI/CD workflow for Blazor and AI projects is about more than choosing a few tools; it is about creating a disciplined, automated process that respects the distinct needs of interactive .NET front ends and intelligent back ends. Careful planning ensures that every code change triggers reliable builds, rigorous tests, and secure deployments across development, staging, and production. By cataloging components, structuring parallel builds, enforcing security, embracing infrastructure as code, defining branching strategies, selecting deployment targets, and integrating monitoring, you establish a pipeline that accelerates delivery while preserving quality. This deliberate groundwork enables teams to innovate confidently, knowing that from the moment a developer commits code to the instant a user interacts with the live application, a robust, automated system is safeguarding quality, security, and performance.

Automating Builds and Artifact Management

Automating builds and managing artifacts are central pillars of a modern software delivery process, enabling teams to move from manual, error-prone tasks to predictable and repeatable workflows. A build is the process of converting source code and associated resources into a deployable product, such as an executable application, a container image, or a static website bundle. Artifacts are the tangible outputs of that process: compiled binaries, packaged libraries, configuration files, documentation, or machine learning model weights. By automating builds and managing artifacts effectively, organizations achieve faster releases, higher quality, and better collaboration across development, operations, and quality assurance teams.

The need for automation begins with the complexity of modern applications. A typical web solution may contain multiple services written in different languages, rely on numerous third-party dependencies, and require environment-specific configuration. Manually compiling code, resolving dependencies, and packaging results for every update is not only tedious but also inconsistent; human operators may forget a step or use slightly different tool versions. Automation enforces a single source of truth for how a build is performed. By describing the process as code, usually in pipeline definitions such as YAML files for GitHub Actions, GitLab CI, or Azure DevOps, the team ensures that every build runs the same way, whether triggered by a developer's commit, a nightly job, or a production hotfix.

A fully automated build pipeline starts when changes are pushed to a version control system. A trigger, often a commit to a main or develop branch or a pull request, kicks off the pipeline on a build server or cloud runner. The pipeline checks out the latest source code, installs dependencies, compiles the code, runs unit tests, and performs static analysis or linting. Because these steps run in a clean, reproducible environment such as a container or virtual machine, the outcome is consistent regardless of where the build occurs. Teams can specify exact versions of compilers, SDKs, and libraries to eliminate "works on my machine" issues.

Artifact management enters the picture once a build succeeds. The build outputs are valuable assets that need to be stored, versioned, and distributed reliably. In simple scenarios, artifacts might be .NET assemblies, Java JAR files, or zipped static websites. For containerized deployments, the artifact is typically a Docker image. In AI projects, it could include trained model files, tokenizers, or feature engineering pipelines. Managing these outputs requires using the appropriate type of artifact repository based on the artifact class. For example, compiled application packages and libraries can be stored in package repositories such as Azure Artifacts or GitHub Packages, while container images are typically managed in container registries like Azure Container Registry (ACR). This separation ensures proper versioning, distribution, and governance for each artifact type. The repository serves as a single, authoritative source from which downstream stages such as testing, staging, and production retrieve the exact build artifact. To ensure reliability and governance, artifacts should be immutable once published, governed by appropriate retention policies to manage storage and compliance, and protected with role-based access controls to restrict who can publish, modify, or consume them.

Versioning is a critical element of artifact management. Each artifact should carry a unique identifier that ties it to the source code state, often using semantic versioning or build numbers derived from Git tags and commit hashes. This makes rollbacks and audits straightforward: if a bug appears in production, the team can immediately locate and redeploy the exact artifact that was previously working. Treat artifacts as immutable once published; they should not be overwritten. In practice, this means using immutable version tags, content digests (such as SHA-based identifiers), or other content-addressable identifiers to ensure that the exact artifact can be reliably referenced and reproduced across environments, ensuring that a version label always points to the same binary.

Security and integrity checks further enhance artifact management. Build pipelines should sign artifacts or generate checksums so downstream systems can verify integrity and detect tampering. In addition, modern supply chain practices include generating provenance metadata, producing software bills of materials (SBOMs), and attaching attestations that describe how and where the artifact was built. These measures improve traceability, support compliance requirements, and strengthen trust in the software delivery process. For container images, scanning for vulnerabilities in base layers and dependencies is essential before publishing to a registry. Storing artifacts in repositories with access control and encryption protects sensitive code and proprietary models from unauthorized access.

Another important aspect of automated builds is the ability to enforce quality gates as part of the pipeline. These gates act as decision points, ensuring that code quality, test results, security checks, and compliance requirements are validated before progressing to subsequent stages such as packaging and deployment. Before an artifact is published, the pipeline can run automated tests ranging from unit tests to integration or end-to-end scenarios. Code coverage thresholds, static analysis results, and security scan outputs can all act as gates that must be passed before an artifact is deemed releasable. This ensures that only code meeting predefined standards reaches the artifact repository, reducing defects that might surface later in staging or production.

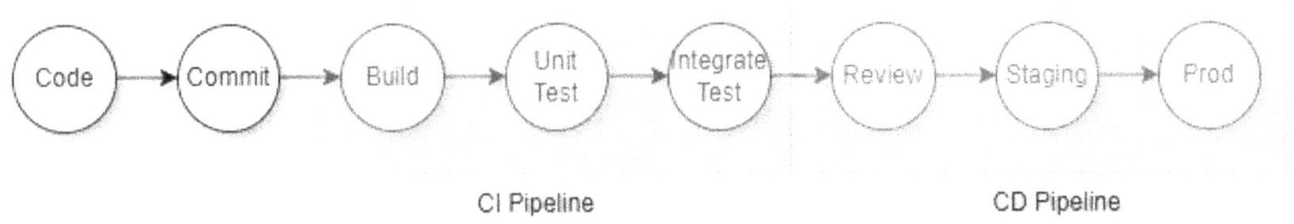

Figure 10-2. *CI/CD Pipeline*

Efficient artifact management also improves collaboration across environments. Development, testing, and operations teams can all pull from the same repository, confident that they are working with identical bits. The release pipeline can automatically promote artifacts from one environment to the next development, staging, and production without requiring a rebuild. This separation of build and deployment is a best practice: build once, deploy many times. It eliminates the risk of subtle differences that could arise if each environment compiled its own build.

Caching and incremental builds are additional considerations when optimizing automated builds. Many build systems support caching intermediate results so that unchanged components do not need to be recompiled, significantly reducing build times for large projects. Artifact repositories can also serve as dependency caches, hosting internal libraries or third-party packages to ensure faster, more reliable retrieval than fetching from public sources each time.

Infrastructure-as-code (IaC) workflows integrate naturally with artifact automation, enabling consistent and repeatable environment provisioning alongside application delivery. In practice, IaC definitions may be versioned alongside the application code and released together or managed through a separate infrastructure pipeline, depending on organizational governance, team boundaries, and compliance requirements. When deployment environments themselves—servers, databases, or Kubernetes clusters—are defined in code, the pipeline can package and version these definitions alongside application artifacts. The result is a complete, reproducible snapshot of both the software and the infrastructure on which it runs, enabling consistent deployments across cloud regions or disaster recovery sites.

Monitoring and feedback close the loop. Build pipelines should emit logs and metrics about build duration, success rates, and artifact sizes. Dashboards and alerts help teams spot slowdowns or failures early, while historical trends reveal opportunities for optimization, such as parallelizing steps or pruning obsolete dependencies. Over time, these insights drive continuous improvement of the automation process itself.

For organizations embracing AI or machine learning workloads, automated builds and artifact management take on extra nuance. Training a model may produce large binary checkpoints or need GPU-specific dependencies. Pipelines can extend beyond traditional application CI/CD to support AI workflows such as model training and evaluation. In practice, these are often handled through separate model training pipelines, while the application CI/CD pipeline focuses on building, testing, and deploying the Blazor application and its supporting services. Coordinating these pipelines ensures that validated models are versioned, approved, and integrated into the application lifecycle in a controlled manner and packaged into a deployable format like ONNX or a Docker image with preloaded weights. The resulting artifacts are versioned and stored so that experiments can be reproduced and models can be rolled back if accuracy degrades. Managing these larger, data-heavy artifacts typically involves specialized storage, but more importantly, a governed model lifecycle is achieved through a model registry. A model registry provides versioning, metadata tracking, approval workflows, and traceability for trained models. Underlying storage may still rely on services such as Azure Blob Storage or ML-oriented artifact stores, but the registry acts as the control plane for promoting, auditing, and deploying models in a structured and compliant manner; the same core principles—automation, versioning, integrity, and access control—apply.

Ultimately, automating builds and managing artifacts transform software delivery from a manual craft into an engineering discipline. Every successful run of the pipeline produces a traceable, deployable package with minimal human intervention. Teams gain the confidence that what they tested is exactly what they release. When paired with continuous integration and continuous deployment practices, this automation shortens release cycles, reduces errors, and frees developers to focus on features rather than repetitive tasks. In an era where users expect frequent, reliable updates and where security and compliance demands are ever tighter, automated builds and robust artifact management are not optional extras; they are fundamental to professional software engineering.

Messaging in Blazor Apps

Messaging and reactive event patterns form the communication backbone of modern distributed applications, and their relevance becomes even more pronounced when you build interactive client experiences with Blazor. In a traditional monolithic web application, components usually communicate through direct method calls or tightly coupled services. While this can suffice for smaller applications, it quickly becomes unwieldy when the system must scale, handle real-time updates, or integrate with microservices, cloud-based resources, or Internet-of-Things (IoT) endpoints. Messaging decouples components by introducing an intermediary message that **represents** data or instructions exchanged between independent parts of the system. This can refer to both in-process communication (such as events within the same application) and brokered messaging (using external systems like queues or topics), depending on the architectural context. Reactive event patterns, in turn, allow those components to respond to events asynchronously, often in real time, producing a user experience that feels immediate and dynamic. In a Blazor application that needs to operate seamlessly across clients and services, these two concepts work hand in hand to create responsive, maintainable, and scalable architectures.

Integrating Continuous Testing and Quality Gates

Continuous testing and the use of quality gates have become central practices for ensuring that software delivered through modern CI/CD pipelines meets high standards of reliability, security, and maintainability. In traditional development cycles, testing was often a distinct phase performed after coding and before deployment, leading to long feedback loops and late discovery of defects. In contrast, continuous testing embeds automated tests throughout the development process so that every code change is validated as soon as it is committed. Quality gates then act as automated checkpoints in the pipeline, enforcing predefined criteria that must be satisfied before software is allowed to advance to the next stage. Together, these practices provide a proactive approach to risk management and ensure that only high-quality artifacts reach production.

The essence of continuous testing lies in running the right tests at the right time. Each time a developer pushes a change to version control, the CI system triggers a pipeline that compiles the code, executes unit tests, and provides immediate feedback. These unit tests verify small, isolated pieces of functionality and are typically fast, making them ideal for early detection of logic errors. Over time, the pipeline can expand to include integration tests that check interactions between modules, API tests that validate contract compliance, and end-to-end tests that simulate realistic user scenarios. In Blazor applications, for example, automated UI tests might confirm that component rendering and state transitions behave correctly across different browsers, while back-end tests verify that .NET APIs respond as expected. Because these tests run automatically with every commit or pull request, developers receive near-real-time alerts if their changes break existing functionality, dramatically reducing the cost and effort of bug fixing.

Implementing continuous testing effectively requires a carefully designed infrastructure. Test code must be maintained with the same discipline as production code: stored in the same repository, reviewed during code reviews, and refactored when necessary. Test data management is another critical concern. Stable and representative data sets allow for repeatable results and meaningful coverage. For AI-driven or data-heavy Blazor applications, this may involve generating synthetic data or masking sensitive records, as well as using mocks, stubs, or recorded responses to simulate external AI service calls during testing. This approach improves test reliability, reduces dependency on live services, and helps control cost and variability in AI-driven workflows. Running tests in parallel across containerized environments or virtual machines further accelerates feedback, ensuring that even large suites complete quickly enough to keep pace with frequent commits.

Quality gates add an additional layer of governance by acting as automatic pass-fail checkpoints in the pipeline. A quality gate defines measurable thresholds that the build must meet before it can be promoted to subsequent stages, such as staging or production. Common quality metrics include minimum code coverage percentages, acceptable levels of code complexity, and adherence to style and security guidelines. Static analysis tools such as SonarQube can evaluate code for maintainability issues, duplication, and potential vulnerabilities. Pipeline orchestrators like Azure DevOps or GitHub Actions then execute these analyses as part of the workflow and report pass or fail status based on the results. If any metric falls below the required threshold, the quality gate blocks the release, prompting developers to correct issues immediately. This approach prevents the accumulation of technical debt and reduces the likelihood of defects escaping into later environments.

An effective quality gate strategy is both strict and pragmatic. Setting thresholds too high early in a project can cause unnecessary friction and frequent pipeline failures, discouraging developers. Instead, team-defined baseline thresholds often start with attainable targets such as 60% code coverage and gradually raise them as the code base matures. Gates can also be tuned to focus on new code rather than legacy code, ensuring that while existing issues are tracked, they do not paralyze progress. For example, a rule might require that all new or modified files achieve at least 80% coverage, even if the overall project coverage is lower. This incremental approach steadily improves quality without creating overwhelming rework.

Security considerations are a vital component of modern quality gates. Static application security testing (SAST) tools can be integrated to scan for vulnerabilities like SQL injection, cross-site scripting, or insecure cryptographic usage. Dependency scanning checks for known vulnerabilities in third-party libraries. In Blazor and .NET projects, integrating modern security tooling ensures that each build is evaluated for potential risks before deployment. Static application security testing (SAST) can be performed using tools such as GitHub Advanced Security (CodeQL), while dependency and software composition analysis (SCA) can be handled using tools like OWASP Dependency-Check or built-in dependency scanning in Azure DevOps. Together, these approaches help identify both code-level vulnerabilities and risks introduced through third-party libraries. For AI applications that may incorporate external data sources or pre-trained models, additional checks may include validation for data integrity, licensing compliance, and model explainability, along with AI-specific safeguards such as prompt safety controls, output schema validation, latency thresholds, and cost-budget enforcement to ensure predictable and responsible operation can be incorporated into the gates, providing an extra safeguard against operational or legal issues.

The combination of continuous testing and quality gates offers several strategic benefits. First, it shortens the feedback loop, allowing developers to fix defects almost as soon as they are introduced. This prevents small problems from compounding into complex, costly failures. Second, it fosters a culture of shared responsibility for quality. Because tests run automatically and gates enforce consistent standards, developers, testers, and operations staff all work with the same expectations and data. Third, it creates a living documentation of application behavior. A well-maintained suite of automated tests effectively describes what the software is supposed to do, while gate metrics provide a clear record of code health over time.

To maximize effectiveness, teams often implement a multi-stage testing strategy tied to their quality gates. The first stage focuses on fast, critical validations running unit tests, basic integration checks, and lightweight AI validations such as prompt tests and schema validation on every commit. The second stage, typically triggered on pull requests, expands coverage to broader integration, API, and contract tests, along with AI safety checks, regression datasets, and output consistency validation.

A final stage, executed after successful merges to the main branch, runs full end-to-end and performance tests, deeper security analysis, and advanced AI evaluations such as latency thresholds, cost-budget checks, and robustness testing. This stage should also include release-readiness gates, such as rollback verification, deployment health checks, and performance budget validation.

Each stage applies progressively stricter gates, ensuring that only code and models meeting functional, performance, and governance criteria are promoted through the pipeline.

Because all these processes are automated, they occur without manual intervention, freeing developers to focus on feature development rather than repetitive validation.

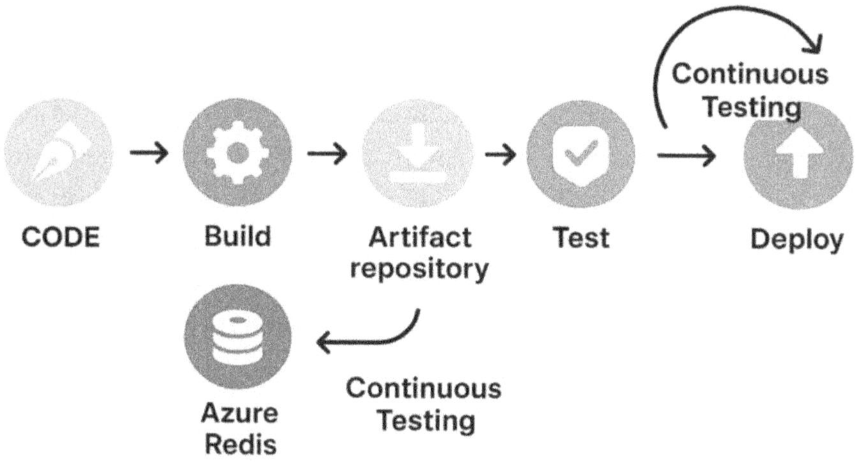

Figure 10-3. *CI/CD Pipeline with Continuous Testing*

In practice, integrating these concepts into a CI/CD pipeline for Blazor or AI applications involves selecting appropriate tools and services. Azure DevOps provides pipelines that can orchestrate builds, run test suites across multiple platforms, and enforce gates before deployment to Azure App Service or Kubernetes clusters. GitHub Actions offers similar capabilities, with workflows that can spin up containerized test environments, execute .NET test commands, and call out to external analysis services. For teams using cloud-based AI features such as Azure OpenAI, automated tests can also include API-based validations to ensure that machine learning endpoints respond with expected accuracy or latency and gates can verify that model versions match approved baselines.

Continuous testing and quality gates are not set-and-forget mechanisms; they require ongoing refinement. As the application grows and new technologies or dependencies are introduced, test coverage goals may need to increase, and additional gates may be added to address new risks. For example, a team might initially skip performance testing but later introduce a gate that requires response times to remain under a certain threshold. Metrics gathered from pipeline runs such as average build duration, failure rates, and coverage trends inform these adjustments. Regular retrospectives can help the team identify bottlenecks, optimize test suites, and retire obsolete checks.

Perhaps the most important cultural shift that comes with continuous testing and quality gates is the move toward prevention rather than detection. Instead of catching defects late in the cycle or in production, teams design their processes so that poor-quality code simply cannot progress. This mindset aligns perfectly with DevOps principles of fast feedback, shared ownership, and continuous improvement. For organizations building complex web applications, integrating Blazor front ends with AI-driven back ends, this approach reduces downtime, protects user trust, and accelerates the path from idea to deployment.

Integrating continuous testing and quality gates transforms software delivery from a linear, reactive process into a dynamic, automated system of continuous assurance. Every code change is automatically validated through an escalating series of tests, and each pipeline stage enforces objective quality standards before allowing progression. This tight integration not only improves code reliability and security but also builds a culture of accountability and excellence. By adopting these practices, development teams can confidently release Blazor and AI applications at high velocity, secure in the knowledge that rigorous, automated safeguards are protecting both their users and their reputation.

Securing and Deploying to Azure Environments

Securing and deploying applications to Azure environments is a critical stage in modern CI/CD workflows, particularly for solutions that combine Blazor front-end interfaces with AI-powered back ends. The deployment phase is more than simply moving code from one environment to another; it involves ensuring the integrity, confidentiality, and availability of application components while maintaining a seamless user experience. Azure provides a rich ecosystem of services and tools that facilitate secure deployments, but success requires careful planning, integration with CI/CD pipelines, and adherence to best practices in security, access control, and infrastructure management.

At the core of securing Azure deployments is identity and access management. Azure Active Directory (AAD) serves as the central authority for authentication and authorization, enabling fine-grained control over who can access resources and what actions they can perform. CI/CD pipelines authenticate to cloud resources using mechanisms such as service principals, federated credentials, or managed identities, rather than relying on embedded or long-lived credentials. Rather than embedding credentials in source code or configuration files, pipelines authenticate using service principals, managed identities, or security tokens issued by Azure AD. This approach ensures that build agents and automation tools have only the permissions required to perform their tasks, following the principle of least privilege. By defining roles such as contributor, reader, or owner, administrators can prevent unauthorized changes to critical resources, protecting the production environment from accidental or malicious modifications.

Secrets management is another essential security practice. Modern applications rely on a variety of sensitive information, including database connection strings, API keys, AI service credentials, and encryption keys. Azure Key Vault provides a centralized, secure repository for these secrets, allowing CI/CD pipelines and applications to retrieve them at runtime without exposing them in plain text. Integrating Azure Key Vault with Azure DevOps or GitHub Actions involves two distinct concerns: securely retrieving secrets at pipeline runtime and managing secret rotation independently within Key Vault. Pipelines are configured to access secrets dynamically, while rotation policies and updates are handled centrally to avoid disrupting deployments. This strategy mitigates the risk of leakage and simplifies compliance with regulatory standards, such as GDPR or HIPAA, which are often relevant for AI solutions handling personal or sensitive data.

When it comes to deploying Blazor applications specifically, there are several hosting options within Azure, each with its own security considerations. Blazor WebAssembly applications, which are static by nature, can be hosted using Azure Static Web Apps or Azure Blob Storage with Azure CDN, but these options differ significantly in architecture and operational capabilities. Azure Static Web Apps provides built-in routing, integrated authentication/authorization, and close coupling with back-end APIs, offering a more streamlined developer experience. In contrast, hosting via Azure Blob Storage with CDN is a more basic static hosting approach, requiring separate configuration for routing, authentication, and API integration, but offering greater flexibility in certain scenarios. In these cases, HTTPS is enforced by default, and role-based access control can protect management operations. Server-side Blazor applications and .NET APIs including those serving AI workloads require more robust runtime environments, such as Azure App Service, Azure Container Apps, or AKS. Azure App Service is well suited for standard web workloads with minimal operational overhead, Container Apps are a good fit for event-driven or containerized services with managed scaling, and AKS is appropriate for complex, highly scalable systems that require full control over orchestration and infrastructure. By using infrastructure-as-code tools like Bicep or Terraform, teams can define and version resource configurations, ensuring consistent, repeatable deployments across staging, testing, and production environments.

Pipeline orchestration is critical for coordinating secure deployments. A typical CI/CD pipeline is divided into stages: build, test, artifact management, and deployment. The deployment stage integrates directly with Azure resource management APIs to provision or update infrastructure, configure networking, and deploy application artifacts. At this stage, quality gates and automated approvals can enforce concrete checks such as minimum test coverage thresholds, successful unit and integration test results, static code analysis and security scan pass criteria, and AI-specific validations (e.g., prompt safety checks or schema validation). Approvals may also require sign-off from designated reviewers or environments before promotion, ensuring that only verified and compliant changes reach production. For example, an approval step might require security scans to pass, including vulnerability assessments of container images or compliance checks on AI model inputs. Deployment slots, available in Azure App Service, allow for blue-green or canary deployments, where new versions of an application are first exposed to a limited user set. This minimizes risk and ensures that if a problem arises, the previous version can be quickly reinstated without downtime.

Networking and data security are also paramount. Azure provides tools such as Virtual Networks (VNets), network security groups (NSGs), and Private Endpoints to isolate applications from public networks while still allowing necessary access. For AI workloads, securing the data path between services is especially critical. Sensitive datasets and model inference requests should be transmitted over secure channels using HTTPS with TLS 1.2 or higher (preferably TLS 1.3), and access should be restricted to authorized endpoints through proper authentication and network controls. Deployments can incorporate automated configuration of firewalls and access policies to enforce these protections. Additionally, logging and monitoring should be integrated into the deployment process. Azure Monitor, Application Insights, and Log Analytics capture operational metrics, performance data, and security events, providing visibility into both application health and security posture. Pipelines can be configured to verify that these monitoring agents are deployed and configured correctly before a release is finalized.

Containerized deployments introduce further considerations. Many AI services are packaged in Docker containers for portability and scalability. Pushing these images to Azure Container Registry (ACR) and deploying them via Azure Kubernetes Service (AKS) or Azure Container Apps enables teams to take advantage of orchestration features such as autoscaling and load balancing. AKS provides full Kubernetes control and flexibility for complex, large-scale deployments, while Container Apps offers a more managed, serverless experience with simpler operations but less granular control over the underlying infrastructure. Security best practices include scanning container images for vulnerabilities, applying role-based access control in ACR, and ensuring that secrets and credentials are never baked into images. Automated CI/CD pipelines can enforce these practices by performing image scans, signing images, and verifying compliance with organizational policies before deployment.

Compliance and auditability are also integral to secure deployments. Every action performed by a CI/CD pipeline whether provisioning resources, deploying code, or updating configuration should be logged and traceable. Azure provides native support for activity logs, policy enforcement, and resource locks, allowing organizations to demonstrate compliance with internal governance and external regulations. This traceability extends to AI workloads as well: pipelines can document which model version was deployed, what training data was used, and which security or compliance checks were executed. Such transparency is crucial for organizations deploying AI applications that have a direct impact on users, such as decision-making tools, healthcare apps, or financial analytics platforms.

Finally, ongoing maintenance and iterative improvement are essential components of securing and deploying to Azure. Pipelines should be continuously reviewed to incorporate updated security practices, new service features, and lessons learned from operational experience. Automated alerts for failed deployments, unusual traffic patterns, or unauthorized access attempts enable rapid response to incidents. Incorporating rollback procedures and disaster recovery strategies ensures that even in the event of failure, applications remain resilient and the user experience is minimally impacted.

Securing and deploying applications to Azure environments involves a comprehensive strategy that integrates identity management, secrets handling, secure artifact deployment, network isolation, monitoring, and compliance. For Blazor front ends and AI-driven back ends, these practices are essential to maintain the integrity, availability, and trustworthiness of applications. By leveraging Azure's native services and embedding security checks within automated CI/CD pipelines, teams can confidently release software at high velocity while minimizing risk. Proper planning and disciplined execution of these deployment and security strategies ensure that both the user experience and organizational assets remain protected throughout the software lifecycle.

CHAPTER 11

Cloud-Native Observability and Resilience

Comprehensive Monitoring and Metrics Collection

Comprehensive monitoring and metrics collection form the backbone of any cloud-native observability strategy, ensuring that applications running in distributed, dynamic environments operate efficiently, reliably, and securely. In modern cloud architectures, especially those combining Blazor front-end interfaces with AI-driven back ends, the system introduces multiple telemetry sources, scaling signals, and distinct failure domains that must be managed cohesively. Components may span multiple microservices, serverless functions, containerized workloads, databases, and external APIs. Monitoring in such environments is no longer a passive activity; it is an active, continuous process that enables teams to gain real-time insight into the behavior of applications, detect anomalies early, and drive informed operational decisions. Effective monitoring begins with understanding the types of metrics to collect, the tools for gathering and analyzing these metrics, and how to integrate this process into both development and production workflows.

At its core, metrics collection is about capturing quantifiable information regarding the health, performance, and utilization of system components. Metrics can broadly be classified into several categories: infrastructure metrics, application performance metrics, business metrics, and user experience metrics. Infrastructure metrics cover resource consumption such as CPU usage, memory utilization, disk I/O,

A. Prasad and H. Singh, *Advanced Blazor Architecture with .NET 10 and Azure OpenAI*,
https://doi.org/10.1007/979-8-8688-2518-7_11

network latency, and container resource limits. These metrics provide visibility into the underlying platform and allow operations teams to detect resource contention, bottlenecks, or failing instances before they impact end users. Application performance metrics, on the other hand, measure how well software components perform in their functional role, including request latency, error rates, throughput, and database query performance. For AI-driven components, it is useful to distinguish between runtime metrics and evaluation metrics. Runtime metrics such as inference latency, throughput, and error rates can be measured directly in production and provide immediate insight into system performance. In contrast, evaluation metrics like model accuracy or prediction quality often require ground truth data and are typically assessed through offline evaluation, delayed feedback loops, or curated validation datasets. Understanding this distinction helps teams design appropriate monitoring and validation strategies for AI systems.

Business metrics provide insight into application outcomes and user interactions. For instance, in a Blazor ecommerce application, metrics such as the number of successful transactions, shopping cart abandonment rates, or feature usage statistics reveal how well the system supports business objectives. Similarly, in an AI-powered recommendation engine, tracking conversion rates, recommendation accuracy, and click-through rates enables product teams to measure the impact of algorithmic changes. User experience metrics, such as page load times, responsiveness of UI components, or perceived latency, are increasingly important in cloud-native applications where performance is a direct factor in user satisfaction and retention. By combining these categories, teams can achieve end-to-end observability, linking infrastructure health to business outcomes and user experience.

```
Dashboard: Blazor-AI-Observability

Row 1: Requests | Failures | Latency
Row 2: Dependencies | CPU/Memory | AI Latency
Row 3: Logs (live stream)
```

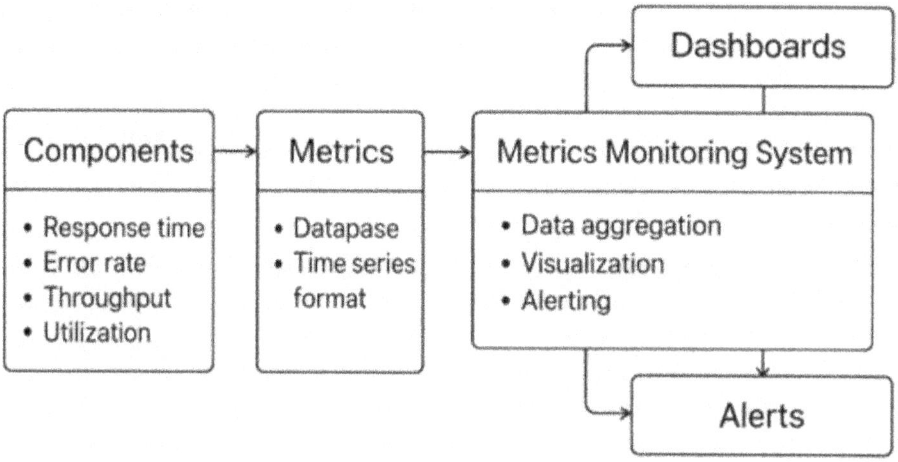

Figure 11-1. *Metrics Monitoring System*

To implement comprehensive monitoring, selecting the right tools and instrumentation techniques is critical. Modern cloud platforms such as Azure provide a set of integrated monitoring services, each with a distinct role. Azure Monitor acts as the central platform for collecting and aggregating metrics and logs across resources. Application Insights focuses on application-level telemetry, including request tracking, dependencies, and exceptions. Log Analytics enables querying and analyzing collected data using a powerful query language, supporting deeper diagnostics and operational insights. These tools provide out-of-the-box telemetry for .NET and Blazor applications, including request rates, response times, exception tracking, dependency calls, and custom event logging. Application components can be instrumented with lightweight SDKs that automatically capture telemetry, while developers can define custom metrics for application-specific events or AI model performance indicators. For distributed systems, metrics should also capture interactions between services, such as API request counts, queue lengths, or event processing latency, to ensure a holistic understanding of system behavior.

An essential aspect of comprehensive monitoring is the establishment of baselines and thresholds. Baselines represent the normal operating range for a metric, established through historical data analysis or expected system performance. Thresholds define the points at which metrics indicate potential problems, triggering alerts or automated responses. For example, sustained CPU utilization above a certain threshold (such as 80%) may indicate the need to scale out resources or investigate performance issues. However, such thresholds should not be treated as fixed values; they should be defined based on service baselines, SLOs, and observed workload behavior to ensure meaningful and reliable scaling decisions. Similarly, if AI model inference latency increases beyond an acceptable threshold, it could indicate underlying infrastructure problems, inefficient algorithms, or network congestion. Continuous monitoring with clearly defined thresholds enables proactive management of cloud-native applications, reducing downtime and improving reliability.

Data collection and aggregation are also critical for effective monitoring. In large-scale distributed systems, metric data is generated at a high velocity from multiple sources. Prometheus, for example, is widely used in Kubernetes environments to scrape metrics from containerized applications, storing time-series data efficiently for query and analysis. Combined with Grafana for visualization, it enables teams to build detailed dashboards showing real-time system health, performance trends, and historical comparisons.

In Azure-centered architectures, these tools are often used alongside or integrated with Azure Monitor, either by forwarding Prometheus metrics to Azure Monitor managed services or by using Azure-native monitoring for platform-level insights, providing a unified observability strategy across cloud and Kubernetes resources.

Instrumentation is the process of embedding code or configuration hooks that generate telemetry. In Blazor applications, instrumentation may include monitoring UI events, tracking API calls, and measuring component render times. For AI components, instrumentation might capture processing time, response characteristics, and confidence indicators. However, teams should exercise caution with client-side telemetry, as excessive event collection can impact performance and may include privacy-sensitive user interactions.

Additionally, logging raw prompts, model inputs, or outputs should only be done under strict redaction, access control, and governance policies to avoid exposing sensitive or personally identifiable information (PII). Instrumentation should be designed to minimize overhead and avoid introducing latency or resource consumption that could affect production performance. Sampling and aggregation techniques help manage the volume of telemetry data while preserving actionable insights. By strategically choosing which metrics to capture in detail vs. in summary, teams can maintain observability without overwhelming storage or processing systems.

Alerting and automated responses are natural extensions of comprehensive monitoring. Metrics themselves are only valuable if deviations are detected and acted upon. Modern observability platforms allow teams to configure alerts based on thresholds, trends, or anomaly detection. Alerts can be routed to email, messaging platforms, incident management systems, or automation scripts. For example, if a web service experiences a sudden spike in request failures, an automated response could scale up additional instances or trigger a rollback of a recent deployment. Incorporating alerting into the monitoring strategy ensures that teams are not merely collecting data but are actively using metrics to maintain application reliability.

Long-term analysis and reporting also play a significant role. Continuous monitoring generates large volumes of data that, over time, reveal trends, usage patterns, and recurring issues. By analyzing historical metrics, teams can make informed decisions about capacity planning, performance optimization, and infrastructure investments. For AI applications, long-term metrics analysis helps identify model drift, degradation in accuracy, or data inconsistencies, which can then trigger retraining processes or algorithmic adjustments. These insights inform both operational management and strategic business decisions, demonstrating the value of comprehensive monitoring beyond immediate incident response.

Integrating monitoring into the CI/CD pipeline brings observability into the development lifecycle from the outset. Pipelines can capture key signals during build and test stages such as test coverage, build duration, and deployment success rates, providing early insight into code quality, performance trends, and release reliability. Performance tests executed in staging environments can feed metrics back into dashboards, providing early warning for potential issues before code reaches production. By embedding monitoring practices in continuous delivery workflows, organizations ensure that every release is accompanied by visibility into performance and reliability, supporting a proactive approach to quality assurance.

Cloud-native architectures, with their reliance on microservices, containerization, and serverless functions, introduce additional challenges for monitoring. Services may be ephemeral, dynamically scaled, and distributed across regions, making it difficult to maintain consistent visibility. Comprehensive monitoring strategies must account for these characteristics by including service discovery integration, automated instrumentation of new instances, and correlation of metrics across distributed components. Techniques such as distributed tracing, where individual requests are tracked across services, complement metrics collection by providing a clear picture of interactions and latency sources.

Finally, cultural and organizational alignment is essential, but it must be reflected in clear, shared responsibilities. In practice, this means development teams own instrumentation and code-level telemetry, operations teams define monitoring standards and alerting policies, and data/AI teams manage model validation, evaluation, and governance. Establishing these roles and shared ownership of reliability metrics, incident response, and deployment quality ensures that observability and system health are maintained collaboratively across the lifecycle. Comprehensive monitoring is most effective when teams adopt observability as a shared responsibility. Developers, operations engineers, and data scientists must collaborate to define meaningful metrics, maintain instrumentation, and respond to alerts promptly. By fostering a culture where monitoring is part of the development and operational workflow rather than an afterthought, organizations can achieve higher reliability, faster incident response, and continuous improvement. Observability thus becomes not just a technical capability, but a key enabler of agile, cloud-native development practices.

In summary, comprehensive monitoring and metrics collection provide the visibility necessary to operate, optimize, and secure cloud-native applications. By capturing infrastructure, application, business, and user experience metrics, teams can achieve full-stack observability. Instrumentation, aggregation, alerting, and analysis form an integrated system that informs both operational response and strategic decision-making. For applications combining Blazor front ends and AI-driven back ends, these practices ensure that both interactive interfaces and intelligent services perform reliably and efficiently. Properly planned and executed monitoring strategies empower teams to detect issues proactively, maintain high availability, optimize performance, and continuously evolve cloud-native applications to meet business objectives and user expectations.

Centralized Logging and Real-Time Analysis

Centralized logging and real-time analysis are essential components of cloud-native observability. Logging represents one of the core observability pillars and complements metrics and distributed tracing by providing detailed, contextual information that helps correlate requests, diagnose issues, and understand system behavior across components. In complex systems that combine Blazor front-end interfaces with AI-driven back ends, logs are more than just error records; they are a rich source of information about system health, user interactions, transaction flows, and AI model performance. Centralizing logs allows development and operations teams to aggregate, analyze, and correlate data from multiple sources, turning raw logs into meaningful intelligence that supports troubleshooting, performance optimization, and proactive incident management.

In traditional applications, logs were often scattered across individual servers, local files, or siloed databases. This approach becomes impractical in cloud-native environments where applications are distributed across microservices, containers, serverless functions, and multiple cloud regions. Without centralization, it is nearly impossible to trace issues across services, identify patterns, or correlate events in real time. Centralized logging addresses this challenge by aggregating log data from all components into a unified access layer, even if the underlying storage spans multiple back ends, tiers, and retention policies. This approach enables consistent querying and analysis while accommodating different storage classes for cost, performance, and compliance needs. This repository can be queried, filtered, and visualized to provide comprehensive insights into the system's operation.

The types of logs generated in cloud-native applications are diverse, and consistency in log structure is critical for effective analysis. Each log entry should follow a defined schema that includes fields such as severity level, event type, source service, and correlation ID to enable end-to-end tracing. Additionally, logs should incorporate a redaction or sensitivity classification to ensure that sensitive data is handled appropriately and in compliance with privacy requirements. System logs capture events from operating systems, containers, and cloud infrastructure, providing information about CPU usage, memory allocation, network activity, and service availability. Application logs capture events from the code itself, such as function calls, database queries, error messages, and user interactions. Security logs track authentication attempts, access control decisions, and potential threats, while audit logs document configuration changes and administrative actions. In AI-powered applications, additional logs may include model inference requests, processing times, prediction confidence scores, and data transformation steps. Centralizing these logs ensures that all relevant information is available in a single view, enabling cross-functional teams to analyze the system holistically.

```
app.Use(async (context, next) =>
{
    var correlationId = context.TraceIdentifier;

    using (logger.BeginScope(new Dictionary<string, object>
    {
        ["CorrelationId"] = correlationId
    }))
    {
        await next();
    }
});
```

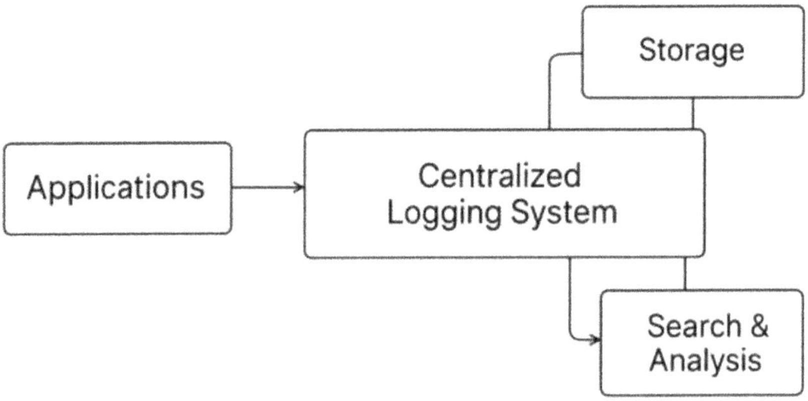

Figure 11-2. *Centralized Logging*

Real-time log analysis enhances the value of centralized logging by enabling immediate detection of issues and anomalies. Azure provides a set of complementary tools for end-to-end logging and observability. Azure Monitor handles log and metric ingestion from various sources, Log Analytics serves as the storage and query layer for analyzing collected data, and Application Insights focuses on application-level telemetry and diagnostics. Together, these services enable real-time dashboards and insights, allowing teams to monitor system behavior as it happens. Real-time analysis can highlight performance degradation, error spikes, failed transactions, or unusual AI model behavior before these issues impact users. By combining automated alerts with thresholds or anomaly detection, teams can respond rapidly, scaling resources, rolling back deployments, or triggering incident response workflows as needed. This proactive approach reduces downtime and improves reliability in production environments.

Effective centralized logging requires a well-designed log aggregation strategy. Logs should be structured, consistent, and enriched with metadata to make searching and correlation easier. Structured logs, often formatted in JSON or other machine-readable formats, allow automated systems to parse and filter data efficiently. Metadata such as timestamps, service names, instance identifiers, request IDs, user identifiers, and transaction types helps correlate events across distributed components. However, user identifiers should be minimized, pseudonymized, or governed according to applicable privacy and compliance requirements to avoid exposing sensitive information. For example, a single user action may trigger requests in multiple microservices, generate database queries, and invoke an AI model inference. By tagging logs with a common correlation ID, teams can reconstruct the sequence of events and pinpoint where failures or delays occur.

Scalability is a key consideration in centralized logging. Cloud-native applications can generate massive volumes of logs, particularly in high-traffic environments or when processing AI workloads. Log aggregation platforms must support horizontal scaling to handle data ingestion, storage, and query loads. Techniques such as partitioning, indexing, and compression optimize storage and retrieval performance. In addition, retention policies should balance compliance requirements with cost considerations by applying tiered strategies. For example, high-volume debug or trace logs may be retained for a short period (such as a few days), while audit and security logs are preserved for longer durations to meet regulatory and forensic requirements. Older data can be archived to lower-cost storage tiers, while recent and frequently accessed logs remain readily available for analysis.

Integration with monitoring and alerting systems is another critical aspect. Centralized logs should feed into dashboards that visualize key performance indicators, error trends, and user behavior. Alerts can be configured to trigger when specific patterns or thresholds are detected, such as a sudden spike in HTTP 500 errors, failed authentication attempts, or latency exceeding acceptable limits. Real-time alerting enables rapid response, often automated through CI/CD pipelines or infrastructure orchestration tools, to scale resources, restart services, or mitigate faults. For AI components, alerts may include model performance degradation, inference failures, or abnormal input distributions, allowing teams to maintain both reliability and accuracy.

Security and compliance considerations are tightly coupled with centralized logging. Logs often contain sensitive information, including user data, authentication tokens, or AI model inputs. Proper access controls, encryption at rest and in transit, and role-based permissions are essential to protect this data. Azure provides native integration with Key Vault, Azure Active Directory, and managed encryption, ensuring that only authorized personnel and services can access log data. For organizations subject to regulatory standards such as GDPR, HIPAA, or SOC 2, centralized logging supports auditing by maintaining tamper-evident records of system activity and administrative actions.

Automation plays a key role in extracting value from centralized logs. Beyond manual inspection, logs can be ingested by analytics engines, machine learning pipelines, or anomaly detection algorithms to identify patterns and trends. AI-driven log analysis can detect subtle deviations from normal behavior, predict potential failures, or optimize resource allocation. For example, in a Blazor application serving a global user base, real-time log analysis may reveal region-specific latency issues, guiding traffic routing or autoscaling decisions. Similarly, AI service logs may indicate gradual model drift, prompting retraining or adjustment of thresholds to maintain predictive accuracy.

Centralized logging also enhances collaboration across development, operations, and data science teams. By providing a single source of truth, all teams can investigate incidents, review trends, and analyze performance metrics without relying on fragmented data sources. For developers, access to detailed application logs supports debugging and feature validation. Operations teams use system and security logs for monitoring and incident response. Data scientists and AI engineers can analyze inference logs, data preprocessing, and feature extraction metrics to maintain model performance and detect biases. This shared visibility fosters a culture of accountability and continuous improvement.

Finally, maintaining an effective centralized logging strategy requires ongoing evaluation and refinement. As applications evolve, new services, AI models, or microservices may be introduced, generating additional logs and requiring updated correlation strategies. Regular reviews ensure that critical events are captured, log verbosity remains appropriate, and storage policies balance operational needs with cost efficiency. Dashboards and alerts should be periodically updated to reflect changing priorities, system growth, and emerging risks. By continuously adapting the logging infrastructure, organizations can sustain comprehensive observability while supporting agile development and high-velocity deployments.

Centralized logging and real-time analysis provide the visibility necessary to operate complex cloud-native applications effectively. By aggregating logs from diverse sources, enriching them with metadata, and analyzing them in real time, teams gain actionable insight into system performance, user interactions, security events, and AI model behavior. Integration with alerting, automation, and monitoring frameworks ensures rapid detection and response to anomalies. Scalable, secure, and structured logging supports operational excellence, compliance, and collaboration across teams. For applications that combine Blazor interfaces with AI-driven back ends, centralized logging is indispensable for maintaining reliability, performance, and trust, enabling proactive decision-making and continuous improvement in a dynamic cloud environment.

Designing Fault-Tolerant Cloud Applications

Designing fault-tolerant cloud applications is a fundamental requirement for achieving reliability, availability, and resilience in modern distributed systems. Cloud-native architectures, such as those supporting Blazor front-end interfaces with AI-driven back ends, are inherently complex, often comprising microservices, serverless functions, containerized workloads, and multiple external dependencies. While the cloud offers elasticity and managed infrastructure, applications must still be architected to withstand component failures, network issues, hardware outages, and unexpected load spikes. Fault tolerance ensures that when a failure occurs, the system continues to function correctly, maintaining service availability and minimizing impact on users.

At the heart of fault-tolerant design is redundancy. Redundancy involves duplicating critical components or services so that if one instance fails, another can seamlessly take over. In cloud environments, this often takes the form of multiple virtual machines, container replicas, or serverless function instances running across different availability zones or regions. For example, deploying a Blazor front end to Azure App Service with multiple instances ensures that if a single instance becomes unavailable, incoming user requests are automatically routed to healthy instances. Similarly, AI services deployed as containerized microservices on Azure Kubernetes Service (AKS) can be scaled horizontally with multiple replicas, allowing the system to handle failures gracefully without interrupting inference requests. Redundancy not only improves reliability but also supports load balancing, distributing traffic efficiently to prevent overload on individual nodes.

Another key principle is decoupling and modularity. Fault-tolerant applications are designed such that the failure of one component does not cascade to others. Microservices and serverless architectures inherently support decoupling by isolating functionality into independent units with clearly defined interfaces. For instance, in a cloud-native ecommerce application, payment processing, product catalog, and recommendation services can operate independently. If the recommendation service fails, the payment and catalog functions continue uninterrupted, preserving core business operations. Message queues and event-driven architectures further enhance decoupling by providing asynchronous communication between services. Systems such as Azure Service Bus and Azure Event Grid support different messaging patterns. Azure Service Bus provides queue-based buffering, enabling reliable message storage and eventual delivery when downstream services are temporarily unavailable. In contrast, Azure Event Grid follows an event distribution model, delivering notifications to multiple subscribers with minimal buffering, making it better suited for reactive, event-driven scenarios rather than durable message queuing.

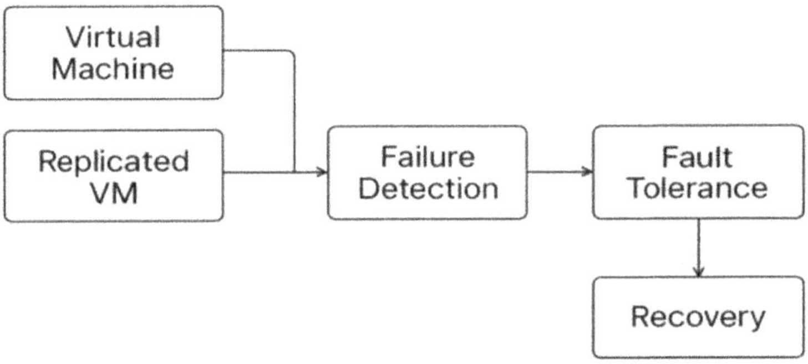

Figure 11-3. *Fault-Tolerant Mechanism in Cloud Computing*

Resiliency patterns such as retries, circuit breakers, and bulkheads are also essential for fault-tolerant design. Retries help handle transient failures such as brief network interruptions or temporary database unavailability by attempting operations again without manual intervention. However, retries should be bounded and implemented with exponential backoff and jitter to avoid overwhelming dependent services. Additionally, operations should be designed to be idempotent so that repeated attempts do not produce unintended side effects. Circuit breakers prevent repeated attempts to call failing services, reducing system load and avoiding cascading failures. When a breaker opens, subsequent requests are short-circuited for a defined period and can return fallback responses or error messages. After a cooldown interval, the system transitions to a half-open state to test if the dependency has recovered, allowing limited requests before fully restoring normal operation if successful. Bulkheads partition resources so that failures in one subsystem do not exhaust shared resources, ensuring that healthy components continue to operate. For example, isolating memory and thread pools for different AI inference services prevents a memory leak in one model from affecting the availability of others.

State management is a critical consideration in fault-tolerant cloud applications. Stateless components are inherently more resilient, as they can be restarted or replaced without losing critical information. Blazor WebAssembly front-end components can remain stateless by storing session data in browser storage or external distributed caches, such as Azure Cache for Redis or Azure Managed Redis. For server-side Blazor components or AI services that require stateful operations, state replication and persistence are necessary. Techniques such as database replication, distributed caches, and durable queues ensure that state is preserved even when individual nodes fail. Event sourcing can be used to record state-changing events in an immutable log, allowing services to reconstruct state in the event of a failure. This approach can be valuable for scenarios that require strong auditability or reproducibility such as certain AI workflows, but it introduces additional complexity in design, storage, and operational management. As such, it should be applied selectively rather than treated as a default pattern for resilience.

Monitoring and automated recovery are integral to fault-tolerant design. Continuous monitoring detects failures quickly, triggering automated responses such as scaling, failover, or restart actions. Azure Monitor, Application Insights, and Log Analytics provide real-time telemetry and alerting, enabling systems to respond proactively to anomalies. Automated recovery mechanisms can restart failed services, provision new instances, or reroute traffic to healthy nodes. For AI components, monitoring model performance metrics and latency is equally important, as degraded performance can be indicative of resource exhaustion or service failure. Automated failover processes can switch inference requests to backup models or replicated services to maintain availability.

Designing for fault tolerance also requires careful consideration of dependencies. External services, third-party APIs, and cloud-managed components can introduce points of failure. To mitigate these risks, applications should employ strategies such as graceful degradation, where non-critical functionality is temporarily disabled while core services continue operating. For instance, if an external recommendation API fails, a Blazor application can continue serving product catalog and checkout functionalities while displaying a default recommendation message. Dependency monitoring and health checks allow pipelines and orchestration systems to detect failures early and take corrective action, such as rerouting requests or triggering service restarts.

Load balancing and traffic management are additional mechanisms to improve fault tolerance. By distributing requests across multiple instances or availability zones, applications can avoid overloading any single node and reduce the risk of performance degradation. Cloud-native services like Azure Front Door or Azure Application Gateway provide global load balancing, health probes, and failover routing to ensure uninterrupted access. For AI workloads, routing inference requests across multiple model instances or GPU nodes prevents any single failure from affecting overall system performance and maintains a consistent user experience.

Testing fault tolerance is equally critical. Simulating failures, network latencies, and resource exhaustion in staging or pre-production environments allows teams to validate that redundancy, failover, and recovery mechanisms function as intended. Chaos engineering techniques, popularized by frameworks such as Chaos Monkey, can help validate system resilience by intentionally introducing controlled failures. However, these practices should be implemented with strict guardrails such as scoped experiments, environment isolation (e.g., non-production or carefully controlled production segments), monitoring thresholds, and automated rollback mechanisms to ensure that testing does not cause unintended disruption to users or critical services. In a cloud-native Blazor application integrated with AI services, testing might involve simulating node failures, network partitioning, or database outages to verify that both front-end and back-end services maintain availability and data consistency.

Finally, documentation and operational practices support fault-tolerant design. Teams must define clear recovery procedures, escalation paths, and incident management workflows. Runbooks, automated scripts, and orchestration templates ensure that recovery actions are repeatable and reliable. Observability and logging should provide enough detail to reconstruct the sequence of events leading to a failure, supporting post-incident analysis and continuous improvement. By combining architectural principles, automation, monitoring, and operational rigor, organizations can build cloud-native applications that deliver consistent, reliable, and resilient services, even in the face of unpredictable failures.

Designing fault-tolerant cloud applications requires a holistic approach that spans architecture, infrastructure, automation, and operations. Redundancy, decoupling, resiliency patterns, and state management form the structural foundation, while monitoring, automated recovery, and dependency management ensure operational effectiveness. Load balancing, traffic management, and rigorous testing validate system behavior under adverse conditions, while documentation and operational practices sustain long-term reliability. For complex cloud-native solutions combining Blazor front ends and AI-driven back ends, fault tolerance is not an optional feature but a critical requirement, enabling applications to maintain availability, protect user experience, and deliver continuous value in dynamic and distributed cloud environments.

Scalable Architecture and Autoscaling Strategies

Scalable architecture and autoscaling strategies are central to achieving performance, reliability, and cost efficiency in cloud-native applications. Modern applications, particularly those combining Blazor front-end interfaces with AI-driven back ends, must handle highly variable workloads, unpredictable traffic spikes, and resource-intensive operations such as real-time analytics or machine learning inference. Scalability ensures that the application can adapt to these demands without degrading user experience, while autoscaling strategies allow resources to dynamically adjust in response to demand, optimizing both performance and operational costs. Designing a scalable cloud architecture involves multiple layers, including application design, infrastructure orchestration, load balancing, and intelligent resource management.

At the foundation of scalable architecture is the principle of horizontal scaling, also known as scaling out. Unlike vertical scaling, which involves adding more CPU, memory, or storage to a single instance, horizontal scaling distributes workloads across multiple instances of an application or service. This approach is particularly suitable for cloud-native deployments, as it aligns with containerized and microservice-based architectures. For example, a Blazor WebAssembly front end hosted in Azure Static Web Apps or an Azure App Service can serve users from multiple instances running in different regions. Similarly, AI inference workloads running on Azure Kubernetes Service (AKS) or Azure Container Apps can be distributed across several container replicas. Horizontal scaling improves fault tolerance as well, since if one instance fails, traffic can be routed to healthy instances without service disruption.

Microservices and modular architecture support scalability by isolating functionality into independently deployable units. By decoupling services, each component can scale according to its specific demand rather than scaling the entire application monolithically. For example, in a cloud-native ecommerce platform, product catalog services may require minimal resources, while payment processing or recommendation AI services might need significantly more compute power during peak periods. Using microservices allows teams to scale these components individually, ensuring optimal resource utilization and reducing operational costs. This modular approach also simplifies maintenance, testing, and deployment, making it easier to implement scaling policies without affecting unrelated components.

Load balancing is a critical element of scalable architecture, ensuring that requests are efficiently distributed across available instances. Cloud-native environments offer a variety of load balancing options, including Azure Front Door, Azure Application Gateway, and internal load balancers within AKS clusters. These services monitor the health of instances, route traffic away from unhealthy nodes, and provide global distribution of requests. Load balancing combined with horizontal scaling creates a system capable of responding to sudden spikes in user activity or AI inference demand, maintaining consistent response times, and avoiding bottlenecks. Additionally, health probes and monitoring ensure that traffic is only sent to fully operational instances, further enhancing reliability.

Autoscaling strategies enable systems to dynamically adjust the number of instances or the allocated resources based on predefined metrics or real-time analysis. There are several approaches to autoscaling, including reactive, predictive, and scheduled scaling. However, without proper controls such as cooldown periods, stabilization windows, and well-defined thresholds, autoscaling policies can oscillate, leading to unnecessary cost and unstable system behavior. Reactive scaling adjusts resources in response to real-time metrics such as CPU utilization, memory consumption, request latency, or queue depth. For example, if the CPU usage of AI inference containers exceeds a threshold, additional replicas can be automatically provisioned, but for AI workloads, CPU or memory utilization is not always the best proxy for user-facing performance. Predictive scaling uses historical data and machine learning models to forecast demand and adjust resources proactively, preventing performance degradation before it occurs. Scheduled scaling leverages known traffic patterns, such as increased user activity during business hours, to preemptively allocate resources. Combining these strategies allows applications to handle variable loads efficiently while controlling costs.

Metrics-driven scaling relies on monitoring and telemetry data to inform scaling decisions. Metrics can be infrastructure-focused, such as CPU, memory, and disk I/O, or application-focused, such as request throughput, error rates, queue lengths, and AI model inference latency.

```yaml
apiVersion: autoscaling/v2
kind: HorizontalPodAutoscaler
spec:
  minReplicas: 2
  maxReplicas: 10
  metrics:
  - type: Resource
    resource:
      name: cpu
      target:
        type: Utilization
        averageUtilization: 70
```

Figure 11-4. *Sample Autoscaling Rule*

Azure Monitor, Application Insights, and custom telemetry pipelines enable teams to collect, aggregate, and analyze these metrics. Autoscaling rules can then be defined based on thresholds, trends, or anomaly detection, ensuring that resources are scaled up or down in a timely and automated manner. For example, a rule might scale out the application by one replica when average CPU utilization exceeds 70% for five consecutive minutes, and scale in when it drops below 40% over a similar interval. By continuously analyzing performance metrics, organizations can optimize scaling policies, improve application responsiveness, and reduce the risk of over-provisioning.

For AI workloads, additional considerations apply. Model inference can be computationally intensive and often varies depending on input complexity and concurrency. Autoscaling policies for AI services must account for GPU or specialized hardware usage, memory consumption, and batch processing requirements. Container orchestration platforms such as AKS support GPU-enabled nodes for real-time inference workloads, allowing scaling policies to add or remove nodes based on demand. In contrast, training-oriented compute such as Azure Machine Learning clusters is typically designed for batch or scheduled workloads, where resources are provisioned for model training jobs rather than continuously serving live requests. Predictive scaling can leverage usage patterns, such as time-of-day inference peaks or seasonal trends, to provision the necessary resources in advance, ensuring uninterrupted performance for AI-driven applications.

Serverless and event-driven architectures further enhance scalability by decoupling compute resources from infrastructure management. Services such as Azure Functions and Azure Logic Apps both support event-driven patterns, but they serve different architectural roles. Azure Functions provides code-based execution for handling events and scaling compute dynamically (including scaling from zero), while Azure Logic Apps focuses on workflow orchestration and integration across services using a declarative approach. Both can scale with demand, but they are typically used for different types of event-driven workloads. This pay-per-use model ensures that applications remain responsive even under unpredictable loads while minimizing costs during periods of low activity. Serverless components are particularly effective for background processing, AI model scoring, or asynchronous tasks in a Blazor front-end workflow, where the computational load can vary significantly over time.

State management is a key consideration when designing scalable applications. Stateless components are easier to scale because any instance can handle incoming requests without relying on local state. For Blazor WebAssembly, client-side session data is typically stored in browser storage (such as localStorage or sessionStorage), with optional use of back-end APIs for persistence. In contrast, shared or server-managed state used across users or services is maintained in external systems such as distributed caches or cloud-based stores like Azure Cache for Redis or Azure Managed Redis.

For Blazor Server, circuit state is maintained on the server and tied to a user's SignalR connection, which requires strategies such as session affinity or external state storage to ensure consistency and resilience across instances. For AI model inference pipelines and other stateful back-end components, replication or persistent storage mechanisms are necessary to maintain consistency, durability, and fault tolerance. Techniques like distributed caching, database replication, or event sourcing enable state to be maintained across scaled instances, allowing horizontal scaling without loss of data integrity.

Scalable architecture also involves designing for failure tolerance. Autoscaling policies should be integrated with monitoring and alerting systems to detect unhealthy instances or degraded performance and trigger recovery actions. Horizontal scaling not only handles increased load but also provides redundancy for fault tolerance. By combining scalable architecture with fault-tolerant design patterns, applications can maintain high availability even during infrastructure failures, network disruptions, or unanticipated traffic surges.

Finally, cost optimization is a critical aspect of scalable architecture and autoscaling strategies. While scaling ensures performance, over-provisioning can lead to unnecessary expenditure. Cloud providers like Azure offer tools for cost monitoring and optimization, enabling teams to analyze usage patterns, adjust scaling thresholds, and select the most cost-efficient resource types. Autoscaling ensures that resources are allocated dynamically based on demand, balancing performance with budget constraints. Predictive scaling can further reduce costs by provisioning resources ahead of anticipated demand rather than always maintaining excess capacity.

Scalable architecture and autoscaling strategies are essential for maintaining the performance, availability, and cost-efficiency of cloud-native applications. Horizontal scaling, microservices, modular design, and load balancing provide the structural foundation for scaling, while metrics-driven autoscaling ensures resources adapt dynamically to workload fluctuations. For AI-driven workloads, GPU allocation, batch processing, and predictive scaling are critical to maintaining consistent inference performance. Stateless design, distributed state management, serverless components, and failure-aware scaling enhance both responsiveness and resilience. By combining these principles, organizations can build cloud-native Blazor and AI applications that handle variable demand gracefully, optimize costs, and deliver a reliable, high-quality user experience under dynamic conditions.

CHAPTER 12

Optimizing Performance in Blazor Apps

Profiling and Performance Analysis Techniques

Profiling and performance analysis are fundamental steps in optimizing Blazor applications, but the nature of performance challenges differs significantly between hosting models. In Blazor Server, performance is closely tied to network latency, SignalR circuit behavior, and server resource utilization, whereas Blazor WebAssembly focuses more on payload size, client-side execution, and browser runtime constraints.

Profiling and performance analysis provide developers with deep insights into how their code executes, how resources are utilized, and where performance bottlenecks occur. Blazor applications often integrate complex UI components, asynchronous operations, and API- or AI-driven back ends, making it essential to monitor performance systematically. Profiling refers to the process of collecting data about an application's execution such as CPU usage, memory consumption, method call frequency, and response times, while performance analysis involves interpreting this data to identify inefficiencies, optimize code, and improve overall user experience.

In Blazor applications, profiling can begin at the component level. Each UI component may trigger rendering cycles, bind data, and perform calculations that impact overall performance. Tools like Visual Studio Profiler or JetBrains dotTrace allow developers to measure the time spent in each component, identify expensive render operations, and detect excessive re-rendering. Profiling at this granularity ensures that developers can pinpoint specific UI elements or data-binding operations that slow down the application. For server-side Blazor, additional profiling of SignalR connections is

A. Prasad and H. Singh, *Advanced Blazor Architecture with .NET 10 and Azure OpenAI*,
https://doi.org/10.1007/979-8-8688-2518-7_12

crucial, as latency in real-time communication can degrade responsiveness. Metrics such as round-trip time for hub messages, server processing time, and network delays provide visibility into performance across the client-server boundary.

Memory usage is another key aspect of performance analysis. Blazor WebAssembly runs within the browser's memory space, and inefficient memory usage can lead to slower execution, increased garbage collection, and potential instability. In addition, performance is influenced by the initial download size of the application; larger payloads increase startup time, while runtime trade-offs, such as AOT compilation vs. IL interpretation, impact execution speed, memory usage, and build size. These factors must be balanced carefully to deliver a responsive and efficient user experience. Profiling tools can track allocations, identify memory leaks, and highlight objects retained longer than necessary. Developers can also monitor JavaScript interop calls, which are often used to interact with browser APIs, as these calls may introduce overhead if executed excessively. For server-side Blazor, monitoring memory consumption on the server ensures that application scaling and responsiveness remain optimal, particularly under high user load.

Application profiling extends beyond code execution to include network performance. For client-side Blazor applications, resources such as WebAssembly binaries, CSS, JavaScript files, and images must be efficiently loaded. Profiling network requests using browser developer tools or Azure Application Insights can reveal large payloads, slow endpoints, and caching inefficiencies. By analyzing request frequency, payload sizes, and latency, developers can make informed decisions about compressing resources, optimizing API responses, and minimizing redundant data transfers. Profiling network traffic is especially important in AI-driven applications where large datasets or model results are transmitted between client and server.

Profiling is also critical for identifying performance issues in data access and database interactions. Blazor applications often rely on REST APIs, gRPC services, or direct database queries to fetch and update data. Measuring query execution times, tracking database connection usage, and monitoring API response times help identify slow endpoints or inefficient queries. Techniques such as logging query execution plans, using ORM profiling tools, or integrating middleware for performance metrics can reveal areas where optimization is possible. By reducing database latency and streamlining API interactions, overall application responsiveness improves, enhancing user satisfaction.

Automated profiling and continuous performance monitoring are becoming increasingly important in modern development workflows. Integrating performance validation into CI/CD pipelines enables automated regression testing, benchmarking, and load testing, ensuring that performance degradations are detected early during development or before deployment. Tools like Application Insights, New Relic, or Dynatrace can automatically capture performance metrics, visualize trends, and alert teams when thresholds are exceeded. For Blazor applications that involve complex AI computations or heavy user interaction, automated monitoring provides real-time visibility into CPU load, memory usage, request latency, and component render times, enabling proactive optimization.

In addition to measuring performance, profiling techniques often provide actionable insights for optimization. Identifying hotspots in the code allows developers to refactor inefficient algorithms, reduce unnecessary computations, or simplify data-binding operations. Profiling may reveal frequent component re-renders that can be mitigated by using ShouldRender overrides or more efficient state management. Memory profiling can suggest the use of object pooling or structuring data to minimize allocations. Network profiling can guide developers to implement compression, batching, or lazy loading strategies, reducing load times and bandwidth consumption. For AI integrations, profiling inference time, model size, and data transfer helps optimize both server-side computation and client-side responsiveness.

Profiling tools also support comparison of different application versions or deployment configurations. By establishing a performance baseline, developers can measure the impact of new features, updates, or optimizations. For example, comparing rendering times before and after introducing a new UI component or library ensures that enhancements do not introduce regressions. Baselines can also guide resource allocation, determining whether additional compute, memory, or caching strategies are necessary to maintain performance under expected user loads.

Ultimately, profiling and performance analysis are continuous processes rather than one-time activities. As Blazor applications evolve, with new components, API integrations, or AI features added, performance characteristics change. Regularly profiling applications, monitoring trends, and acting on insights ensures that the application remains responsive, efficient, and scalable. By combining detailed component-level profiling, memory and network analysis, database and API monitoring, and automated performance tracking, development teams gain the visibility needed to identify optimization opportunities. In practice, this should be followed by targeted improvements such as applying Blazor rendering best practices, using UI virtualization for large datasets, reducing unnecessary re-renders, and optimizing WebAssembly payload size and runtime trade-offs (e.g., trimming, compression, and selective AOT). These optimization levers help translate performance insights into measurable improvements in responsiveness and user experience.

In conclusion, profiling and performance analysis in Blazor applications provide the foundation for systematic optimization. By identifying hotspots, measuring memory and network usage, monitoring database and API interactions, and integrating continuous performance tracking, teams can make data-driven decisions that improve responsiveness, efficiency, and scalability. Effective profiling ensures that both server-side and client-side Blazor applications, including AI-integrated solutions, deliver seamless performance, robust user experience, and operational excellence in cloud-native environments.

Caching Strategies for Blazor Applications

Caching strategies are essential for optimizing the performance of Blazor applications, reducing latency, lowering server load, and improving the overall user experience. In both client-side Blazor WebAssembly and server-side Blazor applications, efficient caching ensures that frequently accessed data, computational results, and static assets are stored closer to the user or application logic, minimizing the need for repeated computation or remote data fetching. Caching is especially important in cloud-native architectures where applications often rely on multiple APIs, databases, and AI services, each introducing potential latency and variability. By implementing caching effectively, developers can significantly enhance responsiveness and scalability.

There are several levels of caching that can be leveraged in Blazor applications. On the client side, Blazor WebAssembly applications can leverage both browser storage and HTTP caching mechanisms. Browser storage options such as localStorage, sessionStorage, and IndexedDB are used for persisting application state or data, while browser and HTTP caching (e.g., cache-control headers and service workers) help reduce network requests and improve load performance by reusing previously fetched resources. Local storage allows data to persist across browser sessions, enabling offline access or faster retrieval of static datasets. However, it should not be used to store sensitive information such as access tokens or personally identifiable data, as it is accessible from client-side scripts. Additionally, developers should account for data staleness by implementing expiration or refresh strategies to ensure that cached business data remains accurate and up to date. Session storage is suitable for temporary data that only needs to exist for the duration of a browser session. IndexedDB, a more sophisticated browser-based storage option, supports larger datasets and structured storage, making it suitable for caching complex objects, AI inference results, or pre-fetched API responses. By strategically caching data on the client, applications can reduce network calls, lower server load, and improve perceived performance, especially for users on slower connections.

Server-side Blazor applications rely on caching strategies implemented on the server or at intermediary layers. In-memory caching is a common approach, where frequently accessed objects, computation results, or database query results are stored in the application memory for fast retrieval. The .NET platform provides built-in support for in-memory caching through classes such as MemoryCache, as well as a distributed caching abstraction via IDistributedCache. It is important to note that IDistributedCache is not a concrete cache implementation, but an interface that can be backed by providers such as Azure Cache for Redis or SQL-based caches, allowing developers to choose an appropriate distributed store for their deployment needs. In-memory caching is ideal for high-speed access to ephemeral data, but it is limited to a single server instance and does not persist across application restarts. To overcome these limitations in distributed environments, developers often use distributed caches such as Azure Redis Cache, which provide high availability, fault tolerance, and consistent data access across multiple instances of an application.

Caching is also critical for static assets, such as CSS, JavaScript, images, and WebAssembly binaries. For Blazor WebAssembly applications, these assets can be cached using HTTP caching headers, content delivery networks (CDNs), and service workers. By leveraging CDNs like Azure CDN or Cloudflare, static files are served from geographically distributed nodes, reducing latency for users worldwide. HTTP caching headers such as Cache-Control, ETag, and Expires instruct browsers and intermediaries to store resources for specified durations, minimizing repeated downloads. Service workers enable advanced caching strategies for progressive web applications (PWAs), allowing offline access, background synchronization, and prefetching of critical resources. Proper configuration of these mechanisms ensures that the application loads quickly, even under constrained network conditions.

Data caching strategies are particularly relevant for API-driven Blazor applications. Frequently accessed datasets, such as user profiles, configuration settings, or AI model results, can be cached to reduce repeated database or service calls. Techniques such as memoization, where the result of a computation is stored for subsequent calls with the same inputs, improve efficiency in both UI components and server-side operations. Developers can also implement time-based caching, setting expiration intervals for cached data to ensure consistency while balancing performance. Sliding expiration policies, where cached items are renewed based on access frequency, help keep active data available while removing stale entries automatically.

Distributed caching is critical for cloud-native scalability and reliability. In environments with multiple server instances or containerized deployments, local in-memory caches are insufficient, as each instance maintains its own copy of cached data. Distributed caches provide a shared store that multiple application instances can access to maintain consistency and improve performance. In managed cloud environments, services such as Azure Cache for Redis or Azure Managed Redis offer fully managed, scalable caching with built-in high availability. In contrast, self-managed solutions like Memcached require teams to provision, operate, and scale the cache infrastructure themselves, offering flexibility but with additional operational overhead. This approach ensures data consistency, supports failover in case of node failure, and allows horizontal scaling without cache fragmentation. For AI-driven applications, distributed caching can store precomputed inference results, model parameters, or intermediate computation outputs, reduce latency, and avoid redundant calculations across multiple requests.

Caching also interacts closely with state management in Blazor applications. Server-side Blazor applications maintain circuit states for each connected client, which can consume significant memory and affect performance under high concurrency. By caching frequently used data outside the circuit state, such as in memory or Redis, developers can reduce memory consumption and improve scalability. Similarly, client-side caching in Blazor WebAssembly reduces repeated server calls for data that rarely changes, minimizing round trips and improving responsiveness. Effective caching strategies balance the need for freshness with the performance benefits of storing data close to the application.

Advanced caching strategies include layered or multi-tier caching, combining client-side, server-side, and distributed caches. This approach ensures that data is retrieved from the nearest and fastest source, falling back to slower layers only when necessary. For example, a Blazor WebAssembly application may first check browser storage for cached results. If the data is not available, it calls a back-end API, where the server can then follow a cache hierarchy such as checking in-memory cache, then a distributed cache (e.g., Azure Cache for Redis or Azure Managed Redis), and finally the database if needed. By intelligently layering caches, applications can achieve both low latency and high consistency.

Monitoring and maintaining cache health is also essential. Cached data must be invalidated or refreshed appropriately to prevent serving outdated or inconsistent information. Cache invalidation strategies include time-based expiration, event-driven updates, or explicit manual refresh triggered by changes in underlying data sources. Tools such as Azure Monitor and Application Insights can provide visibility into performance characteristics like latency and resource utilization. However, cache-specific metrics such as hit/miss ratios typically require explicit instrumentation or integration with cache provider telemetry. By collecting and analyzing these signals, developers can fine-tune caching policies while ensuring that performance improvements do not come at the expense of data accuracy or user experience.

In conclusion, caching strategies are a cornerstone of optimizing Blazor application performance. By leveraging client-side storage, server-side memory caches, distributed caching, static asset caching, and layered approaches, developers can significantly reduce latency, improve responsiveness, and optimize resource utilization. Proper management of cache expiration, consistency, and monitoring ensures that applications remain accurate, reliable, and performant under varying workloads. For Blazor applications integrated with AI or API-driven back ends, caching not only improves UI responsiveness but also reduces server and computation load, enabling scalable, efficient, and high-performing cloud-native solutions.

Load Optimization and Resource Management

Blazor Load and resource management are critical components of performance tuning in Blazor applications. As web applications grow in complexity and user base, efficiently handling concurrent requests, managing server resources, and distributing workload becomes essential to maintain responsiveness and reduce latency. In cloud-native environments, especially when integrating AI-driven services, Blazor applications often encounter dynamic workloads that vary by time, user activity, or computational demand. Optimizing how the application handles load and resources ensures scalability, improves user experience, and reduces operational costs.

One of the primary considerations in load optimization is understanding the application's workload patterns. Profiling tools and monitoring services, such as Azure Monitor or Application Insights, can provide detailed metrics on request volume, response times, CPU and memory usage, and user behavior. By analyzing these metrics, developers can identify peak usage periods, long-running requests, and bottlenecks in the application pipeline. For instance, an AI recommendation service integrated with a Blazor front end may experience high inference requests during certain hours. Understanding these patterns allows teams to plan scaling strategies, prefetch data, and optimize resource allocation in advance.

Load distribution remains an important technique for handling high traffic, but in Blazor Server applications, it must account for connection-oriented behavior. Traditional load balancers, such as Azure Front Door or Application Gateway, can distribute incoming requests across instances, but Blazor Server relies on persistent SignalR circuits that are tied to server-side state.

As a result, scaling strategies often incorporate Azure SignalR Service to offload connection management and enable more effective horizontal scaling. This approach reduces pressure on individual application instances and avoids issues related to circuit affinity while still allowing load balancers to manage overall traffic distribution. This prevents any single instance from being overwhelmed and ensures that response times remain consistent. In server-side Blazor applications, distributing SignalR hub connections evenly across server instances is particularly important, as each hub maintains a connection state that consumes server memory. For AI services, distributing inference requests across multiple GPU or CPU nodes ensures that no single instance becomes a performance bottleneck, improving both throughput and reliability.

Optimizing request handling is another critical aspect of load management. Techniques such as asynchronous programming, request batching, and throttling help prevent server resources from being consumed inefficiently. Asynchronous operations allow the server to handle multiple requests concurrently without blocking threads, which is particularly important for I/O-bound operations like database queries or external API calls. However, this model primarily benefits I/O-bound workloads; CPU-intensive operations such as certain AI inference tasks require different optimization strategies, including parallel processing, scaling compute resources, or offloading to specialized services. Batching requests, such as combining multiple data retrieval operations into a single call, reduces network overhead and database load. Throttling limits the number of requests processed simultaneously, ensuring that resource-intensive operations do not overwhelm the system and degrade performance for other users.

Caching plays a complementary role in load optimization. By storing frequently accessed data, computational results, or static resources in memory or distributed caches, applications can reduce repeated processing and database queries. This not only improves response times but also reduces CPU and memory consumption under heavy loads. For example, a Blazor application that caches AI inference results or precomputed recommendations can serve subsequent requests directly from cache, dramatically reducing the load on back-end AI services. Coupled with proper cache invalidation strategies, caching ensures both high performance and data consistency.

Resource management involves allocating computing, memory, and storage efficiently to meet performance requirements while minimizing cost. In cloud environments, scaling resources dynamically based on load ensures that the application can handle spikes without over-provisioning. Horizontal scaling adds additional instances of services, while vertical scaling increases the capacity of individual nodes. For AI workloads, resource management must consider GPU utilization, batch processing, and memory-intensive model operations. In addition, scaling decisions should be informed by signals such as queue depth, request latency, and concurrency levels to ensure that inference services remain responsive under varying demand. Kubernetes clusters, Azure App Services, or serverless platforms like Azure Functions provide mechanisms to manage resources automatically based on metrics such as CPU load, request queue length, or custom telemetry.

Connection and session management are also critical in load optimization. Server-side Blazor maintains circuit states for each connected client, which consumes memory and can affect scalability under high concurrency. Optimizing circuit lifetime, offloading state to distributed caches, and limiting simultaneous connections per server instance are effective strategies for resource management. For client-side Blazor WebAssembly, efficient management of API calls, background operations, and local state ensures that the browser does not become a bottleneck, particularly on devices with limited resources.

Network optimization is another important consideration. Minimizing latency, reducing payload sizes, and optimizing API endpoints help applications handle higher loads efficiently. Techniques such as data compression, content minification, and bundling reduce the amount of data transmitted over the network. Lazy loading and on-demand fetching prevent unnecessary data from being retrieved, improving perceived performance for end users. For applications with AI components, optimizing data transfer between client and server, such as sending only essential features for inference rather than entire datasets, reduces network load and accelerates response times.

Monitoring and adaptive management are essential for continuous optimization. Real-time metrics provide visibility into how resources are consumed under varying load conditions. Autoscaling policies can be adjusted dynamically to add or remove instances based on CPU usage, memory consumption, or request queue length. Predictive scaling, leveraging historical usage patterns and AI-driven forecasts, allows applications to preemptively allocate resources before traffic spikes occur. However, it is most effective when workload patterns are relatively stable and predictable; highly variable or bursty traffic can reduce the accuracy of forecasts and limit their effectiveness. This ensures that applications remain responsive while controlling operational costs by avoiding over-provisioning during low-demand periods.

Load testing is a critical practice in evaluating performance under stress. Simulating high concurrency, peak traffic, and resource-intensive operations in a controlled environment reveals system limitations and identifies bottlenecks before production deployment. Tools like Apache JMeter and Azure Load Testing allow developers to simulate realistic workloads, measure response times, and validate autoscaling policies. By performing iterative testing and analysis, teams can fine-tune resource allocation, optimize request handling, and ensure that both Blazor front-end and AI back-end components maintain performance under extreme conditions.

Finally, designing for graceful degradation ensures that the application continues to function under resource constraints or partial failures. Non-critical features can be temporarily disabled, while essential services continue operating, maintaining core functionality for users. For example, optional AI recommendation features can be deprioritized during peak load, ensuring that checkout and browsing functionality in a Blazor ecommerce application remain responsive. Graceful degradation, combined with intelligent load management and resource allocation, improves user experience even under challenging conditions.

In conclusion, load optimization and resource management are essential practices for ensuring that Blazor applications perform reliably under variable workloads. By understanding traffic patterns, distributing requests efficiently, optimizing request handling, leveraging caching, and dynamically managing resources, developers can maintain responsiveness and scalability. Network optimization, connection management, and load testing further enhance performance, while adaptive scaling and predictive resource allocation ensure cost efficiency. For applications integrating AI-driven back ends, these strategies are critical for balancing computational demand, latency, and throughput. By systematically applying load optimization and resource management techniques, development teams can deliver high-performing, resilient, and user-friendly Blazor applications in dynamic cloud environments.

CHAPTER 13

Zero-Trust and Enterprise Security

Authentication and Authorization in Zero-Trust Environments

The Zero-Trust security model has become a modern standard in enterprise cybersecurity, moving away from traditional perimeter-based defenses. It is grounded in the principle of "never trust, always verify," where every user, device, and application is continuously authenticated and authorized before accessing resources. Unlike legacy approaches that granted implicit trust once inside the network, Zero-Trust assumes that every entity, internal or external, may already be compromised. This principle is especially critical in today's threat landscape marked by ransomware attacks, credential theft, insider threats, and supply chain exploits.

Authentication and authorization represent the core enforcement pillars of Zero-Trust. Authentication validates the identity of users and devices, while authorization determines what level of access they are granted. Together, these mechanisms create a dynamic, adaptive, and context-aware security posture, minimizing attack surfaces and reducing the risks of unauthorized lateral movement [22].

Why Traditional Perimeter-Based Security Fails

Legacy enterprise security models relied on perimeter defenses such as firewalls, intrusion prevention systems, and VPNs. Once authenticated at the "gate," users were implicitly trusted to access internal systems. However, this model has several shortcomings in the modern enterprise ecosystem:

A. Prasad and H. Singh, *Advanced Blazor Architecture with .NET 10 and Azure OpenAI*,
https://doi.org/10.1007/979-8-8688-2518-7_13

1. **Cloud Migration**: With data and applications distributed across cloud providers (AWS, Azure, GCP), the corporate perimeter has dissolved.
2. **Remote Work**: Employees, contractors, and partners access resources from diverse locations and devices.
3. **IoT and Mobile Devices**: Billions of heterogeneous devices introduce unpredictable attack vectors.
4. **Credential Theft and Lateral Movement**: High-profile attacks (e.g., SolarWinds) demonstrated how, once inside, attackers can move laterally across systems with little resistance.

Traditional trust boundaries are no longer sufficient. Attackers can exploit a single compromised account to bypass internal defenses, making Zero-Trust's identity-centric and continuous verification approach essential.

Role of Identity As the New Perimeter

In a Zero-Trust model, access decisions are no longer driven by network location but by a combination of identity and context. This includes who the user is, the posture of the device they are using, the sensitivity of the resource being accessed, and real-time signals such as location or risk level. Together, these factors shape a more adaptive and reliable approach to authorization.

- Identity is verified using IAM, MFA, and federated protocols such as SAML and OpenID Connect, while OAuth is used for delegated authorization.
- **Device Identity**: Checked for compliance (e.g., patched OS, antivirus running, disk encryption enabled).
- **Contextual Attributes**: Location, time, role, risk score, and behavioral analytics.

This shift from network perimeter to identity perimeter allows enterprises to enforce fine-grained, adaptive access controls, ensuring that trust is never static but continuously validated.

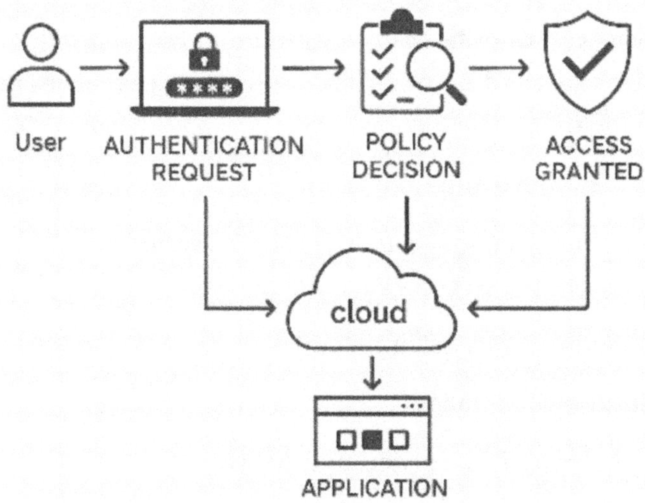

Figure 13-1. *Zero-Trust Authentication Flow*

Authentication is the first gatekeeper in Zero-Trust. Key mechanisms include

1. Multi-factor Authentication (MFA)

   MFA strengthens login security by requiring at least two independent factors:

   - Something you know (password/PIN)
   - Something you have (smartphone, token, security key)
   - Something you are (biometrics such as fingerprint or face recognition)

   Enterprise Example: Microsoft mandates MFA in Azure AD Conditional Access, reducing risks of credential theft by 99.9%.

2. Passwordless Authentication

   Passwordless methods eliminate weak or reused passwords:

   - Biometrics (Windows Hello, Apple FaceID)
   - FIDO2 hardware keys (YubiKey, Titan Security Key)

- Push notifications (Okta Verify, Duo Mobile)
- **Enterprise Example**: Many organizations are adopting passwordless and BeyondCorp-style access approaches to reduce phishing risks.

3. Risk-Based Adaptive Authentication

   Adaptive authentication dynamically adjusts verification requirements based on contextual risk factors:

   - Device posture (secure/insecure)
   - Geolocation anomalies
   - Login behavior (time of day, unusual IPs)

   Enterprise Example: Okta Identity Cloud implements adaptive MFA [23], triggering step-up authentication only under suspicious conditions, balancing security with usability.

Authorization Mechanisms in Zero-Trust

Authorization ensures that authenticated entities are granted only the minimal privileges required.

1. Role-Based Access Control (RBAC)
   - Users receive permissions based on organizational roles (e.g., HR Manager, Database Admin).
   - Simple but rigid in dynamic, cloud-native environments.
2. Attribute-Based Access Control (ABAC)
   - Access decisions based on attributes such as user department, data sensitivity, time, or device type.
   - Enables fine-grained, context-aware access.

   Enterprise Example: AWS IAM uses ABAC policies, granting access only when conditions match defined attributes.

3. Policy-Based Access Control (PBAC): Access decisions are evaluated against defined policies and rules. AI/ML, where used, can complement this by contributing to risk scoring rather than directly enforcing access decisions. Uses AI and machine learning to evaluate risk scores and enforce policies in real time.

   - Adapts dynamically to evolving threats.

   Enterprise Example: Palo Alto Networks integrates PBAC into Prisma Cloud, adjusting permissions based on real-time analytics.

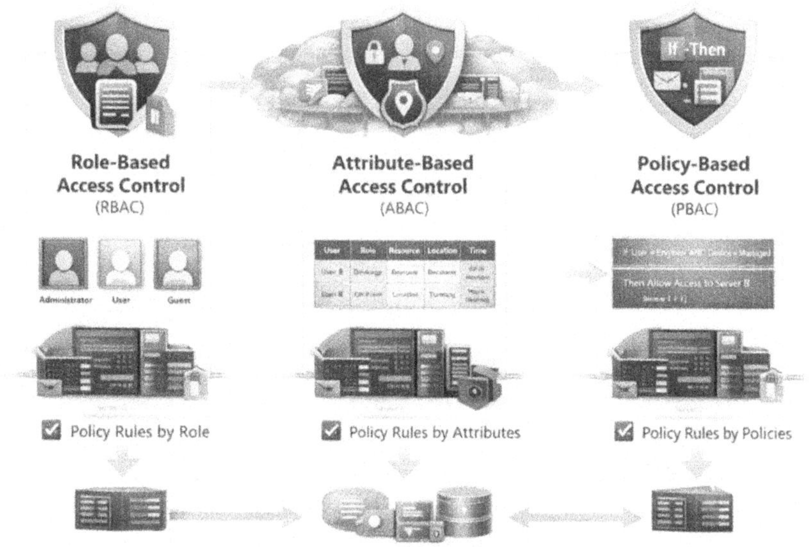

Figure 13-2. *Zero-Trust Authorization Mechanisms in Cloud Environments*

IAM Integration with Zero-Trust Principles

Identity and Access Management (IAM) platforms unify authentication and authorization in a Zero-Trust framework:

- **Microsoft Azure AD**: Conditional Access enforces continuous verification using risk-based signals.
- **Google BeyondCorp**: Eliminates VPN reliance by enforcing device trust + user identity for application access.
- **Okta**: Provides centralized IAM with adaptive MFA, passwordless login, and real-time monitoring.

These platforms highlight how IAM, when integrated with Zero-Trust, enables enterprises to protect cloud, hybrid, and on-premises assets without relying on static perimeters.

Challenges and Trade-Offs

While authentication and authorization in Zero-Trust enhance resilience, enterprises face challenges:

1. **Usability vs. Security**: Frequent MFA prompts can frustrate users, requiring a balance through adaptive methods.
2. **Legacy Integration**: Older systems may not support modern IAM or Zero-Trust policies.
3. **Cost and Complexity**: Deploying identity federation, adaptive risk scoring, and continuous monitoring requires significant investment.

Future Trends in Authentication and Authorization

- **Continuous Authentication**: Behavioral biometrics (typing rhythm, mouse movement) and session monitoring continuously validate user legitimacy.
- **AI-Driven Identity Verification**: Machine learning models detect anomalies and automate risk scoring in real time.
- **Decentralized Identity (DID) [23]**: Blockchain-based identity solutions give users ownership of credentials, reducing reliance on centralized IAM providers.

Example Code: Adaptive Authorization in Zero-Trust

```
// Zero-Trust Authorization (RBAC + ABAC + PBAC) — short .NET 10 / Blazor snippet
// Plug-in to ASP.NET Core Authorization so you can use:
//   [Authorize(Policy = "ZeroTrustReadClaims")]
//
// Notes:
// - RBAC: roles (Admin/Employee)
// - ABAC: claims (department, clearance, data_domain)
// - PBAC: adaptive rules (risk score, device compliance, MFA recency)

using System.Security.Claims;
using System.Threading.Tasks;
using Microsoft.AspNetCore.Authorization;

public sealed class ZeroTrustRequirement(string action, string sensitivity) : IAuthorizationRequirement
{
    public string Action { get; } = action;           // "read" | "write"
    public string Sensitivity { get; } = sensitivity; // "confidential" | "restricted"
}

public interface IRiskSignalProvider
{
    int GetRiskScore(ClaimsPrincipal user);        // 0..100
    bool IsDeviceCompliant(ClaimsPrincipal user);  // posture signal
    bool IsMfaRecent(ClaimsPrincipal user);         // step-up satisfied recently?
}

public sealed class ZeroTrustHandler(IRiskSignalProvider risk)
    : AuthorizationHandler<ZeroTrustRequirement>
{
    protected override Task HandleRequirementAsync(
        AuthorizationHandlerContext ctx,
        ZeroTrustRequirement req)
    {
        // ===== RBAC (role baseline) =====
        var isAdmin = ctx.User.IsInRole("Admin");
        var isEmployee = ctx.User.IsInRole("Employee");

        if (req.Action is "read" && !(isAdmin || isEmployee)) return Task.CompletedTask;
        if (req.Action is "write" && !isAdmin) return Task.CompletedTask;

        // ===== ABAC (claims/attributes) =====
        // Example: finance domain requires Finance department
        var domain = ctx.User.FindFirstValue("data_domain");   // e.g., "finance"
        var dept = ctx.User.FindFirstValue("department");   // e.g., "Finance"
        if (domain is "finance" && dept is not "Finance") return Task.CompletedTask;
```

```
        // Example: restricted sensitivity requires high clearance
        var clearance = ctx.User.FindFirstValue("clearance"); // e.g., "high"
        if (req.Sensitivity is "restricted" && clearance is not "high") return Task.CompletedTask;

        // ===== PBAC (adaptive policies) =====
        var riskScore = risk.GetRiskScore(ctx.User);

        // Hard deny for very high risk
        if (riskScore > 80) return Task.CompletedTask;

        // Require compliant device for restricted resources
        if (req.Sensitivity is "restricted" && !risk.IsDeviceCompliant(ctx.User))
            return Task.CompletedTask;

        // Step-up MFA for elevated risk (or unknown contexts, etc.)
        if (riskScore >= 50 && !risk.IsMfaRecent(ctx.User))
        {
            // In real apps you might return a challenge/redirect flow.
            // With ASP.NET Authorization, we simply do not succeed the requirement.
            return Task.CompletedTask;
        }

        // All checks passed
        ctx.Succeed(req);
        return Task.CompletedTask;
    }
}
```

```
// --- Registration (Program.cs, .NET 10 minimal hosting) ---

builder.Services.AddSingleton<IRiskSignalProvider, YourRiskSignalProvider>();
builder.Services.AddSingleton<IAuthorizationHandler, ZeroTrustHandler>();

builder.Services.AddAuthorization(options =>
{
    options.AddPolicy("ZeroTrustReadClaims",
        p => p.Requirements.Add(new ZeroTrustRequirement("read", "confidential")));

    options.AddPolicy("ZeroTrustWriteClaims",
        p => p.Requirements.Add(new ZeroTrustRequirement("write", "restricted")));
});
```

This snippet simulates policy-based Zero-Trust authorization by combining role, device posture, MFA, and risk scoring to enforce dynamic, context-aware access.

Authentication and authorization serve as the backbone of Zero-Trust security. By implementing MFA, passwordless authentication, adaptive risk-based checks, and context-aware authorization (RBAC, ABAC, PBAC), enterprises strengthen defenses against credential theft, insider threats, and advanced attacks.

Case studies from Microsoft Azure AD, Google BeyondCorp, and Okta show real-world adoption, demonstrating Zero-Trust's practicality. Future directions such as continuous authentication, AI-driven anomaly detection, and decentralized identity will further enhance enterprise resilience. Ultimately, Zero-Trust authentication and authorization enable organizations to protect critical assets in an increasingly borderless, cloud-driven digital world.

Securing AI Usage Within Enterprise Zero-Trust Frameworks

Importance of AI in Enterprise Operations

Artificial intelligence (AI) is now a practical part of modern enterprise systems, with its security and governance implications becoming increasingly important. Today's organizations rely on AI to optimize nearly every aspect of business operations, from automating customer service interactions with chatbots to enabling predictive analytics in supply chain management. For example, HR teams deploy AI-driven virtual assistants to streamline recruitment processes, while financial institutions use AI-powered fraud detection systems that analyze transaction patterns in real time. In manufacturing, predictive maintenance powered by AI reduces downtime and operational costs by forecasting equipment failures before they occur. Major cloud platforms such as Amazon Web Services (AWS), Microsoft Azure, and Google Cloud have integrated AI services into their ecosystems, enabling enterprises to embed intelligence across hybrid and multi-cloud infrastructures seamlessly. Yet, this widespread integration of AI comes with an expanded attack surface. The more enterprises depend on AI for critical decisions, the more attractive these systems become to attackers. As a result, Zero-Trust, which eliminates the assumption of inherent trust in any user, device, or system, becomes an essential paradigm for ensuring that enterprise AI operates securely, ethically, and reliably.

Risks of AI Adoption in Enterprise Environments

Despite its benefits, the adoption of AI introduces several new and unique risks that enterprises must carefully address. One major concern is adversarial machine learning attacks, in which attackers subtly manipulate inputs to trick AI models into making incorrect predictions. For instance, researchers have demonstrated how placing stickers on a stop sign can cause an autonomous vehicle's vision system to misclassify it as a speed limit sign, potentially leading to dangerous outcomes. Beyond adversarial inputs, data poisoning and model manipulation present another significant risk. If attackers manage to corrupt training datasets, they can bias AI models to behave in ways that serve malicious goals. In financial services, poisoned datasets could trick credit risk models into approving fraudulent applications, exposing institutions to financial and reputational damage. Additionally, the rise of unauthorized AI model access and shadow AI usage creates hidden vulnerabilities. Shadow AI occurs when employees deploy unapproved AI tools without enterprise oversight, leading to compliance risks and potential data leakage. Unauthorized access to proprietary AI models may also result in theft of intellectual property, undermining competitive advantage. These risks collectively illustrate why AI cannot be secured with traditional perimeter-based defenses and why Zero-Trust principles must be integrated into AI usage.

Applying Zero-Trust Principles to AI

The Zero-Trust model provides a blueprint for securing enterprise AI by enforcing authentication, authorization, and continuous monitoring at every stage of interaction. Strong authentication for AI models and APIs ensures that only verified entities can access critical systems. This may involve secure API keys, OAuth-based tokens, or even certificate-based authentication. Multi-factor authentication (MFA) can be extended to administrative dashboards where AI models are configured or deployed, reducing the risk of unauthorized access. Beyond authentication, access authorization for datasets and machine learning pipelines [21] is crucial. By applying attribute-based access control (ABAC), organizations can ensure that only specific roles, such as data scientists or auditors, are permitted to access sensitive datasets or initiate model deployments. Granular access rules prevent unverified or malicious models from entering production environments. To complement these safeguards, enterprises must implement continuous monitoring of AI behavior and outputs. Just as networks are monitored for anomalies, AI systems should be observed for unusual predictions, bias, or sudden changes in performance. For example, if an AI chatbot begins producing toxic or nonsensical outputs, Zero-Trust systems can automatically flag and restrict access until the issue is resolved. Finally, securing the AI lifecycle from dataset curation, training, and validation, through deployment and ongoing maintenance, is vital. Provenance checks verify dataset integrity, adversarial testing validates model robustness, and post-deployment monitoring ensures sustained trustworthiness. Together, these Zero-Trust principles create a security-first foundation for enterprise AI.

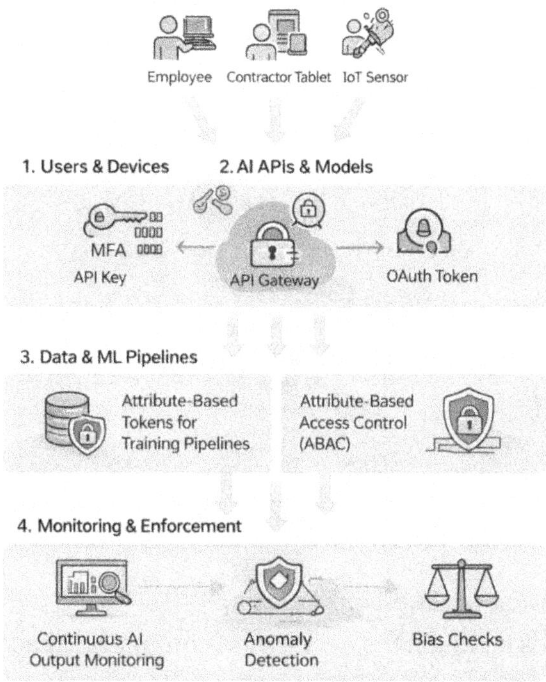

Figure 13-3. *Zero-Trust AI Ecosystem Flowchart*

AI Governance and Policy Frameworks

Beyond technical safeguards, enterprises must adopt robust governance frameworks to ensure that AI deployment remains ethical, transparent, and compliant. Policies addressing model explainability, fairness, accountability, and auditing are critical to building trust not only with regulators but also with customers and stakeholders. The US National Institute of Standards and Technology (NIST) has developed the AI Risk Management Framework (AI RMF), which provides structured guidance on managing AI risks. When integrated with Zero-Trust principles, such frameworks ensure that enterprises not only secure AI from external threats but also prevent internal misuse. For instance, enterprises may require explainability reports for every deployed AI model, documenting decision-making logic to prevent opaque "black box" risks. Regular audits can further verify whether AI systems align with ethical guidelines and compliance requirements, especially in sensitive sectors like healthcare or finance. By embedding governance into AI operations, organizations establish a culture of accountability, reducing the likelihood of misuse while aligning with Zero-Trust's principle of "never trust, always verify."

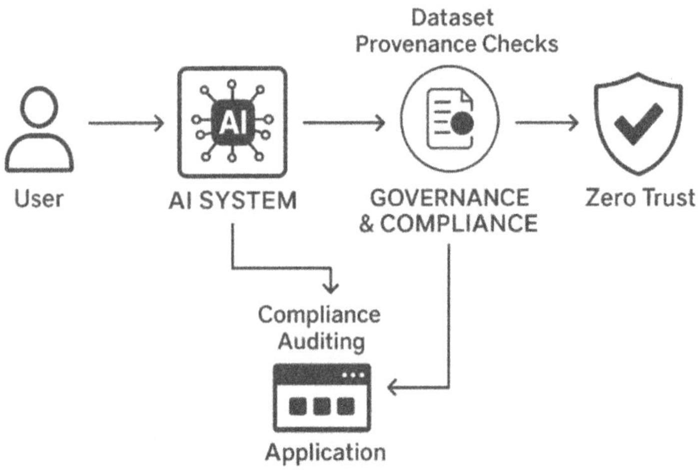

Figure 13-4. *AI Governance and Compliance Within Zero-Trust*

Case Studies of AI Misuse and Lessons Learned

Real-world case studies highlight the necessity of combining AI adoption with Zero-Trust principles. One notable example is the misuse of generative AI tools like GPT within enterprises. Several organizations discovered that employees were pasting sensitive corporate data into public AI chatbots, unintentionally creating data leaks. In response, enterprises enforced Zero-Trust-aligned Data Loss Prevention (DLP) policies to restrict unauthorized AI use and monitor data movement. Similarly, research on adversarial image attacks [21] demonstrated how imperceptible pixel-level changes could trick AI classifiers into producing entirely wrong predictions. These findings underscore the importance of adversarial training and continuous monitoring of AI outputs. Such case studies provide tangible lessons: AI is powerful but fragile, and without Zero-Trust guardrails, enterprises risk exploitation of these weaknesses.

Zero-Trust AI Integration with Cloud Platforms

Cloud providers have recognized these risks and begun embedding Zero-Trust principles into AI services. AWS SageMaker, for example, uses Identity and Access Management (IAM) policies and Virtual Private Cloud (VPC) isolation to control AI training and deployment. Microsoft Azure Machine Learning integrates conditional access policies, private endpoints, and encrypted pipelines to ensure that only authenticated users can interact with sensitive datasets. Google Cloud AI applies its BeyondCorp Zero-Trust model to AI APIs, emphasizing secure, identity-driven access. These features demonstrate how cloud-based Zero-Trust integrations empower enterprises to manage AI securely, even across distributed environments.

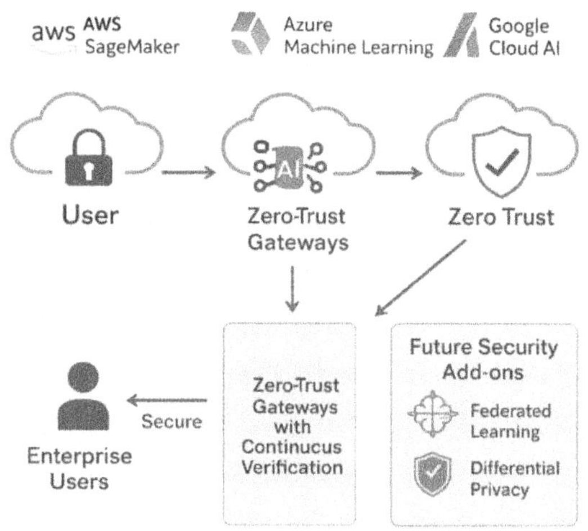

Figure 13-5. *Secure Integration of Enterprise Users with Cloud-Based AI Platforms*

Looking forward, several promising directions will further secure AI within Zero-Trust frameworks. Federated learning enables decentralized model training across multiple devices while preserving local data privacy, reducing centralized attack surfaces. Differential privacy techniques ensure that models cannot be reverse-engineered to reveal individual data points, protecting sensitive user information. Meanwhile, confidential computing enclaves provide runtime protection for AI models, shielding them even while they are being executed in cloud environments. Together, these innovations signal a future in which enterprises can harness AI's power while remaining resilient against evolving threats.

Example Code: AI API Access with Zero-Trust Policy

```
// Zero-Trust AI API Access using an AuthorizationHandler (.NET 10 + Blazor)
// Use in Blazor:
//   [Authorize(Policy = "AiApi.Train")]
//   [Authorize(Policy = "AiApi.ReadOnly")]
// Notes:
// - RBAC: roles (DataScientist, Auditor)
// - ABAC: dataset sensitivity claim (dataset_sensitive=true/false)
// - Zero-Trust: default deny + token is assumed validated by ASP.NET authentication middleware
```

```
using System.Security.Claims;
using System.Threading.Tasks;
using Microsoft.AspNetCore.Authorization;

public sealed class AiApiAccessRequirement(string mode) : IAuthorizationRequirement
{
    public string Mode { get; } = mode; // "train" or "readonly"
}

public sealed class AiApiAccessHandler : AuthorizationHandler<AiApiAccessRequirement>
{
    protected override Task HandleRequirementAsync(
        AuthorizationHandlerContext context,
        AiApiAccessRequirement requirement)
    {
        // 0) Zero-Trust: ensure the identity is authenticated (token validated by middleware)
        if (context.User?.Identity?.IsAuthenticated != true)
            return Task.CompletedTask; // deny (no ctx.Succeed)

        // ABAC input: dataset sensitivity (could come from token claim, route data, or resource metadata)
        // For a short snippet, we read it from a claim: dataset_sensitive = "true"/"false"
        var sensitiveClaim = context.User.FindFirstValue("dataset_sensitive");
        var datasetSensitive = bool.TryParse(sensitiveClaim, out var s) && s;

        // 1) TRAIN mode policy
        // - DataScientist can train ONLY when dataset is NOT sensitive
        if (requirement.Mode == "train")
        {
            if (context.User.IsInRole("DataScientist") && !datasetSensitive)
                context.Succeed(requirement);

            return Task.CompletedTask;
        }

        // 2) READ-ONLY mode policy
        // - Auditor can read regardless of sensitivity
        if (requirement.Mode == "readonly")
        {
            if (context.User.IsInRole("Auditor"))
                context.Succeed(requirement);
            return Task.CompletedTask;
        }
                // 3) Default deny (unknown mode)
        return Task.CompletedTask;
    }
}
```

```
// ------------------------------
// Registration (Program.cs, .NET 10)
// ------------------------------

builder.Services.AddAuthorization(options =>
{
    options.AddPolicy("AiApi.Train",
        p => p.Requirements.Add(new AiApiAccessRequirement("train")));

    options.AddPolicy("AiApi.ReadOnly",
        p => p.Requirements.Add(new AiApiAccessRequirement("readonly")));
});

builder.Services.AddSingleton<IAuthorizationHandler, AiApiAccessHandler>();
```

```
// -----------------------------
// Example: Blazor component usage
// -----------------------------

@attribute[Authorize(Policy = "AiApi.Train")]
< h3 > Training UI </ h3 >

@* A separate page/component could use: *@
@* @attribute [Authorize(Policy = "AiApi.ReadOnly")] *@
```

This illustrates how Zero-Trust principles enforce role, token validity, and dataset sensitivity checks before AI usage.

AI has become central to enterprise strategy, offering unprecedented insights and efficiencies. However, its adoption widens the attack surface, exposing organizations to adversarial attacks, data poisoning, and unauthorized access. By embedding Zero-Trust principles—authentication, authorization, monitoring, governance, and lifecycle security—enterprises can transform AI from a vulnerability into a strategic advantage. With cloud providers incorporating Zero-Trust features and emerging innovations such as federated learning and confidential computing, enterprises are well-positioned to adopt AI responsibly. The future of secure enterprise AI lies not in trust by default but in trust continually earned and verified.

Compliance Frameworks and Zero-Trust Adoption in Enterprises

Need for Regulatory Compliance in Enterprise Security

Enterprises today operate in an environment where data is one of the most valuable assets, but also one of the most regulated. Governments and industry bodies enforce strict compliance requirements to protect sensitive information, ensure consumer trust, and establish accountability for digital operations. Whether it is safeguarding patient health records, processing millions of financial transactions, or storing personal identifiers of citizens, organizations must comply with evolving regulatory landscapes.

Traditional perimeter-based security models often assumed that threats could be kept outside while trusted entities inside were granted broad access. This approach falters in a world where cloud adoption, mobile devices, remote work, and third-party integrations dissolve the notion of a clear perimeter. Compliance frameworks now require organizations to demonstrate continuous, proactive control over every access request, every dataset, and every system interaction [21]. This is where Zero-Trust security provides the structural foundation: it enforces verification at every step, minimizes privileges, and integrates monitoring and auditing directly into system workflows.

By embedding Zero-Trust into enterprise security, compliance shifts from being a reactive checklist exercise to a proactive, ongoing operational principle. Instead of bolting on audits at the end, enterprises align daily operations with compliance expectations. This ensures that organizations are not just avoiding penalties but also building digital trust with regulators, partners, and customers.

Overview of Key Compliance Frameworks

GDPR (General Data Protection Regulation)

The European Union's GDPR remains one of the most influential data protection regulations globally. It emphasizes data minimization, explicit user consent, the right to be forgotten, and strict rules on data transfer outside the EU. Non-compliance leads to severe fines up to 4% of global annual revenue. Zero-Trust principles naturally support GDPR: continuous monitoring ensures that personal data access is logged and attributable, while least-privilege access prevents employees from unnecessarily viewing or exporting personal data. Encryption for data in transit and at rest further ensures compliance with GDPR's requirement for strong safeguards.

HIPAA (Health Insurance Portability and Accountability Act)

HIPAA governs the handling of protected health information (PHI) in the United States. Healthcare enterprises must secure PHI against unauthorized access while maintaining accessibility for legitimate care delivery. Zero-Trust aligns closely with HIPAA by requiring multi-factor authentication (MFA) for healthcare providers, enforcing attribute-based access control (ABAC) so only authorized clinicians can view patient records, and maintaining auditable logs of every access request. With telemedicine and digital health services expanding, Zero-Trust ensures that PHI remains protected even across distributed digital platforms.

PCI DSS (Payment Card Industry Data Security Standard)

Financial enterprises processing credit and debit card data must comply with PCI DSS, which requires encryption, regular vulnerability assessments, and intrusion detection systems. Zero-Trust strengthens PCI DSS compliance by ensuring that only authorized applications and users can access payment systems. Continuous authorization prevents stolen credentials from being reused, while detailed logging provides auditors with a verifiable record of every transaction and system interaction.

NIST Cybersecurity Framework and Zero-Trust Guidelines

The NIST Cybersecurity Framework (CSF) 2.0 defines six core functions: Govern, Identify, Protect, Detect, Respond, and Recover. Building upon this, NIST's Zero-Trust Architecture (SP 800-207) [20] explicitly recommends identity-centric security, micro-segmentation, and continuous verification. Enterprises adopting Zero-Trust through the lens of NIST guidelines create systems that are not only compliant but also resilient against advanced persistent threats. By mapping enterprise security controls to these frameworks, organizations demonstrate maturity in compliance management.

Figure 13-6. *Zero-Trust Integration with GDPR, HIPAA, and PCI DSS*

How Zero-Trust Aligns with Compliance Requirements

Zero-Trust aligns with compliance mandates because it embodies principles that regulatory frameworks demand.

- **Encryption for Data at Rest and Transit**: GDPR, HIPAA, and PCI DSS all mandate strong encryption. Zero-Trust enforces encryption as the default for all communications.

- **Identity Verification**: Every access request, whether from a user, device, or application, requires authentication. This directly supports HIPAA and PCI DSS.
- **Logging and Monitoring**: Zero-Trust ensures that every access event is recorded, enabling full auditability, which is a cornerstone of GDPR and HIPAA compliance.
- **Dynamic Policy Enforcement**: Policies adapt to context, such as user role, device health, or geolocation, aligning with compliance expectations of "reasonable safeguards."

By automating these controls, Zero-Trust transforms compliance from a periodic burden into a continuous security practice.

Role of Auditing, Monitoring, and Logging

Audit logs are the backbone of compliance. Without them, enterprises cannot demonstrate accountability or investigate potential breaches. Zero-Trust architectures inherently produce granular, tamper-resistant logs of every access decision, device posture, and transaction. These logs enable

- GDPR compliance through traceable accountability for data handlers
- HIPAA auditing, ensuring healthcare providers can verify every PHI access
- PCI DSS reporting [21], where every payment system interaction is logged for fraud analysis

Moreover, centralized monitoring platforms use AI to analyze these logs in real time, detecting anomalies such as sudden spikes in data access or suspicious login patterns. This not only supports compliance but also strengthens security posture.

Enterprise Strategies for Achieving Compliance

1. Encryption and data residency controls help protect sensitive data and support compliance with regulations such as GDPR and PCI DSS. Encrypting datasets safeguards them in transit and at rest, while regional storage options ensure that data remains within approved jurisdictions.

2. **Continuous Risk Assessments**: Zero-Trust requires continuous risk evaluation of users, devices, and applications. For example, a login attempt from a new device in a foreign country triggers additional verification. This aligns with PCI DSS, which mandates ongoing vulnerability assessments.

3. **Automated Compliance Monitoring Tools**: Platforms like Splunk, Microsoft Compliance Manager, and AWS Audit Manager automate compliance checks, generating real-time dashboards for regulators and internal auditors. Automation reduces human error and ensures compliance status is always up to date.

Case Examples of Compliance-Driven Zero-Trust Deployments

- **Financial Sector**: A European bank implemented Zero-Trust with GDPR-compliant encryption and continuous monitoring, leading to a noticeable reduction in unauthorized access incidents and smoother audit outcomes.

- **Healthcare**: A hospital network adopted Zero-Trust IAM solutions with MFA and ABAC policies. This ensured compliance with HIPAA while enabling secure telemedicine services, particularly important during the COVID-19 pandemic.

These real-world cases demonstrate that Zero-Trust is not theoretical; it is actively helping enterprises meet compliance while modernizing operations.

Balancing Innovation with Regulatory Obligations

One of the greatest enterprise challenges is balancing compliance with innovation. Overly restrictive compliance controls may slow digital transformation, while insufficient safeguards risk legal penalties and reputational damage. Zero-Trust helps resolve this tension by enabling context-aware, dynamic access. Instead of blanket restrictions, policies adapt to the user, device, and workload. This means developers can innovate quickly without bypassing compliance controls, and sensitive datasets remain protected without stifling productivity.

The future of compliance is becoming more complex. Alongside GDPR, new regulations such as the EU AI Act are emerging, governing the ethical and secure use of artificial intelligence. Enterprises will soon need to prove not only data protection but also algorithmic accountability. Zero-Trust, combined with AI-driven compliance monitoring, will become the backbone of enterprise governance. The future points toward global harmonization of compliance frameworks, where Zero-Trust can act as the universal operational model that satisfies diverse regulations while enabling enterprises to innovate securely.

Example Code: Logging for Compliance

```
// Example Code: Logging for Compliance (C# / .NET 10)
//
// This snippet demonstrates compliance-ready access logging aligned with
// GDPR, HIPAA, and PCI DSS requirements.
//
// Key principles:
// - Immutable, append-only logs
// - Timestamped access records
// - Who / What / Action / Outcome captured
// - Suitable for Zero-Trust audit trails and SIEM ingestion

using System;
using System.IO;

public static class ComplianceLogger
{
    private static readonly string LogFilePath = "compliance_log.txt";

    /// <summary>
    /// Writes a compliance audit log entry for security and regulatory purposes.
    /// </summary>
    /// <param name="user">User or service identity performing the action</param>
    /// <param name="resource">Target resource (dataset, API, record)</param>
    /// <param name="action">Action performed (Read, Update, Export, Delete)</param>
    /// <param name="status">Outcome (Success, Denied, Failed)</param>
    /// <returns>The formatted log entry</returns>
    public static string LogAccess(
        string user,
        string resource,
        string action,
        string status)
    {
        // ISO 8601 timestamp (recommended for audit logs)
        var timestamp = DateTimeOffset.UtcNow.ToString("o");

        // Structured but human-readable log format
        var logEntry =
            $"{timestamp} | User:{user} | Resource:{resource} | Action:{action} | Status:{status}";

        // Append-only logging (Zero-Trust & compliance-friendly)
        File.AppendAllText(LogFilePath, logEntry + Environment.NewLine);

        return logEntry;
    }
}
```

```
// ------------------------------
// Example usage (Console / API / Blazor)
// ------------------------------

Console.WriteLine(
    ComplianceLogger.LogAccess(
        user: "DoctorA",
        resource: "PatientRecord123",
        action: "Read",
        status: "Success"));
// HIPAA compliance log

Console.WriteLine(
    ComplianceLogger.LogAccess(
        user: "Cashier1",
        resource: "PaymentGateway",
        action: "Update",
        status: "Denied"));
// PCI DSS compliance log

Console.WriteLine(
    ComplianceLogger.LogAccess(
        user: "AnalystB",
        resource: "CustomerDataEU",
        action: "Export",
        status: "Denied"));
// GDPR compliance log
```

This sample script simulates a compliance logging system where every access attempt, successful or denied, is recorded with timestamps. Such auditable logs are essential for GDPR accountability, HIPAA auditing, and PCI DSS transaction tracking. In enterprise deployments, these logs would feed into centralized SIEM systems for real-time monitoring and compliance reporting.

Compliance is no longer optional; it is the foundation of enterprise trust and business continuity. Frameworks such as GDPR, HIPAA, PCI DSS, and NIST provide critical guardrails for handling sensitive data, but enforcing them requires an adaptable, proactive approach. Zero-Trust maps seamlessly to these requirements, embedding encryption, auditing, access control, and monitoring into daily operations. By adopting Zero-Trust, enterprises not only meet compliance obligations but also build resilience against cyber threats. Looking forward, as AI-specific regulations emerge, Zero-Trust will evolve into the scalable compliance backbone of the digital enterprise, ensuring that organizations remain secure, innovative, and trusted in an increasingly regulated world.

CHAPTER 14

Case Study: AI-Enhanced Enterprise App

Designing and Architecting the AI-Enhanced Blazor Enterprise Application

This case study explores a cloud-based enterprise application in a regulated domain, such as financial services or healthcare, detailing its architecture, primary actors (end users, administrators, and external services), data types (transactional, personal, and operational), and key constraints. The solution uses a modern web UI framework with integrated AI capabilities to support real-time insights and decision-making.

From a non-functional perspective, the design emphasizes performance (low-latency interactions), scalability (handling variable workloads), availability (high uptime and fault tolerance), and security (Zero-Trust principles with strict access controls). It also addresses compliance requirements, ensuring data protection, auditability, and adherence to regulatory standards.

A. Prasad and H. Singh, *Advanced Blazor Architecture with .NET 10 and Azure OpenAI*,
https://doi.org/10.1007/979-8-8688-2518-7_14

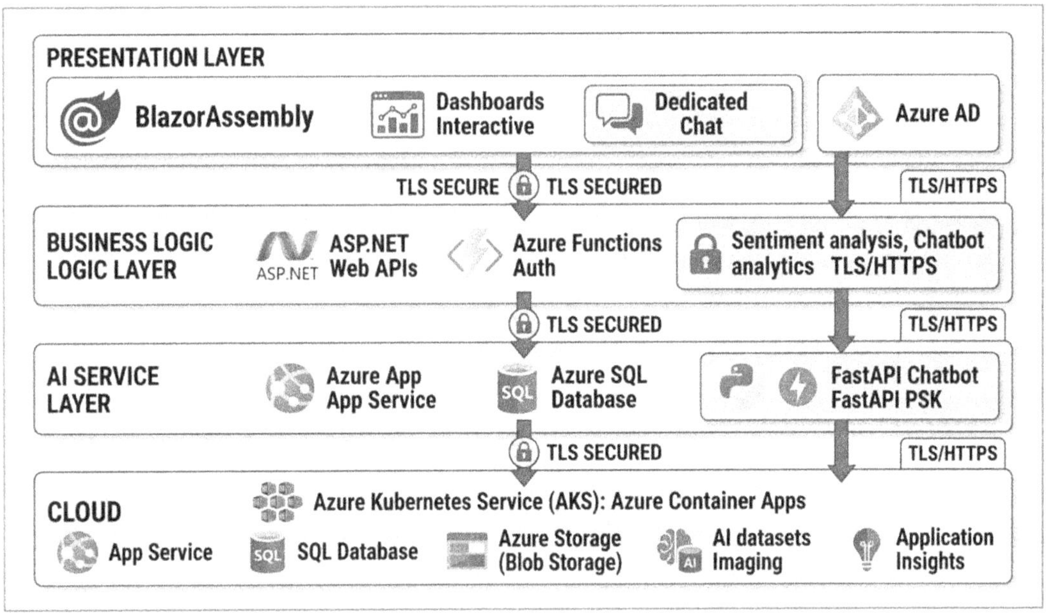

***Figure 14-1.** Overall System Framework*

Why Blazor for Enterprise Applications

Blazor, a framework developed by Microsoft, enables developers to create modern, interactive web applications using C# instead of JavaScript. This approach offers several advantages for enterprises that are heavily invested in the .NET ecosystem.

- **Unified Development Model**: By allowing both front-end and back-end development in C#, Blazor reduces the need for context switching between multiple programming languages.
- **Reusable Components:** Enterprises benefit from modular and maintainable UI designs through Blazor's component-driven architecture.
- **Security Integration**: Blazor provides native authentication and authorization capabilities, seamlessly integrating with Microsoft Entra I.
- **Cross-Platform Support:** It runs on both WebAssembly (WASM) and server-side rendering, providing flexibility for deployment.
- **Cloud Readiness:** Blazor is optimized for Azure hosting models such as Azure App Service and Azure Static Web Apps.

In this architecture, Blazor serves as the presentation layer, while Python-based services power the intelligence layer, integrated through synchronous REST calls for real-time interactions and asynchronous jobs for background processing. Azure provides the backbone for governance, scalability, and compliance.

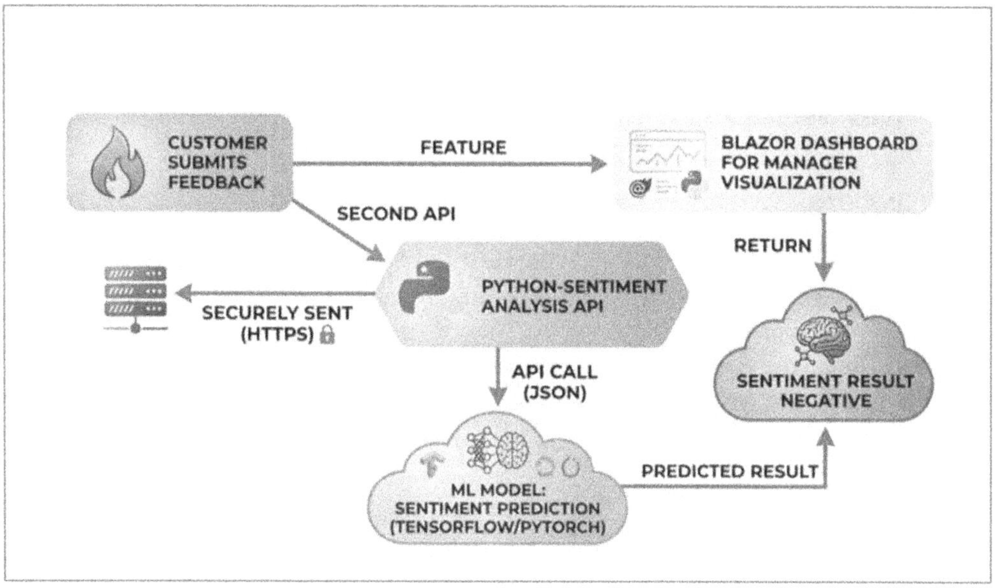

Figure 14-2. *AI Feature Workflow Diagram*

Target AI Features for the Enterprise App

The AI-enhanced enterprise application is designed to integrate three core AI-driven features that address critical business needs:

- **AI Chatbot for Customer Support:** Provides real-time assistance by leveraging NLP models trained on enterprise FAQs, reducing support costs.
- **Predictive Analytics Dashboard**: Implements machine learning models to forecast KPIs such as sales, customer churn, or demand trends. Results are visualized in interactive Blazor dashboards.
- **Sentiment Analysis of Customer Feedback:** Automates the processing of user reviews and feedback, classifying them as positive, negative, or neutral to help management track customer satisfaction.

These features not only enhance user experience but also allow enterprises to make data-driven decisions effectively.

System Architecture Overview

The system architecture is structured into four layers:

- **Presentation Layer (Blazor App):** Provides dashboards, chatbot UI, and reports.
- **Business Logic Layer (ASP.NET Core/Azure Functions):** Manages authentication, authorization, and request orchestration between Blazor and AI services.
- **AI Service Layer (Python APIs):** Implements machine learning models (sentiment analysis, prediction). These APIs are exposed via FastAPI/Flask for integration.
- **Cloud Infrastructure (Azure):** Provides compute, storage, databases, and monitoring using AKS, Azure SQL, Azure Blob Storage, Application Insights, and more.

Security and Zero-Trust Design

Since enterprise applications process sensitive data, security is a cornerstone of the design. Key measures include

- **Authentication and Authorization**: Enforced via AAD and OAuth2.
- **Least Privilege Access**: Enforced with RBAC and ABAC policies.
- **Encryption:** End-to-end encryption with TLS 1.3 for data in transit and AES-256 for data at rest.
- **Zero-Trust:** Every request undergoes identity, device, and context validation.

This design aligns with relevant regulatory requirements, such as data protection and audit controls, based on the needs of the target domain.

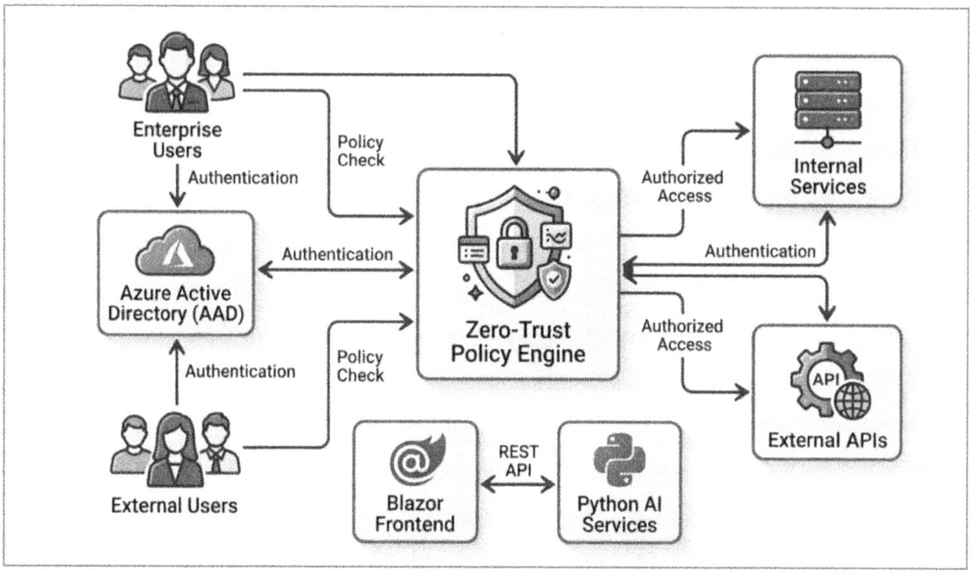

Figure 14-3. Security and Zero-Trust Architecture

Example Workflow

- A customer submits product feedback in the Blazor app.
- The text is securely transmitted through the ASP.NET Core layer to a Python-based sentiment analysis API, ensuring controlled access and consistent enforcement of security policies.
- The API processes the input using a trained ML model and returns the sentiment.
- Results are aggregated and displayed in the Blazor dashboard in real time.

This workflow demonstrates how AI can be embedded into everyday enterprise operations.

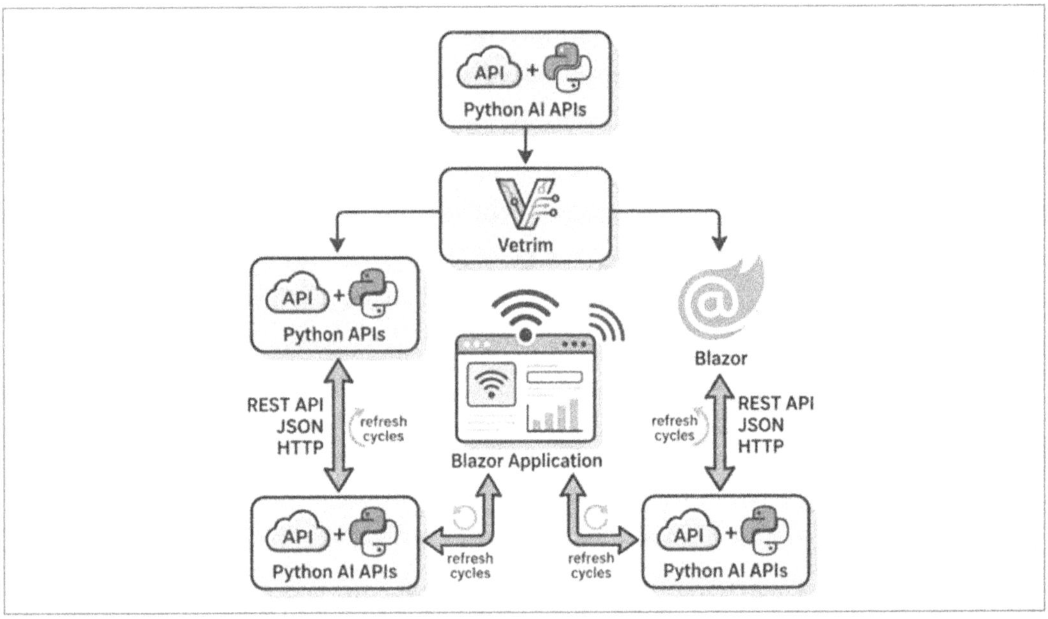

Figure 14-4. *Python AI API Integration*

The diagram illustrates a layered integration between the Blazor application and Python-based AI services. Blazor acts as the central presentation layer, handling user interactions and UI rendering. It communicates with back-end services through REST APIs using JSON over HTTP.

At the core, the Blazor application interacts with multiple Python AI APIs to process intelligence workloads such as analysis and predictions. These interactions occur in two patterns: synchronous calls for real-time responses and refresh cycles for continuous updates.

An intermediary processing layer (e.g., data orchestration or transformation component) coordinates requests between the UI and AI services, ensuring consistent data flow and response handling. This design enables modular scalability, where AI services can evolve independently while the UI remains responsive and secure.

Python Example: Sentiment Analysis Model

```python
# sentiment_model.py
# Import required libraries for data handling, text processing,
# model training, and saving the model
import pandas as pd
from sklearn.feature_extraction.text import TfidfVectorizer
from sklearn.linear_model import LogisticRegression
from sklearn.pipeline import Pipeline
import joblib

# Step 1: Create a small sample dataset of customer feedback with sentiment labels
data = {
    "text": [
        "The product is excellent and works perfectly",
        "Terrible service, I will never buy again",
        "Average experience, nothing special",
        "Loved the quick delivery and quality packaging",
        "The system crashes frequently and frustrates me"
    ],
    "sentiment": ["positive", "negative", "neutral", "positive", "negative"]
}

# Convert the dataset into a DataFrame
df = pd.DataFrame(data)

# Step 2: Build a machine learning pipeline
# TF-IDF converts text into numeric vectors and Logistic Regression performs classification
model_pipeline = Pipeline([
    ("tfidf", TfidfVectorizer()),
    ("classifier", LogisticRegression())
])

# Step 3: Train the model using the dataset
model_pipeline.fit(df["text"], df["sentiment"])

# Step 4: Save the trained model for later use in applications or APIs
joblib.dump(model_pipeline, "sentiment_model.pkl")

# Step 5: Test the model with a sample sentence
sample_text = ["The new update is amazing!"]
prediction = model_pipeline.predict(sample_text)

# Print the predicted sentiment
print("Prediction:", prediction[0])
```

This model uses TF-IDF for feature extraction and Logistic Regression for classification. The trained model is saved and later deployed as a REST API for integration with Blazor.

Benefits of the Proposed Design

- **Scalability**: AI APIs hosted on Azure can autoscale independently.
- **Security**: Azure AD ensures enterprise-grade identity management.
- **Flexibility:** The architecture allows new AI modules (e.g., fraud detection) to be added.

- **Compliance**: Monitoring and logging ensure regulatory alignment.
- **Developer Efficiency:** Using C# for UI and Python for AI enables cross-team collaboration.

Designing an AI-enhanced enterprise application using Blazor and Azure requires balancing innovation, security, and scalability. This architecture demonstrates how enterprises can leverage Blazor for a unified UI experience while harnessing Python AI services for intelligence. With Zero-Trust principles and cloud-native deployment, the design ensures compliance, security, and extensibility. This lays the foundation for implementing and integrating AI APIs in the next stages of the case study.

Implementing AI Services and APIs in Python for Blazor Integration

In the modern enterprise ecosystem, artificial intelligence (AI) is no longer an optional enhancement but a necessity for competitive advantage. By enabling predictive analytics, customer sentiment monitoring, and intelligent recommendations, AI directly contributes to better decision-making, operational efficiency, and improved customer satisfaction. While Blazor provides a robust .NET-based front-end framework for enterprise-grade applications, Python remains the language of choice for AI model development due to its rich ecosystem of machine learning (ML) and natural language processing (NLP) libraries.

This section explores how AI modules such as sentiment analysis, forecasting, and recommendation engines can be built in Python, exposed as versioned RESTful APIs with well-defined schema contracts, secured through standard authentication mechanisms, and integrated with a Blazor front end. We also discuss enterprise workflows that demonstrate real-world use cases and highlight how Azure Machine Learning (AML) can be leveraged for secure deployment at scale.

Building AI Modules in Python

The first step is the development of core AI modules. These modules represent the intelligence layer of the enterprise architecture and can serve multiple business functions.

- **Natural Language Processing (NLP) for Sentiment Analysis:** Sentiment analysis allows enterprises to classify customer feedback into positive, negative, or neutral categories. Using scikit-learn, spaCy, or transformers, the model can process text data and return insights for customer experience management.
- **Forecasting Model for Business KPIs**: Forecasting models built using statsmodels, Prophet, or LSTMs in TensorFlow can predict key business indicators such as sales, churn, or demand. Such models empower managers to take proactive actions based on predictive insights.
- **Recommendation System**: A collaborative or content-based filtering system can recommend products or services to customers based on their past interactions. Libraries like surprise, implicit, or deep learning methods can be applied here.

Each of these models is encapsulated in Python modules that can later be exposed through APIs for consumption by enterprise apps.

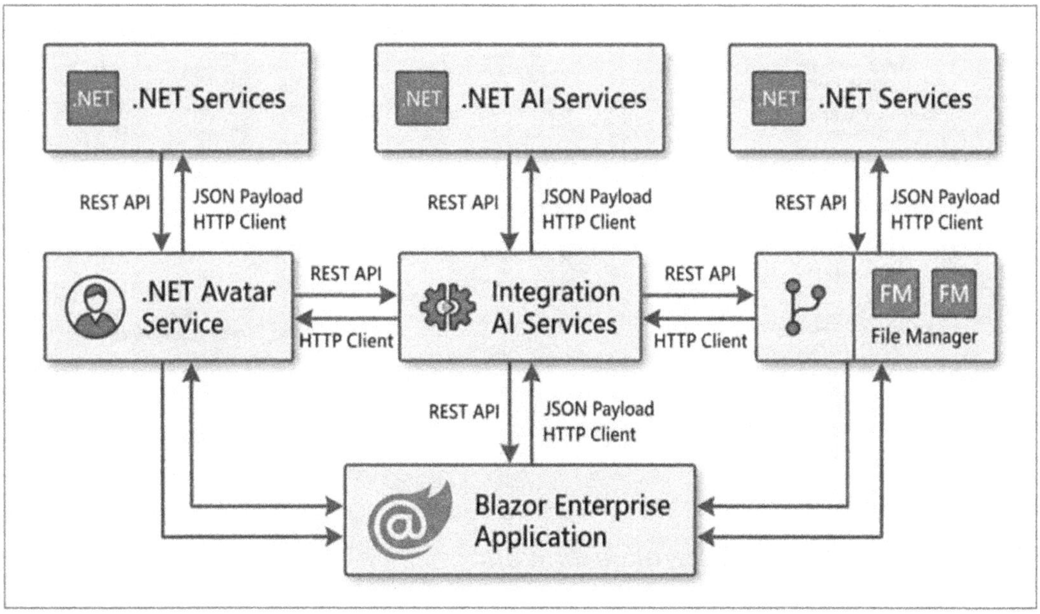

Figure 14-5. *AI Service Layer Architecture*

Wrapping AI Logic As REST APIs

To allow the Blazor application to interact with AI services, Python models must be exposed as RESTful endpoints. FastAPI is well-suited for this scenario due to its high performance, built-in validation, dependency injection support, schema enforcement, automatic OpenAPI documentation, and seamless handling of asynchronous requests.

For example:

- **POST /predict-sentiment**: Accepts text input and returns sentiment classification
- **POST /forecast-sales:** Accepts CSV/JSON data and returns sales forecasts
- **POST /recommend-products:** Accepts customer ID and returns a ranked list of recommendations

By standardizing all AI services as APIs, enterprises achieve modularity, scalability, and maintainability.

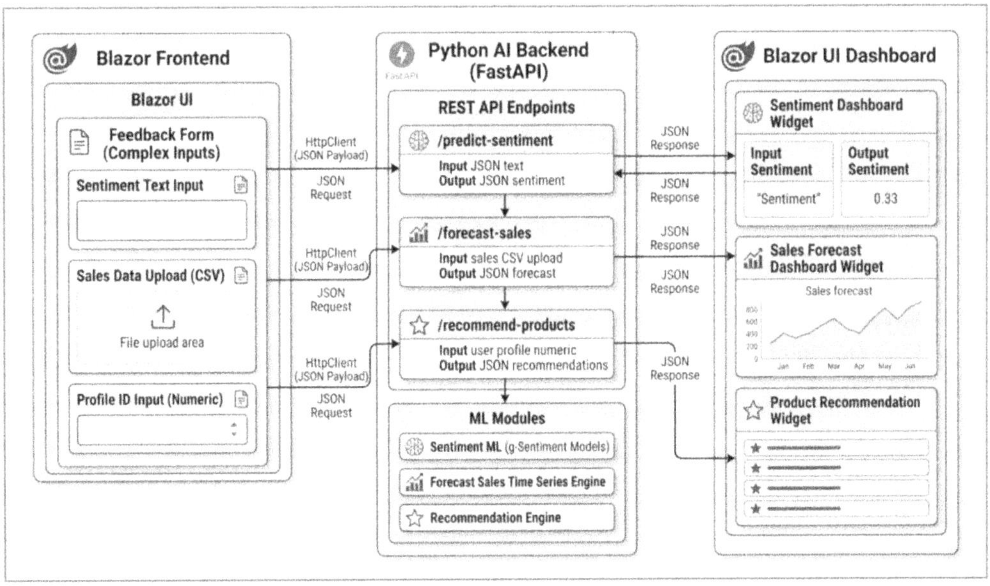

Figure 14-6. *REST API Integration with Blazor*

Connecting Blazor Front End with Python Back-End APIs

In the architecture, Blazor acts as the UI layer, and the Python APIs act as the AI service layer. Integration occurs through standard HTTP requests.

- A Blazor component (e.g., feedback form) captures input and sends it as a JSON payload via HttpClient to the Python API endpoint.
- The Python API processes the input using the ML model and returns a prediction or recommendation as JSON.
- The Blazor component then updates the UI (dashboard, chatbot, recommendation widget) with the returned result.

This approach keeps AI logic separate from the front end, allowing models to evolve independently. It also supports resilience through timeouts, retries, and circuit breaking while enabling backward-compatible API changes without impacting the Blazor app.

Example Enterprise Workflows

1. **Sentiment Analysis of Customer Feedback**
    - A user submits feedback in the Blazor application.
    - The application sends a POST request to /predict-sentiment.
    - The API evaluates the text using an NLP model and returns a label (positive/negative/neutral).
    - The Blazor dashboard displays aggregated customer sentiment to managers in real time.
2. **Predictive Analytics for Sales Forecasting**
    - A business analyst uploads sales data through a Blazor interface.
    - The file is sent to /forecast-sales.
    - The Python API runs a time-series forecasting model and predicts next quarter trends.
    - Results are visualized as charts within Blazor's interactive dashboard.
3. **Recommendation System for Personalized Experiences**
    - A customer logs into the Blazor portal.
    - Their profile ID is sent to /recommend-products.
    - The Python back end computes product recommendations.
    - The Blazor app displays a tailored recommendation list, boosting personalization.

Azure AI Integration

While APIs can run locally or on servers, enterprises benefit from deploying models on Azure Machine Learning (AML) for scalability and governance.

- **Training and Deployment**: Models are trained in Azure ML workspaces and deployed as managed endpoints.
- **Security:** Azure Active Directory integrates with AML to control access.
- **Scalability:** Azure Kubernetes Service (AKS) autoscaling ensures APIs can handle peak loads.
- **Monitoring:** Application Insights captures logs, metrics, and anomalies.

Blazor applications can consume these AML-hosted endpoints the same way as local FastAPI endpoints, ensuring consistent integration.

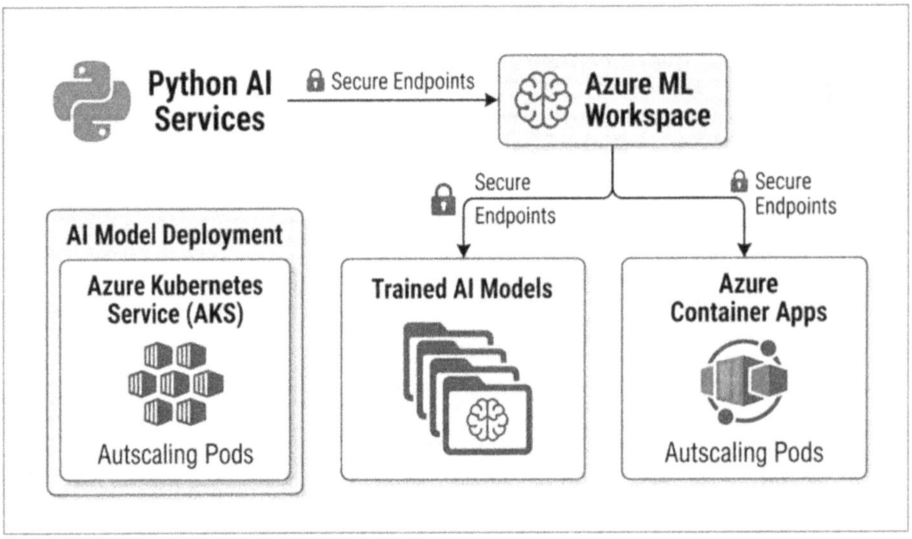

Figure 14-7. *Azure AI Deployment and Monitoring*

Example Python Code: FastAPI REST Service

Below is an example of wrapping a sentiment analysis model into a REST API using FastAPI:

```python
# ai_service.py
from fastapi import FastAPI
from pydantic import BaseModel
import joblib

# Load the trained sentiment model from disk.
# This model is assumed to be created earlier and saved using joblib.
model = joblib.load("sentiment_model.pkl")


# Define the structure of incoming request data.
# Pydantic automatically validates the JSON payload.
class Feedback(BaseModel):
    text: str


# Create the FastAPI application instance.
# The metadata helps generate automatic API documentation.
app = FastAPI(title="Enterprise AI Service", version="1.0")


@app.post("/predict-sentiment")
def predict_sentiment(feedback: Feedback):
    """
    Accept text input and return the predicted sentiment
    using the pre-trained machine learning model.
    """

    # Run inference on the incoming text
    prediction = model.predict([feedback.text])[0]

    # Return both the original input and predicted sentiment
    return {
        "text": feedback.text,
        "sentiment": prediction
    }
```

Benefits of FastAPI Integration

FastAPI has emerged as a preferred framework for building modern AI-driven REST APIs in Python due to its combination of speed, simplicity, and enterprise-readiness. In an enterprise Blazor application architecture, FastAPI serves as the intermediary between AI models and the front-end interface, ensuring that intelligence is delivered in real time while maintaining robustness, security, and scalability.

Speed and Performance: One of the most significant advantages of FastAPI is its high-performance capability, largely due to its asynchronous request handling. Unlike traditional synchronous frameworks such as Flask or Django, FastAPI leverages Python's async capabilities, enabling the API to handle multiple requests concurrently without blocking. In the context of AI, where model inference or data preprocessing can take time, asynchronous execution ensures that requests do not pile up, thus reducing latency and improving the end-user experience. For example, when multiple users submit feedback for sentiment analysis simultaneously, FastAPI can process all incoming requests in parallel, returning predictions efficiently without slowing down the system. This responsiveness is crucial for enterprise applications that require near-real-time analytics, such as predictive dashboards or AI-powered customer support chatbots.

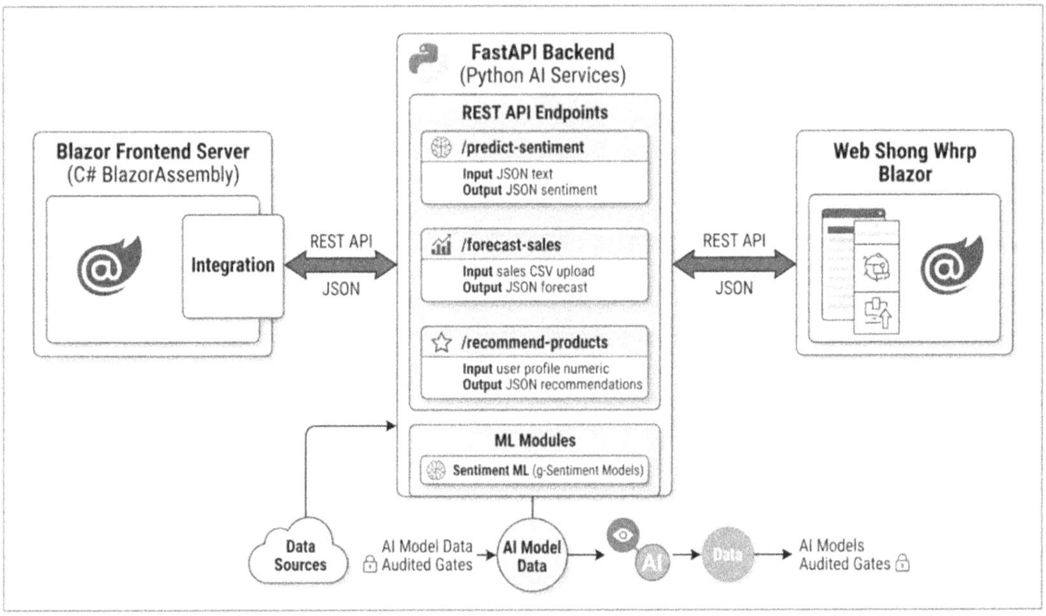

Figure 14-8. *FastAPI Benefits and Enterprise Workflow*

Automatic Documentation with Swagger/Open API: FastAPI automatically generates interactive API documentation using Swagger or ReDoc, a feature particularly beneficial in enterprise settings. These autogenerated documents serve as both a developer guide and a testing platform, allowing teams to validate endpoints without writing extensive manual documentation. This facilitates collaboration between back-end AI engineers and front-end Blazor developers. For instance, a Blazor team integrating a predictive sales API can quickly review expected input formats, response structures, and test sample payloads directly from the documentation interface, reducing miscommunication and speeding up development cycles.

Interoperability with Blazor and JSON Payloads: FastAPI seamlessly integrates with Blazor applications using standard JSON payloads. Since Blazor relies on HTTP-based communication through HttpClient for API calls, FastAPI's JSON serialization ensures that data exchanged between the front end and AI services is clean, structured, and easily consumable. This interoperability allows developers to focus on AI model logic and front-end design independently, without worrying about data format conversion or compatibility issues. Additionally, it enables the creation of reusable APIs that can serve multiple clients, including mobile applications, dashboards, and third-party services.

Scalability and Containerization: FastAPI applications can be easily containerized using Docker and deployed to cloud environments such as Azure Kubernetes Service (AKS) or Azure Container Apps. This supports horizontal scaling, allowing the system to handle increased traffic by deploying additional instances of AI APIs. In an enterprise scenario where usage patterns fluctuate, for instance, during product launches or financial reporting periods, the ability to scale the AI service layer independently from the front end ensures consistent performance and resource optimization. Containerization also simplifies CI/CD pipelines, enabling automated deployment of updated models or API features while maintaining minimal downtime.

Challenges and Mitigations

Despite its benefits, integrating AI services with FastAPI introduces several challenges, particularly in enterprise environments with strict performance, security, and reliability requirements.

Latency: Real-time AI predictions, especially those involving deep learning models or large datasets, can introduce noticeable latency. Users may experience delays while waiting for model inference results, which can impact user experience. Mitigation strategies include implementing caching mechanisms for frequently requested computations and optimizing model inference with asynchronous processing or batch prediction techniques. For example, sentiment predictions for common phrases can be cached, allowing repeated requests to return instantaneously without reprocessing the same text. Additionally, deploying AI models with lightweight architectures or GPU acceleration in Azure ML can further reduce response times.

Model Drift: Predictive AI models are subject to model drift, where the accuracy of predictions declines over time due to changes in input data patterns or evolving business dynamics. For instance, a sales forecasting model trained on historical data may become less accurate during unprecedented market fluctuations. Mitigation involves establishing continuous retraining pipelines in Azure ML that automatically update models using recent data. By implementing version control, monitoring model performance metrics, and triggering retraining when accuracy falls below thresholds, enterprises can maintain high reliability and trust in their AI outputs.

Security Concerns: Exposing AI APIs publicly without safeguards can introduce vulnerabilities, including unauthorized access to sensitive enterprise data or intellectual property. Mitigation strategies focus on implementing OAuth2-based authentication alongside Microsoft Entra ID–based authorization to enforce secure and consistent access control, ensuring that only verified users or services can access APIs. FastAPI supports dependency injection for authentication workflows, allowing seamless enforcement of role-based access control (RBAC) or attribute-based access control (ABAC). Additionally, TLS encryption for all API communications and network isolation via virtual networks in Azure further reduces attack surfaces and aligns with enterprise Zero-Trust security policies.

FastAPI provides a powerful, efficient, and scalable framework for deploying AI services in enterprise Blazor applications. Its asynchronous handling, automatic documentation, and seamless JSON integration enable rapid development and smooth collaboration across teams. Containerization and cloud deployment enhance scalability, while built-in support for security and interoperability addresses enterprise-grade requirements. At the same time, careful consideration of challenges such as latency, model drift, and API security, combined with Azure ML integration and Zero-Trust practices, ensures that the AI services remain performant, reliable, and secure. By leveraging FastAPI effectively, enterprises can unlock real-time AI-driven insights without compromising user experience or operational integrity.

Implementing AI services and APIs in Python for Blazor integration creates a powerful enterprise architecture that blends user-friendly interfaces with intelligent decision-making capabilities. Sentiment analysis, forecasting, and recommendation systems provide immediate business value, while FastAPI ensures scalable, maintainable RESTful integration. By deploying APIs to Azure Machine Learning and securing them with Zero-Trust principles, enterprises achieve compliance, resilience, and scalability.

The workflows outlined here illustrate how AI transforms enterprise operations, turning customer feedback into actionable insights, enabling data-driven forecasts, and delivering personalized experiences. With the foundation laid, the next stage will involve deploying and orchestrating these services securely in Azure Cloud as part of a full enterprise pipeline.

Deploying and Securing the AI-Enhanced Blazor Application on Azure

Once an AI-enhanced Blazor enterprise application is designed and AI services are implemented in Python, the next crucial step is deployment and security. Azure Cloud offers a comprehensive ecosystem for hosting web applications, AI services, and enterprise-grade databases while supporting security, scalability, and observability. Deploying an AI-driven Blazor app to Azure requires careful planning around infrastructure, containerization, CI/CD pipelines, and Zero-Trust security principles to ensure that the system remains performant, compliant, and resilient against cyber threats.

In enterprise contexts, deployment is not just about putting an app live; it also encompasses maintaining high availability, enabling disaster recovery, ensuring data compliance, and securing both user and machine identities interacting with AI APIs.

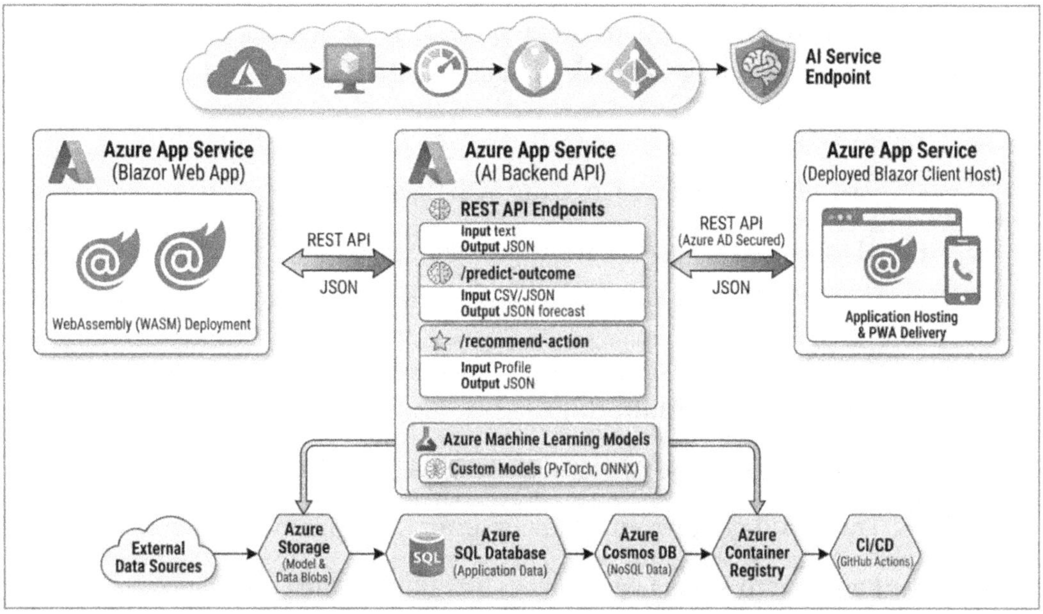

Figure 14-9. *Azure Deployment Architecture for Blazor + AI*

Azure Deployment Architecture

The recommended deployment architecture involves separating the application into distinct layers for flexibility and scalability:

1. **Blazor Presentation Layer**
    - Hosted on Azure App Service (for WebAssembly or server-side Blazor)
    - Enables HTTPS endpoints for secure user interactions
    - Integrates with Azure Active Directory (AAD) for authentication
2. **Python AI Services Layer**
    - Hosted on Azure Kubernetes Service (AKS) or Azure Container Apps
    - Exposes AI endpoints via FastAPI REST APIs
    - Autoscaling enabled to handle spikes in requests, e.g., multiple users submitting feedback simultaneously
3. **Data Layer**
    - Structured data stored in Azure SQL Database
    - AI training datasets and unstructured logs in Azure Blob Storage
    - Encryption at rest using Azure Storage Service Encryption (SSE) with AES-256
4. **Observability and Monitoring**
    - Azure Monitor and Application Insights for telemetry
    - Tracks API performance, latency, error rates, and usage patterns
    - Logs sent to Azure Log Analytics for auditing and compliance reporting
5. **Security Layer**
    - Zero-Trust principles applied to all interactions
    - Every API call and user action authenticated and authorized

- Encryption in transit is secured using modern TLS, enforced end-to-end across communication paths
- Conditional access policies via AAD

Continuous Integration/Continuous Deployment (CI/CD)
Enterprise deployments benefit from automated CI/CD pipelines to ensure consistency, reduce errors, and enable rapid updates:

1. **Repository Structure**
    - Separate directories for Blazor front end, Python AI services, and infrastructure-as-code scripts
    - GitHub Actions or Azure DevOps pipelines used to automate builds
2. **Blazor Deployment**
    - CI pipeline builds the Blazor app and generates WebAssembly assets.
    - CD pipeline deploys the assets to Azure App Service using az webapp deploy commands.
3. **Python AI Services Deployment**
    - Dockerfile created for Python services.
    - CI pipeline builds Docker images and pushes to Azure Container Registry (ACR).
    - CD pipeline deploys containers to AKS with autoscaling and load balancing enabled.
4. **Infrastructure as Code**
    - ARM templates or Terraform scripts define App Service, AKS, databases, and storage resources.
    - Version-controlled infrastructure ensures reproducibility and auditability.

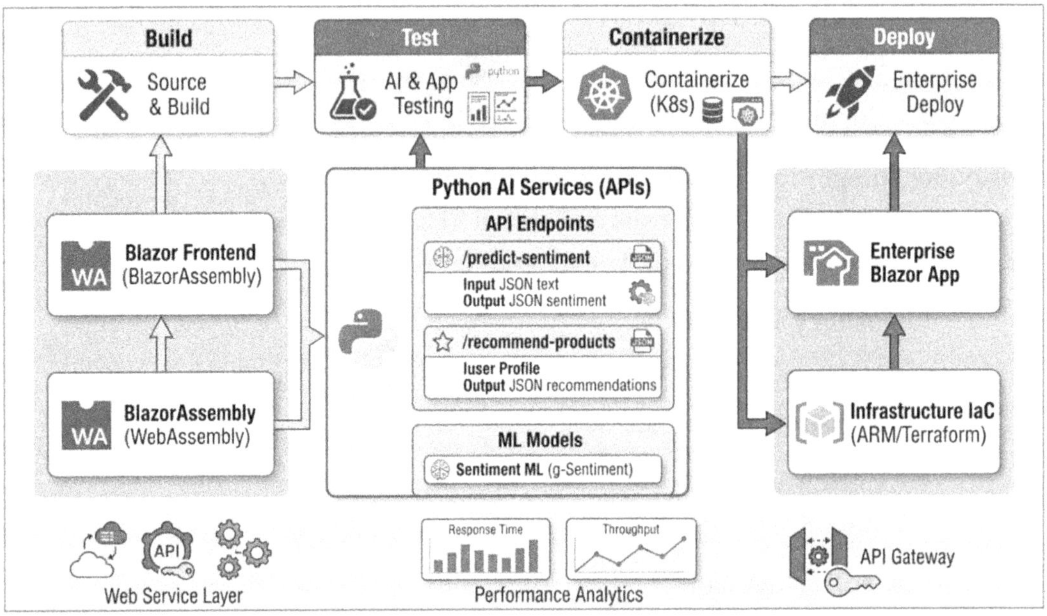

Figure 14-10. CI/CD Pipeline for Enterprise AI Application

Security and Zero-Trust Implementation

Securing the enterprise application is critical, especially for AI-enhanced services that handle sensitive business data.

1. **Identity and Access Management**

    - Microsoft Entra ID integration supports end-user sign-in for the Blazor app and secure workload authentication for the Python APIs.
    - Enforces multi-factor authentication (MFA) for administrative users.
    - Role-based access control (RBAC) and attribute-based access control (ABAC) policies applied to datasets and AI endpoints.

2. **API Security**

    - FastAPI endpoints secured using OAuth2 tokens or certificate-based authentication
    - Each API request validated for user identity, device compliance, and network context (core Zero-Trust principle)

3. **Data Encryption**

    - **At Rest**: Azure SQL Database and Blob Storage encrypted using AES-256
    - **In Transit**: TLS 1.3 enforced for all front-end/back-end communication

4. **Network Security**

    - Private endpoints used to restrict access to databases and AI services
    - Network security groups (NSGs) applied for granular traffic control
    - AKS deployed in Virtual Networks (VNets) for isolation from the public internet

5. **Monitoring and Incident Response**

    - Real-time logging and alerting via Azure Monitor
    - AI model usage monitored for anomalies (e.g., unusual prediction patterns or unauthorized access attempts)
    - Integration with SIEM systems for compliance and forensic investigations

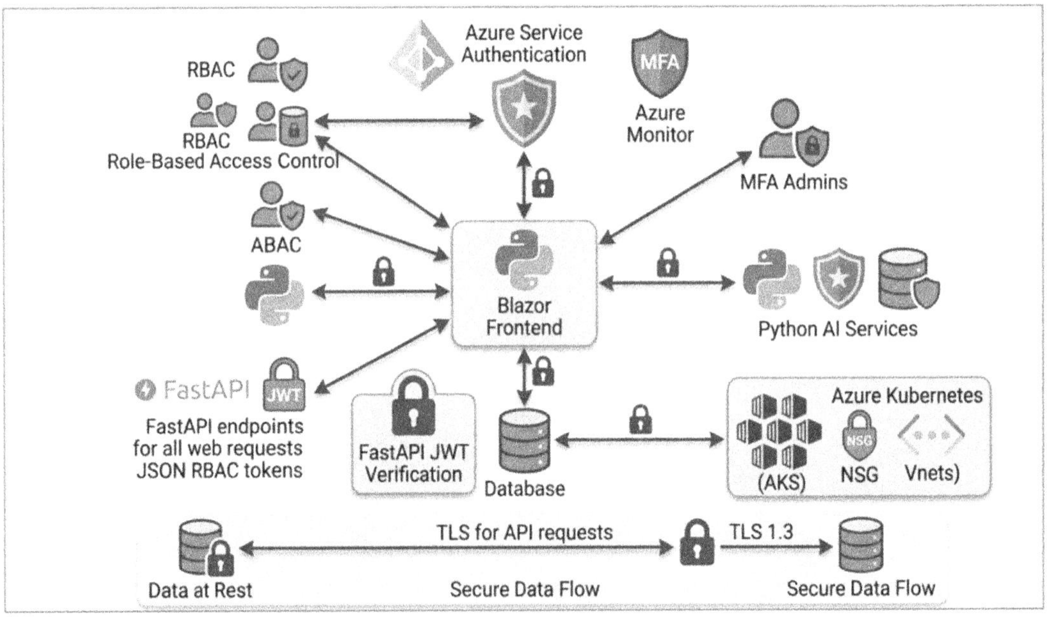

Figure 14-11. *Zero-Trust Security Implementation*

Example: Python REST API Integration with Azure AD

Here's an example of how Python-based FastAPI AI services can validate Azure AD tokens before returning predictions:

```python
# ai_service.py

from fastapi import FastAPI, Header, HTTPException
import jwt  # Library used for decoding JWT tokens

# Create FastAPI application
app = FastAPI()

# Public key used to verify Azure AD issued tokens
AZURE_AD_PUBLIC_KEY = "YOUR_AZURE_AD_PUBLIC_KEY"


def verify_token(token: str):
    # Decode and validate the JWT token
    try:
        payload = jwt.decode(
            token,
            AZURE_AD_PUBLIC_KEY,
            algorithms=["RS256"],
            audience="YOUR_APP_ID"
        )
        return payload
    except jwt.ExpiredSignatureError:
        raise HTTPException(status_code=401, detail="Token expired")
    except jwt.InvalidTokenError:
        raise HTTPException(status_code=401, detail="Invalid token")


@app.post("/predict-sentiment")
def predict_sentiment(text: str, authorization: str = Header(None)):

    # Ensure Authorization header exists
    if not authorization:
        raise HTTPException(status_code=401, detail="Authorization header missing")

    # Extract token from "Bearer <token>"
    token = authorization.split(" ")[1]

    # Validate the token
    verify_token(token)

    # Simple sentiment logic (placeholder for real AI model)
    sentiment = "positive" if "good" in text.lower() else "negative"

    return {"text": text, "sentiment": sentiment}
```

Explanation

- The FastAPI service checks each request for a valid AAD JWT token.
- Unauthorized or expired tokens are rejected (Zero-Trust enforcement).
- Once verified, the API executes AI inference and returns results securely.

Azure AI Integration and Monitoring

Enterprises increasingly rely on advanced machine learning (ML) models to drive actionable insights and automate decision-making processes. Deploying these models effectively in a production environment requires not only robust infrastructure but also secure, monitored, and scalable access. Azure Machine Learning provides a comprehensive platform for managing the entire ML lifecycle from model development and training to deployment, monitoring, and version control. By leveraging Azure's capabilities, enterprises can ensure that their AI services are production-ready while maintaining compliance with security and regulatory standards.

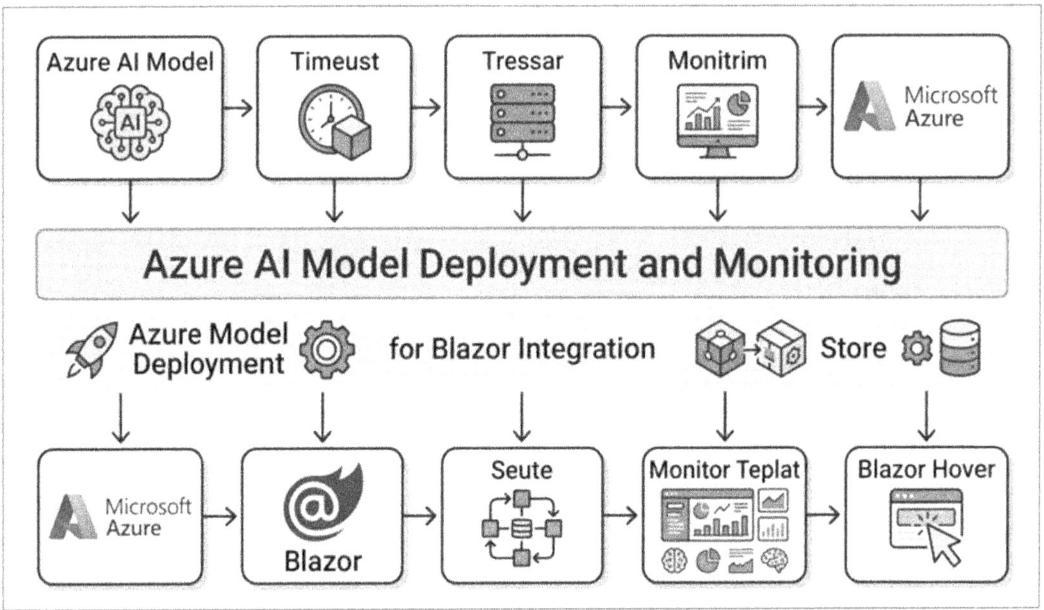

Figure 14-12. Azure AI Integration and Monitoring Workflow

Once ML models are trained, they can be deployed to Azure Machine Learning endpoints, which expose the models through secure REST APIs. These endpoints allow Blazor applications or other client systems to interact with the AI services in real time. For instance, customer feedback submitted via a Blazor UI can trigger a sentiment analysis request to a Python-based ML endpoint, which returns the predicted sentiment to the user interface. Exposing models as APIs decouples the AI logic from the application front end, promoting modularity and enabling independent scaling of the AI services without affecting the user-facing Blazor application.

A key aspect of deploying AI in production is monitoring model performance and usage. Azure Machine Learning provides endpoint logging and versioning, allowing enterprises to track which models are being used, by whom, and how frequently. This not only ensures accountability but also facilitates the detection of model drift, a phenomenon where a model's performance degrades over time due to changes in input data distributions. Monitoring endpoints enables proactive model retraining and tuning, ensuring that predictions remain accurate and reliable. Furthermore, integrating Azure Application Insights provides detailed telemetry on API performance, including request latency, throughput, error rates, and resource utilization. This visibility is crucial for maintaining the quality of service and ensuring a smooth user experience.

Benefits of This Deployment Approach

Scalability: Separating the front-end (Blazor) and back-end AI services allows each layer to scale independently. For example, during peak usage periods, AI endpoints can autoscale without impacting the Blazor application, ensuring consistent performance for all users. Azure's managed services such as App Service and AKS (Azure Kubernetes Service) further facilitate dynamic scaling and load balancing, accommodating enterprise-grade workloads.

Security: Security is a top priority when deploying AI services that interact with sensitive enterprise data. A Zero-Trust approach ensures that every request whether from a user, device, or application is authenticated and authorized. Azure Active Directory (AAD) integration enforces role-based and attribute-based access controls, while all communication channels utilize encryption protocols such as TLS 1.3. FastAPI endpoints in Python can verify JWT tokens issued by AAD, ensuring that only authorized clients can access AI services.

Compliance: Enterprises often operate under strict regulatory requirements such as GDPR, HIPAA, or PCI DSS. The deployment architecture inherently supports compliance through centralized logging, audit trails, and secure access controls. Every API call and data transaction is recorded and monitored, providing verifiable evidence for internal audits or external regulatory inspections.

Resilience: Cloud-native deployment strategies enhance system resilience. Azure's managed services provide built-in redundancy, high availability, and disaster recovery capabilities. Containers deployed on AKS or Azure Container Apps can be automatically redistributed across nodes in the event of failures, minimizing downtime and ensuring continuous availability of AI services.

Maintainability: CI/CD pipelines and containerization simplify model updates, retraining, and version management. Continuous integration pipelines build and validate code, while continuous deployment pipelines push updates to production in a controlled, automated manner. Dockerized Python AI services allow for seamless rollback if issues arise, maintaining system stability.

Deploying an AI-enhanced Blazor enterprise application on Azure requires a carefully orchestrated approach that balances performance, security, compliance, and maintainability. By leveraging Azure App Service, AKS, Azure Active Directory, and Azure Machine Learning, enterprises can provide real-time AI insights to users while adhering to Zero-Trust security principles. Python-based FastAPI endpoints offer high-performance integration with the Blazor front end, creating a modular, maintainable, and secure system architecture.

Through CI/CD pipelines, containerization, identity management, and comprehensive monitoring, organizations can ensure business continuity, regulatory compliance, and operational efficiency. Azure's telemetry and logging capabilities allow proactive detection of anomalies, model drift, and potential security risks, ensuring the AI services remain reliable and trustworthy. This deployment framework empowers enterprises to innovate with AI responsibly, delivering scalable, secure, and intelligent applications capable of meeting modern business demands while safeguarding critical data assets.

CHAPTER 15

Future of Blazor and AI in Enterprise Solutions

State Management Strategies

State management is central to any interactive web application, and in Blazor, it plays a key role in maintaining a consistent and responsive UI. State represents the current condition of the app—such as user preferences, session data, UI selections, and cached results—and must be handled carefully to avoid unnecessary re-renders or inconsistent behavior.

In practice, Blazor supports multiple state patterns, including scoped state containers, PersistentComponentState, browser storage, and server-side circuit persistence. These approaches differ across hosting models: server-side relies on circuit state for continuity, while WebAssembly manages state locally within the browser, requiring explicit persistence strategies.

The enterprise software landscape is undergoing a profound transformation, driven by cloud-native development, artificial intelligence (AI), and the evolution of web frameworks such as Blazor. Traditionally, enterprise applications relied on rigid architectures, monolithic designs, and isolated data analytics. Today, organizations are demanding applications that are not only secure and scalable but also intelligent, adaptive, and responsive to dynamic business environments. Blazor, Microsoft's modern web framework leveraging .NET technologies, enables developers to build interactive, high-performance web applications using C# rather than JavaScript. Its compatibility with AI-driven services and cloud infrastructure positions it as a cornerstone for next-generation enterprise solutions.

A. Prasad and H. Singh, *Advanced Blazor Architecture with .NET 10 and Azure OpenAI*,
https://doi.org/10.1007/979-8-8688-2518-7_15

As enterprises prepare for .NET 10 and beyond, integrating AI capabilities into Blazor applications has become increasingly critical. This chapter explores the emerging trends, best practices, and strategic approaches enterprises should adopt to future-proof their applications.

Emerging Trends in Blazor and AI for Enterprises

1. **Convergence of AI and Web Applications**

   AI capabilities such as natural language processing (NLP), predictive analytics, and recommendation engines are increasingly integrated into enterprise applications. These may be exposed as application features or implemented through embedded inference runtimes that execute models directly within the application environment. The integration of AI with Blazor enables real-time intelligence on the front end, allowing users to make informed decisions and gain actionable insights directly from dashboards or interactive components.

   Modern trends indicate a shift toward hybrid architectures, where the Blazor front end interacts with containerized Python or .NET AI microservices deployed on cloud platforms such as Azure. This separation ensures modularity, scalability, and independent evolution of AI models while maintaining a unified user experience.

2. **Cloud-Native and Microservices Architectures**

   Enterprises are embracing cloud-native designs and microservices to enhance resilience and scalability. AI services are increasingly deployed in containerized environments using Docker or Kubernetes, allowing dynamic scaling and automated orchestration. Blazor applications consume these services through REST or gRPC APIs, ensuring seamless integration.

   The trend toward serverless AI pipelines using Azure Functions or AWS Lambda allows enterprises to process large datasets without managing complex infrastructure, reducing costs and operational overhead.

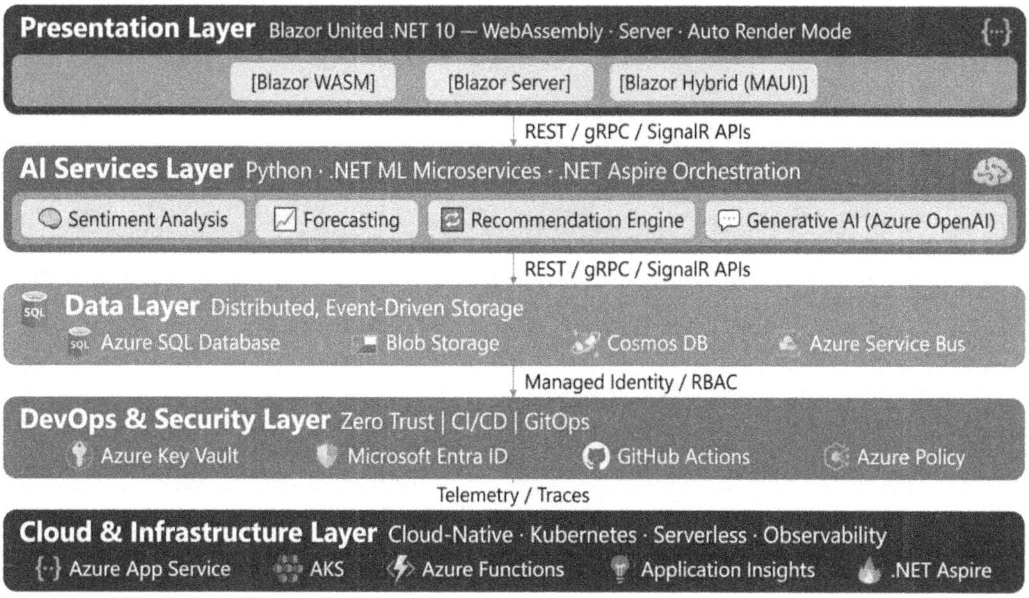

Figure 15-1. *Future Blazor + AI Enterprise Architecture*

3. **Edge AI and Real-Time Processing**

   Edge computing, combined with AI, is gaining traction in enterprises for applications requiring low latency and immediate responses. Blazor applications connected to edge-deployed AI models can deliver near-real-time insights—such as predictive maintenance or sentiment analysis—without relying entirely on centralized cloud processing. Lightweight, latency-sensitive workloads are well suited for edge execution, while compute-intensive training and large-scale inference are typically handled in centralized environments.

4. **Enhanced Security and Compliance**

   As AI processes sensitive data, Zero-Trust security frameworks and compliance regulations like GDPR, HIPAA, and PCI DSS are becoming integral to enterprise solutions. Blazor applications integrated with AI must enforce role-based access, encrypted communications, and continuous auditing. Future trends point toward AI-powered security monitoring, where AI detects anomalies in user behavior or API usage to prevent breaches proactively.

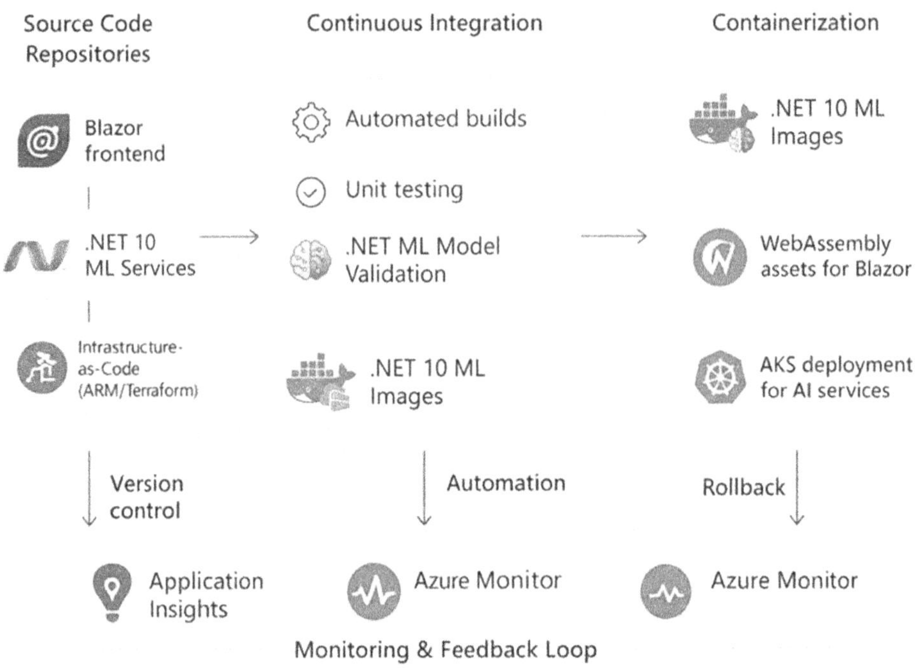

Figure 15-2. *CI/CD Pipeline for AI-Enhanced Blazor Applications*

Best Practices for Integrating AI with Blazor

1. **Modular Architecture**: Separate the front end, back end, and AI components into distinct services to promote maintainability, scalability, and independent evolution of each layer. Use RESTful APIs or gRPC to connect Blazor with AI services, enabling independent scaling, versioning, and maintenance.

2. **CI/CD and Automated Deployment**: Leverage containerization (Docker) and CI/CD pipelines for Blazor and AI services. Automated testing ensures that AI models maintain accuracy while the front end remains responsive and secure.

3. **Asynchronous Processing**: AI inference can introduce latency; adopt asynchronous programming patterns in Blazor and FastAPI/.NET APIs to handle concurrent requests without blocking the user interface.

4. **Monitoring and Observability**: Use Azure Monitor, Application Insights, or Prometheus/Grafana to track API performance, model drift, errors, and latency. Integrate automated alerting for anomalies or degraded AI performance.

5. **Data Governance and Privacy**: Apply strong data governance practices for AI datasets. Mask sensitive data, maintain version-controlled datasets, and ensure compliance with enterprise data policies.

6. **Reusable AI Components**: Design AI capabilities as reusable services with clear API versioning and stable contracts, supported by governance practices such as a model registry and backward compatibility management. For instance, a sentiment analysis API or a demand-forecasting service can be shared across multiple Blazor applications within the organization.

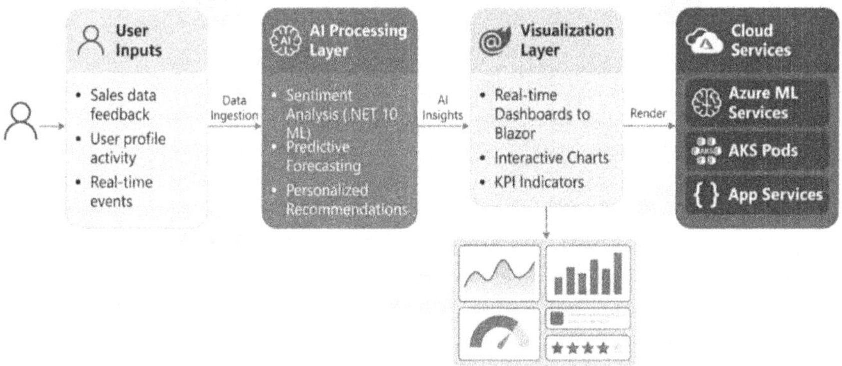

***Figure 15-3.** AI-Driven Real-Time Dashboards and User Interaction*

Preparing for .NET 10 and Beyond

.NET 10 promises new capabilities that will impact how Blazor applications interact with AI:

1. **Performance Improvements**: The runtime delivers improved rendering efficiency, Blazor WebAssembly preloading, enhanced diagnostics, passkey support in identity, and improved state persistence, resulting in more responsive Blazor applications when interacting with AI services.

2. **Enhanced WebAssembly Support**: Blazor WebAssembly (WASM) will benefit from better threading, SIMD support, and near-native performance. This enables client-side inference or preprocessing in the browser for lightweight ML tasks. However, it introduces trade-offs in download size, startup time, memory usage, and AOT or lazy-loading choices, which must be evaluated based on the scenario.

3. **Unified Cloud-Native Development**: The platform supports streamlined deployment of AI-enabled microservices, serverless functions, and containerized workloads through established cloud tooling, helping reduce friction between development and operations.

4. **Interoperability with Python and AI Frameworks**: Blazor applications integrate with AI models built in TensorFlow, PyTorch, or scikit-learn through API-based interoperability, enabling efficient and loosely coupled communication with Python services.

5. **Security Enhancements**: .NET 10 introduces improved cryptography APIs, secure storage for secrets, and stronger authentication mechanisms, ensuring that AI-driven applications remain compliant and resistant to modern cyber threats.

Future Outlook

The combination of Blazor and AI is set to redefine enterprise application development. Enterprises can anticipate

1. **Smarter UIs**: Real-time AI insights embedded directly in user interfaces

2. **Predictive Operations**: Integration of predictive analytics across supply chain, sales, and HR systems

3. **Personalization at Scale**: AI-driven personalization in enterprise portals, chatbots, and dashboards

4. **Autonomous Systems**: AI-enabled automation for repetitive enterprise tasks, reducing manual intervention and operational costs

5. **Sustainable AI Practices**: Cloud-native deployments with AI workloads optimized for energy efficiency and cost-effectiveness

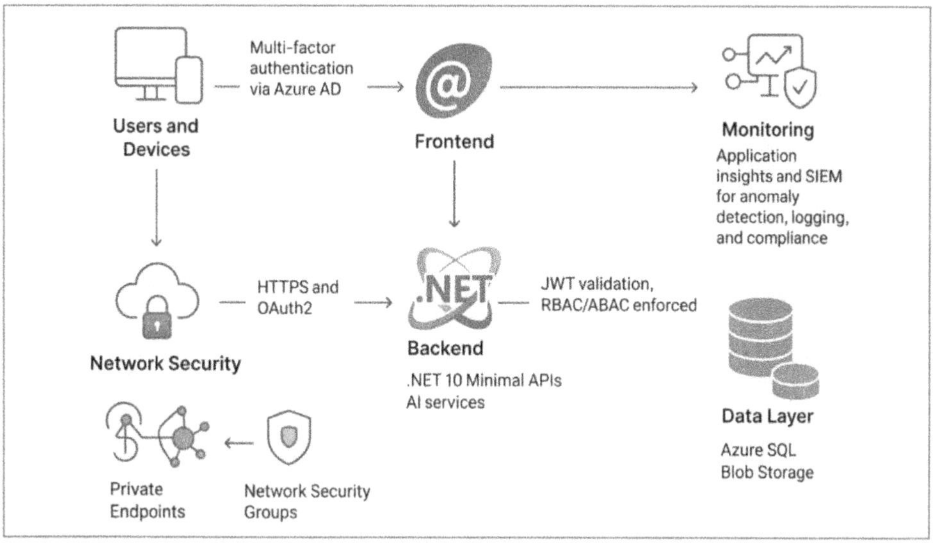

***Figure 15-4.** Security and Zero-Trust in AI-Enhanced Blazor Applications*

Organizations that embrace these trends today will not only achieve operational efficiency but also unlock the full potential of real-time decision-making, predictive insights, and personalized user experiences, ensuring competitiveness in an increasingly data-driven enterprise landscape.

Predictive Analytics with Blazor and Python ML Models

With future enterprise applications, Blazor can integrate advanced predictive analytics using Python machine learning models. By leveraging Python libraries such as scikit-learn, TensorFlow, or Prophet, enterprises can forecast KPIs like sales, churn, and customer engagement. These predictions are exposed as REST APIs using FastAPI and consumed in Blazor dashboards. This modular approach enables real-time insights while keeping front-end and AI services loosely coupled. Enterprises can easily retrain models and update endpoints without changing the UI.

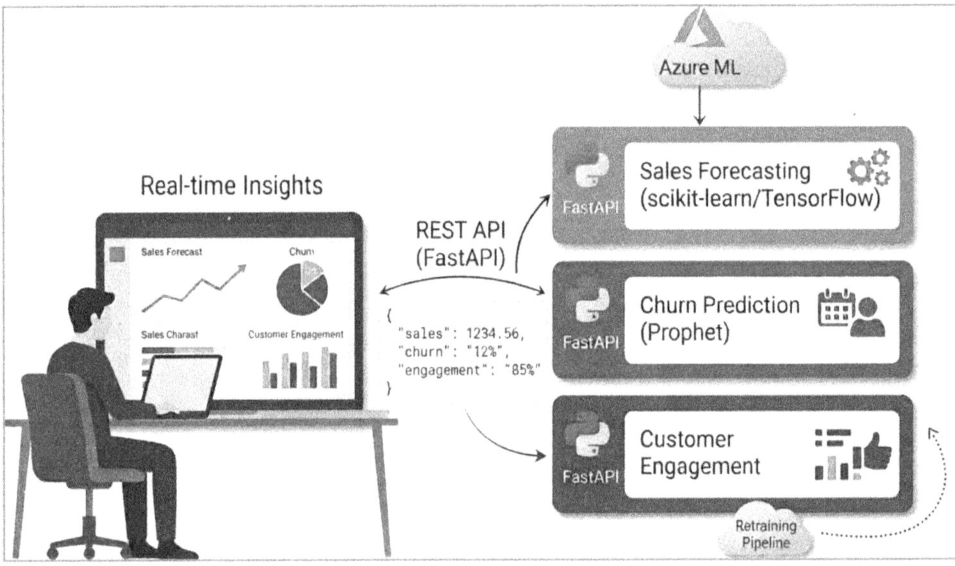

***Figure 15-5.** Blazor Front-End and Python AI Service Integration*

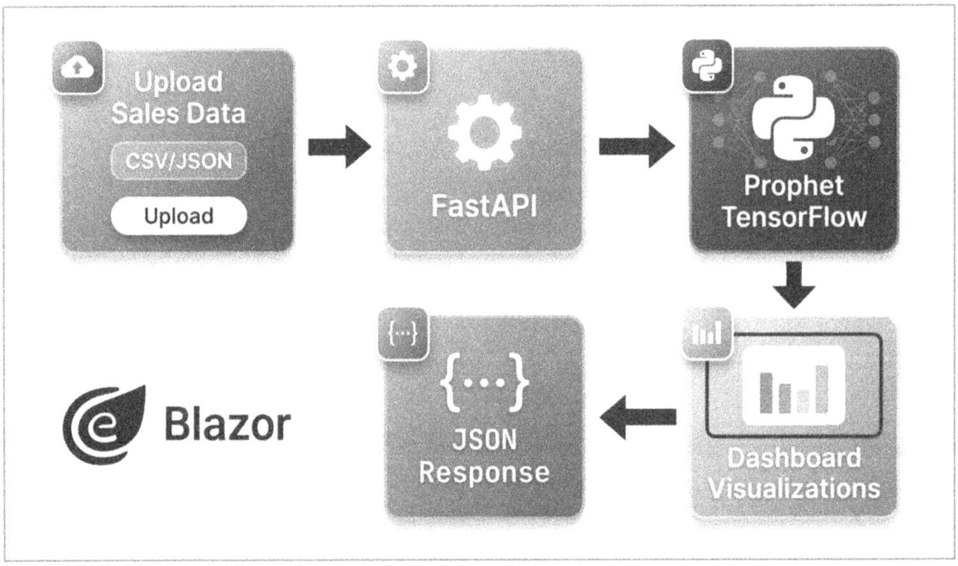

***Figure 15-6.** Predictive Analytics Workflow in Blazor Enterprise App*

Sales Forecasting Using Prophet

```python
# sales_forecast.py
from prophet import Prophet
import pandas as pd

# Read input data. Prophet expects:
#   - ds: date/time column
#   - y : numeric target (sales)
data = pd.read_csv("sales_data.csv")

# Convert and validate types early to avoid silent training issues.
data["ds"] = pd.to_datetime(data["ds"], errors="coerce")
data["y"] = pd.to_numeric(data["y"], errors="coerce")

# Drop invalid rows and sort by date (Prophet assumes a time-ordered series).
data = data.dropna(subset=["ds", "y"]).sort_values("ds")

if data.empty:
    raise ValueError("sales_data.csv has no valid rows after parsing 'ds' and 'y'.")

# Create a baseline Prophet model.
# Defaults work well for many business series (trend + seasonality),
# and can be tuned later (e.g., weekly/yearly seasonality, holidays).
model = Prophet()

# Fit the model to historical data.
model.fit(data)

# Create a future dataframe for the next 30 days.
# Prophet infers frequency from the historical 'ds' values.
future = model.make_future_dataframe(periods=30)

# Predict for both historical and future dates.
forecast = model.predict(future)

# yhat is the point forecast; yhat_lower/yhat_upper provide uncertainty bounds.
print(forecast[["ds", "yhat", "yhat_lower", "yhat_upper"]].tail())
```

Real-Time Sentiment Analysis in Enterprise Applications

Future Blazor apps will increasingly use AI for real-time sentiment analysis. Customer feedback, social media posts, or survey responses can be processed using Python NLP libraries such as transformers or spaCy. By exposing these models via FastAPI endpoints, Blazor UIs can display dynamic sentiment scores, trends, and alerts. This allows enterprises to react proactively to customer needs and market shifts. The approach ensures scalable, maintainable AI integration while keeping the user experience interactive and responsive.

Building a Simple Sentiment Analysis API with FastAPI

```python
# sentiment_api.py

from fastapi import FastAPI
from transformers import pipeline

# Create the FastAPI application instance.
# This will expose REST endpoints that clients can call.
app = FastAPI()

# Load a pretrained sentiment analysis model from Hugging Face.
# The pipeline API abstracts tokenization, model loading, and inference.
sentiment_model = pipeline("sentiment-analysis")


@app.post("/analyze-sentiment")
def analyze(text: str):
    """
    Analyze the sentiment of the provided text.

    The model returns a label (e.g., POSITIVE or NEGATIVE)
    along with a confidence score representing prediction certainty.
    """

    # Run inference using the sentiment model
    result = sentiment_model(text)[0]

    # Return a simple JSON response with the prediction
    return {
        "text": text,
        "label": result["label"],
        "score": result["score"]
    }
```

Personalized Recommendations for Enterprise Users

Blazor applications of the future can leverage AI-driven recommendation engines to personalize content, products, and services. Using Python frameworks like Surprise or TensorFlow, collaborative and content-based filtering can provide recommendations tailored to user behavior. Exposed via FastAPI, these endpoints allow Blazor UIs to fetch personalized suggestions in real time, increasing engagement and revenue. With continuous model retraining on fresh data, enterprises can maintain relevance and improve customer satisfaction.

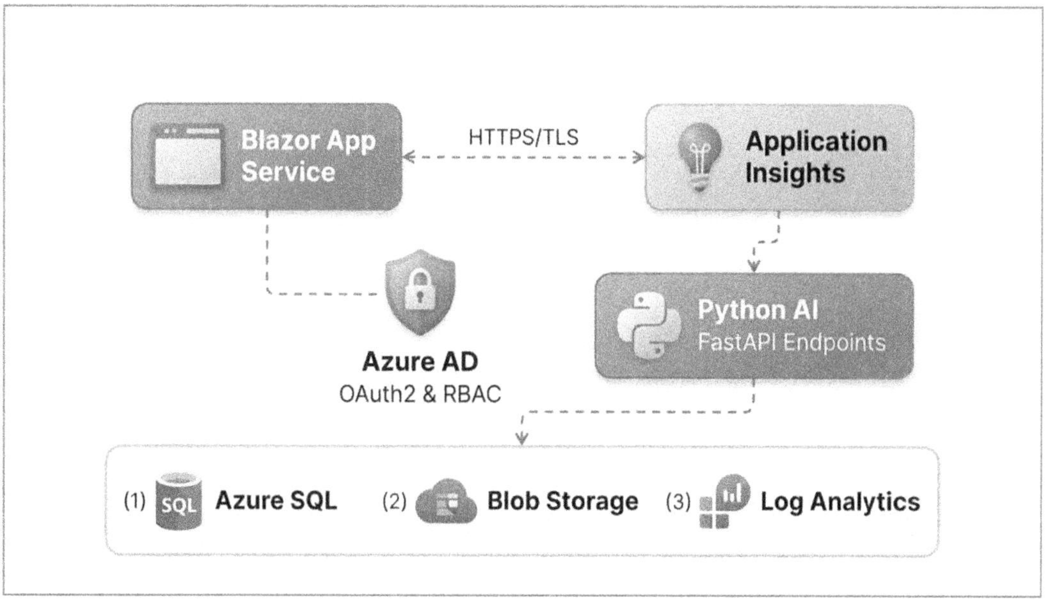

Figure 15-7. *Azure Deployment Architecture with Zero-Trust Security*

Building a Simple Recommendation Model Using Matrix Factorization

```python
# recommendation.py

from surprise import SVD, Dataset, Reader
import pandas as pd

# Load historical user ratings.
# Expected columns: userId, itemId, rating
data = pd.read_csv("ratings.csv")

# Define the rating scale used in the dataset.
# This helps the library interpret the values correctly.
reader = Reader(rating_scale=(1, 5))

# Convert the pandas DataFrame into a Surprise dataset format.
# Only the relevant columns are passed to the model.
dataset = Dataset.load_from_df(
    data[['userId', 'itemId', 'rating']],
    reader
)

# Initialize the recommendation model.
# SVD is a matrix factorization technique commonly used
# in collaborative filtering systems.
model = SVD()

# Build the training dataset from all available records.
trainset = dataset.build_full_trainset()

# Train the model to learn user-item interaction patterns.
model.fit(trainset)

# Predict a rating for a specific user-item pair.
# The model estimates how likely the user is to prefer the item.
pred = model.predict(user_id=1, item_id=101)

# Display the predicted rating score.
print(pred.est)
```

Integrating Computer Vision for Document Processing

Future enterprise apps will integrate computer vision with Blazor UIs for document scanning, invoice processing, and image-based analytics. Python libraries like OpenCV, PyTorch, or TensorFlow can handle image classification, object detection, and OCR. These models, deployed via FastAPI or Azure ML endpoints, allow real-time processing and actionable insights directly in Blazor dashboards. This reduces manual effort and accelerates decision-making.

Building a Simple OCR API for Text Extraction

```python
# ocr_api.py

import cv2
import numpy as np
import pytesseract
from fastapi import FastAPI, UploadFile

# Initialize the FastAPI application
app = FastAPI()


@app.post("/extract-text")
def extract_text(file: UploadFile):
    """
    Accept an uploaded image file and extract readable text using OCR.
    The endpoint expects a standard image format such as PNG or JPEG.
    """

    # Read the uploaded file into memory as a byte array
    file_bytes = file.file.read()

    # Convert raw bytes into a NumPy array so OpenCV can process it
    image_array = np.frombuffer(file_bytes, np.uint8)

    # Decode the image into OpenCV format
    image = cv2.imdecode(image_array, cv2.IMREAD_COLOR)

    # Run Tesseract OCR to detect and extract text from the image
    text = pytesseract.image_to_string(image)

    # Return the extracted text as a JSON response
    return {"extracted_text": text}
```

AI-Driven Chatbots for Enterprise Support

AI chatbots powered by NLP are becoming essential in enterprise applications. Future Blazor apps can integrate Python-based conversational AI models using Hugging Face transformers or Rasa. By exposing these chatbots via FastAPI endpoints, enterprises can offer 24/7 support, ticket automation, and real-time query resolution. Blazor handles UI rendering, while Python services maintain the intelligence behind natural language understanding and response generation.

Building a Simple Conversational Chatbot API

```python
# chatbot_api.py

from fastapi import FastAPI
from transformers import pipeline

# Create the FastAPI application instance.
# This service will expose a REST endpoint for chatbot interactions.
app = FastAPI()

# Load a pretrained conversational model using the Hugging Face pipeline API.
# The pipeline abstracts tokenization, model loading, and response generation.
chatbot = pipeline("conversational")


@app.post("/chat")
def chat(message: str):
    """
    Accept a user message and generate a chatbot response.
    The model processes the input text and returns a generated reply.
    """

    # Send the user message to the conversational model
    response = chatbot(message)[0]['generated_text']

    # Return both the original message and generated response
    return {
        "user_message": message,
        "bot_response": response
    }
```

With .NET 10 and beyond, Blazor will gain better performance, enhanced WebAssembly support, and tighter integration with AI services. Enterprises typically adopt a modular architecture where Blazor consumes AI endpoints via HTTP JSON calls as the default pattern. Alternative approaches are considered only for scenarios requiring lower latency or tighter integration. Python-based AI services can evolve independently, supporting microservices, containerization, and cloud deployment. Enterprises adopting this strategy will achieve agility, scalability, and rapid innovation in AI-enhanced business solutions.

The future of Blazor in enterprise solutions lies in its seamless integration with AI services, cloud infrastructure, and modern security paradigms. By adopting best practices in modular architecture, CI/CD pipelines, asynchronous processing, and observability, enterprises can create applications that are intelligent, scalable, and resilient. Preparing for .NET 10 and beyond ensures that Blazor applications remain performant, secure, and fully capable of leveraging advanced AI technologies.

References

1. André, P. M., Stiévenart, Q., & Ghafari, M. (2022, October). Developers struggle with authentication in Blazor WebAssembly. In 2022 IEEE International Conference on Software Maintenance and Evolution (ICSME) (pp. 389–393). IEEE.
2. Brito, T., Lopes, P., Santos, N., & Santos, J. F. (2022). Wasmati: An efficient static vulnerability scanner for WebAssembly. Computers & Security, 118, 102745.
3. Cabrera-Arteaga, J., Fitzgerald, N., Monperrus, M., & Baudry, B. (2024). Wasm-Mutate: Fast and effective binary diversification for WebAssembly. Computers & Security, 139, 103731.
4. Haryanto, C. Y., Vu, M. H., Nguyen, T. D., Lomempow, E., Nurliana, Y., & Taheri, S. (2024). SecGenAI: Enhancing security of cloud-based generative AI applications within Australian critical technologies of national interest. arXiv preprint arXiv:2407.01110.
5. Microsoft, ".NET Support Policy": `https://dotnet.microsoft.com/platform/support`, accessed Jan 2025.
6. Microsoft, "ASP.NET Core Blazor performance best practices": `https://learn.microsoft.com/aspnet/core/blazor/performance`, accessed Jan 2025.
7. Microsoft, "Host and deploy Blazor apps": `https://learn.microsoft.com/aspnet/core/blazor/host-and-deploy`, accessed Jan 2025.
8. Microsoft, "What's new in .NET": `https://learn.microsoft.com/dotnet/core/whats-new/`, accessed Jan 2025.

A. Prasad and H. Singh, *Advanced Blazor Architecture with .NET 10 and Azure OpenAI*,
https://doi.org/10.1007/979-8-8688-2518-7

9. Autto, H., Haapio, H., & Nuottila, J. (2024). Contracts rethought and redesigned: A new era with AI. International journal of commerce and contracting, 8(1-2), 7-34.

10. Chan, A., Wei, K., Huang, S., Rajkumar, N., Perrier, E., Lazar, S., ... & Anderljung, M. (2025). Infrastructure for AI agents. arXiv preprint arXiv:2501.10114.

11. Buragadda, S., Vamsi, C. D., Jafrin, M., & Ramisetti, A. (2025, April). A Comprehensive System for Diabetes Management and Prediction Using AI-Driven Chatbot and Machine Learning Models. In 2025 International Conference on Inventive Computation Technologies (ICICT) (pp. 97-103). IEEE.

12. Lavanya, B., Kumar, M., & Reddy, S. K. (2024, November). EaseRent: Integrated Web and Mobile Rental Solutions. In International Conference on Evolutionary Artificial Intelligence (pp. 55-71). Singapore: Springer Nature Singapore.

13. Hammond, L., Chan, A., Clifton, J., Hoelscher-Obermaier, J., Khan, A., McLean, E., ... & Rahwan, I. (2025). Multi-agent risks from advanced AI. arXiv preprint arXiv:2502.14143.

14. Rashidi, V., & Segelström, W. (2021). Evaluating Blazor WebAssembly for the Progressive Web Application Front-End: A Comparative Study Using ReactJS as a Baseline.

15. Hadfield, G. K., & Koh, A. (2025). An Economy of AI Agents. arXiv preprint arXiv:2509.01063.

16. Dai, J., Raji, I. D., Recht, B., & Chen, I. Y. (2025). Aggregated Individual Reporting for Post-Deployment Evaluation. arXiv preprint arXiv:2506.18133.

17. Fisher, J., Appel, R. E., Park, C. Y., Potter, Y., Jiang, L., Sorensen, T., ... & Choi, Y. (2025). Political Neutrality in AI Is Impossible-But Here Is How to Approximate It. arXiv preprint arXiv:2503.05728.

18. Dholakia, S. (2021). Zeroing in on Zero Trust Architecture. ISSA Journal, 19(12).

19. Emmanni, P. S. (2024). Implementing a zero-trust architecture in hybrid cloud environments. International Journal of Computer Trends and Technology, 72(5), 33–39.

20. Li, K., Li, C., Yuan, X., Li, S., Zou, S., Ahmed, S. S., ... & Akan, Ö. B. (2025). Zero-trust foundation models: A new paradigm for secure and collaborative artificial intelligence for internet of things. IEEE Internet of Things Journal.

21. Rose, S., Borchert, O., Mitchell, S., & Connelly, S. (2020). *Zero Trust Architecture.* NIST Special Publication 800-207.

22. Arora, P., & Pillai, N. S. (2025). Generative Artificial Intelligence in Teaching, Learning, and Assessment: An Indian Perspective. In Integration Strategies of Generative AI in Higher Education (pp. 71–100). IGI Global.

23. NIST (2023). *Artificial Intelligence Risk Management Framework (AI RMF 1.0).* National Institute of Standards and Technology.

Index

A

A. Prasad and H. Singh, *Advanced Blazor Architecture with .NET 10 and Azure OpenAI*,
https://doi.org/10.1007/979-8-8688-2518-7

B

C

D

E

N

O

P

Q

R

S

T

www.ingramcontent.com/pod-product-compliance
Lightning Source LLC
Chambersburg PA
CBHW080917180826
50016CB00035B/608
* 9 7 9 8 8 6 8 8 2 5 1 7 0 *